THE MOUNTAINEERS ANTHOLOGY S · E · R · I · E · S

VOLUME I

GLORIOUS FAILURES

THE MOUNTAINEERS BOOKS

Published by
The Mountaineers Books
1001 SW Klickitat Way, Suite 201
Seattle, WA 98134

First edition, 2001

Published simultaneously in Great Britain by Cordee, 3a DeMontfort Street, Leicester, England, LE1 7HD

Manufactured in the United States of America

Editors: Cassandra Conyers, Kathleen Cubley, and Donna DeShazo
Cover art, cover design, and book design: Ani Rucki
Layout: Ani Rucki

Library of Congress Cataloging-in-Publication Data
Glorious failures / compiled by the editors at the Mountaineers Books.—
1st ed.
       p. cm. — (The Mountaineers anthology series ; v. 1)
    ISBN 0-89886-825-4
    1. Mountaineering. 2. Mountaineering expeditions. I. Mountaineers Books (Firm)
II. Series.
GV200 .G57 2001
796.52'2—dc21

                                                           2001004525

CONTENTS

Introduction   5
Foreword by John Harlin III   7

"PARKER AND BROWNE REACH TWENTY THOUSAND FEET"   13
FROM
Mt. McKinley: The Pioneer Climbs
BY TERRIS MOORE

"MASTERS OF UNDERSTATEMENT"   27
FROM
Postcards from the Ledge
BY GREG CHILD

FROM
DEBORAH: A WILDERNESS NARRATIVE   35
BY DAVID ROBERTS

FROM
THE LAND THAT SLEPT LATE   67
BY ROBERT L. WOOD

"LIVING DANGEROUSLY"   73
FROM
This Game of Ghosts
BY JOE SIMPSON

"JUNE 14, 1943
FLEISCHBANK EAST FACE, WILDER KAISER"
AND
"FIRST WINTER ASCENT OF THE SOUTH WEST FACE
OF THE MARMOLATA"   89
FROM
Hermann Buhl: Climbing Without Compromise
BY REINHOLD MESSNER AND HORST HÖFLER

FROM
SUMMITS AND SECRETS   99
BY KURT DIEMBERGER

"DISASTER ON NANGA PARBAT" BY ERWIN SCHNEIDER   113
FROM
Peaks, Passes, and Glaciers
BY WALT UNSWORTH

"MUZTAGH ATA"   125
FROM
Two Mountains and a River in *The Seven Mountain-Travel Books*
BY H.W. TILMAN

"GRIM DAYS ON HARAMOSH" BY TONY STREATHER WITH RALPH BARKER   139
FROM
Heroic Climbs: A Celebration of World Mountaineering
CHRIS BONINGTON, EDITOR

"INTERVIEW WITH JEAN-CHRISTOPHE LAFAILLE"   147
FROM
Kiss or Kill: Confessions of a Serial Climber
BY MARK TWIGHT

"THE K2 MYSTERY"   157
FROM
Moments of Doubt and Other Mountaineering Writings of David Roberts
BY DAVID ROBERTS

"NEITHER SAINT NOR SINNER" AND
"STRANGERS AND BROTHERS"   179
FROM
K2: The Story of the Savage Mountain
BY JIM CURRAN

"THE WESTERN APPROACH AND DEFEAT" AND
"ATTEMPT TO REACH THE SUMMIT RIDGE"   205
FROM
Everest 1938 in *The Seven Mountain-Travel Books*
BY H.W. TILMAN

"LAST ATTEMPT"   225
FROM
Ghosts of Everest: The Search for Mallory & Irvine
BY JOCHEN HEMMLEB, LARRY A. JOHNSON, AND ERIC R. SIMONSON

INTRODUCTION

The Mountaineers Anthologies of adventure and mountaineering writing reflect our longstanding role as publishing leaders in the worldwide climbing community. Many of the climbing world's most renowned authors publish through The Mountaineers Books, and it is from their work that we assemble these collections of exploits and expeditions.

Each volume is distinguished by a specific adventuring theme. Annotations to each selection provide the book title and pages where the original material can be found. Some original material may be out of print, making these anthologies the only source now available.

You are about to embark on a reading adventure filled with triumphs, daring feats, and heroics; disappointments, extreme challenges, and tragedies.

We hope you enjoy this journey through the best that mountaineering literature has to offer.

The Editors
The Mountaineers Books

FOREWORD

"Fate, however, was against us."

With those words, Erwin Schneider signaled the turning point in his team's prospects on Nanga Parbat in 1932. Near the summit of Pakistan's unclimbed 8,125-meter giant, Schneider's team was in a festive mood, "quite carefree concerning the following day which was to consummate our victory." But that night "a tremendous snowstorm burst over the tents" ("Disaster on Nanga Parbat," pg. 113). For days the climbers hung on at high camp, waiting for the break that didn't come. Then they started down despite a storm so strong that in a span of 10 feet it dissolved climbing partners into gray ghosts. In their hearts the climbers thought themselves "certain to return in a few days" when the weather cleared. But frostbite and exhaustion set in as the downward battle turned into war. Six Sherpa high-altitude porters and four German climbers died. The author leads us through their struggle for life against death until he can leave us with his concluding thought: "Shall we be lucky enough to fight another round with Nanga Parbat?"

Yes, it's true, that's the heady finale to one of the great mountaineering tragedies of the twentieth century. This numbing lack of reflection reveals all too much about climbers. As H.W. Tilman put it (*Everest 1938,* pg. 225), " . . . the urge, to ascend and to overcome the difficulties standing in his way . . . is the instinctive feeling of every mountaineer." The urge to explore the psychological conundrum wherein a climber seeks out the biggest obstacle he thinks he can overcome, then risks his life in the attempt, is rather more rare. You won't see it here.

I've earned something of a right to make this criticism—not because I have a solution, but because I'm part of the problem. The problem of climbing, whose issues are so much more profound than going another round with a monster made of ice and rock. Maybe I began working on this puzzle as I followed a hearse carrying my father's body after he fell off of the Eiger, in Switzerland. It's hard to remember definitely, as I was only nine. I worked on it more while absorbing my mother's reaction to the news that I'd tried, and failed, to grab my climbing partner as he began his 500-foot deathfall down Mount Robson, in the Canadian Rockies. Age twenty-two. Twenty-one years later, the tears poured from my emotional wreckage as I said goodbye to my three-year-old daughter on my way to climb the Matterhorn and have a look at the Eiger. Will I see her again? Where is this going? What am I doing? I wonder about these things; then I go climbing anyway, only without the full conviction that gives great mountaineers much of their power.

You won't find crippling introspection in this volume. What you will find is example after example of tenacity and strength in the face of overwhelming resistance, the kind of thing that inspires us to try harder next time. "As Professor Parker passed me his lips were dark and his face showed white from cold through his parka hood, but he made no sign of distress," wrote Terris Moore about their attempt at the first ascent of Mount McKinley (*Mt. McKinley: The Pioneer Climbs*, pg. 13). Finally, after concluding it would be suicide to go on in the storm, "I turned to Professor Parker and yelled, 'the game's up; we've got to get down!' And he answered, 'Can't we go on? I'll chop [steps] if I can.' The memory of those words will always wend a wave of admiration through my mind . . ." We love this heroic stuff. "At least we will be able to say we made a good try," wrote David Roberts (*Deborah: A Wilderness Narrative*, pg. 35) after enduring endless storms in Alaska. Roberts is by far the most thoughtful and literary writer in this volume, and one of the psychologically deeper climbers to write about their craft. Perhaps that's why, when finally he and his partner gave up at the foot of an unclimbable wall, he could voice his thankfulness that "The mountain had allowed us pride." H.W. Tilman wasn't so lucky. He was left to lament his partner's badly frostbitten toes with the thought that "Success would have been a very considerable consolation" ("Mustag Ata," pg. 125).

It certainly would have made all the difference to Fritz Wiessner, who wrestled for the next forty-eight years with his decision to bring his fearful Sherpa partner back to high camp rather than untie from him and make the first ascent of K2, solo, in 1939 ("The K2 Mystery," pg. 157). As fate would have it, Wiessner's concern for his partner's safety precipitated one of the twentieth century's infamous mountaineering tragedies. Later, in defending Wiessner against his critics, respected American climber Robert Underhill wrote, "He had the guts—and there is no single thing finer in a climber, or in a man."

Well, guts are good, and there are plenty of them on display in *Glorious Failures.* But guts have to struggle against wisdom, another worthy trait in a human being. Unless we read this collection merely as entertainment—turning us into bemused spectators at a lengthy series of gladiator matches—we are left to wonder what these climbers learned from their defeats. After all, it's old knowledge that a wise person learns more from failure than from success. And each of these headstrong, world-class climbers was defeated by his mountain. The circumstances leading up to such a breakdown, and the final decision to turn tail—when it comes, how it is wrung, whether it was wise—are what test our souls, what define who we are and what we value. This declaration of defeat typically comes hard. On Terris Moore's descent, he remembers "only a feeling of weakness and dumb despair; we had burned up and lived off our own tissue until we didn't care much what happened."

If that sounds like the preamble to an even more serious adventure, it all too often is.

Jean-Christophe Lafaille and his partner Pierre Beghin were descending through storm at about the 7,200-meter level on a new route on the south face of Annapurna ("Interview With Jean-Christophe Lafaille," pg. 147). They had been three days on their extreme climb—a route whose unimaginable difficulty and danger defined state-of-the-art mountaineering in 1992—when a storm stopped them cold. As Mark Twight writes, " . . . muddled by fatigue, the confusion of the storm, and the need to get down quickly, Pierre leaned back on a single anchor without any backup. It failed and he fell," taking the climbing gear and the rappel rope with him into oblivion. Lafaille was left alone on the ledge. Fortunately, he was a renowned soloist, and had the training to "clinically assess each problem, find the solution, and execute it without freaking out." Then a rock smashed into his arm, compound fracturing two bones. "I'd had it," he told Twight, "I was at the end of my reserves . . . I was suffering too much. I had given everything, but I'd lost." The next day he remembered Doug Scott and Joe Simpson, both of whom had endured against all odds. And he concluded to do the same. Five days after watching his partner die, Lafaille made it to the base of the wall.

As a climber, I realize that in these stories, but for the grace of luck, go I. Missing out on the summit is a "a tough bullet to chew," in Tilman's words. But to most of us the real failure is not coming home, as we're reminded by what resulted from George Mallory's pronouncement "I can't see myself coming down defeated . . . " ("Last Attempt," pg. 225). Personally, I'm haunted by this conflict. I'm all too aware of how thin is the line between a fun adventure and the kind I'd rather not consider. Assuming I survive the initial blow—a fall, a stone, an avalanche—do I have what it takes to write one of these stories? Or would I be the victim, falling over and over until he must be abandoned on a frozen face ("Grim Days on Haramosh," pg. 139)? I fear the answer. I've had my troubles in the mountains, but I don't want to find out how I'd manage with Bill Pilling's broken leg on Alaska's Mount Vancouver, knowing that "staying alive was going to be so much work that for a few minutes I didn't know if I wanted to bother" ("Masters of Understatement," pg. 27).

And yet, like these authors, I trust that my luck will continue. Hermann Buhl, during his escape from the southwest face of Marmolata in the Italian Dolomites, reached a point on the overhanging wall where he and his partner stood on a ledge in a thunderstorm and their wet rappel rope could not be pulled down. "It was as if we were stuck in a mousetrap," he wrote (*Hermann Buhl: Climbing Without Compromise,* pg. 89). This is one of my own worst nightmares: a jammed rappel rope. Reading Buhl's matter-of-fact description, I could feel my panic rising. And then, slowly, the rope began to move. His luck had held; I could breathe again. Seven years later, Buhl walked off a corniced ridge in a storm. His body was never found (*Summits and Secrets,* pg. 99).

"Where are we?" "What are we doing here?" You might expect survivors to ask these questions, but the only person to voice them in this collection is Charlie Houston in a concussed delirium while regaining consciousness in a storm on K2 (*K2: The Story of the Savage Mountain,* pg. 179). His old friend Bob Bates looked him in the eye to break through the surface confusion and reach the man inside. "Charlie," he told him, "if you ever want to see Dorcas and Penny [his wife and daughter] again, climb up there *right now!*"

You won't learn the answer to "What are we doing here?" in this, or almost any collection of writings by climbers. What you will learn is what must be done "right now," including the degree of suffering you'll endure and the indomitable willpower you'll have to pull from somewhere inside yourself if things go wrong, as someday they just well might.

For those of us who climb, or who are fascinated by what mountains demand of human nature, these questions are the mystery that keeps us awed, sometimes disgusted, but always enthralled.

John Harlin III

"PARKER AND BROWNE REACH TWENTY THOUSAND FEET"

FROM
Mt. McKinley: The Pioneer Climbs
BY TERRIS MOORE

ALASKA'S MAGNIFICENT MOUNT MCKINLEY, AT 20,320 FEET THE HIGH-
est point on the North American continent, had been the focus of eight
ascent attempts by 1912, when, in one of the greatest heartbreakers in
mountaineering history, Belmore Browne came within 150 feet of the
storm-lashed summit before admitting defeat. Accompanying Browne was
Professor Herschel C. Parker; this was the third expedition to the peak
by the pair.

Both Browne, a noted writer, artist, and outdoorsman, and Parker, of Columbia University's physics department, had been with the notorious Dr.
Frederick Cook on the latter's exploration of McKinley in 1906. Only after
the majority of his companions had left for home on the abortive 1906 adventure did Cook make another try. He then announced to world acclaim
that he had reached the summit. Browne and Parker, extremely skeptical of
Cook's news, returned to the mountain in 1910 to sleuth out the peak that
Cook had photographed to support his claim. Thus, by the time of their own
well-conceived expedition in 1912, Browne and Parker had an excellent
overview of the route possibilities.

The Parker-Browne party left their steamer in Seward, Alaska, on February 1, 1912, traveled overland, and began their climb early in June. It was late
in that month when, climbing through one of McKinley's horrendous storms,
they reached a point above 20,000 feet. This excerpt from Chapter VIII of
Moore's *Mt. McKinley: The Pioneer Climbs* includes major extracts from Browne's
book about the climb, *The Conquest of Mount McKinley* (1913). Browne is eloquent in conveying both the determination and sorrow felt in this record-
breaking near-miss.

The summit of McKinley was finally reached a year later, by Archdeacon
Hudson Stuck.

An interesting historical footnote: It was the same Parker and Browne,
both members of the American Geographical Society and the Explorers Club,
who in 1907 had tried to beat The Mountaineers (Seattle) to a first ascent
of Mount Olympus, using a trail that the local club had had constructed for
its own attempt later that summer. Parker and Browne made the summit—
but it was the wrong summit!

Professor Parker and Belmore Browne, for their 1912 attempt, had decided on a completely new approach to the north slopes of the mountain—by dog-team, in the winter, from the south. Convinced by their explorations of 1906 and 1910 that the south slopes of the mountain were impossible, they were now ready to try the northeast side of the mountain via the Muldrow Glacier. They had studied the photographs made by their friend Charles Sheldon in 1906, 1907 and 1908 during his explorations with Harry Karstens in the Kantishna, when Sheldon had pointed out the possibilities of the northeast ridge to Lloyd and his friends. And from Lloyd's published photographs made in 1910, Parker and Browne were satisfied that the Sourdough party of that year had found a successful route up this northeast ridge at least to the edge of the High Basin between the north and south peaks.

> *"The next question," Browne writes, "was how we were to reach the northeast ridge. Fairbanks on the Tanana River is the nearest town to Mt. McKinley, and with the aid of dogs in winter time, the journey offers no difficulties, consisting as it does of only 160 miles of excellent snow travel. This was our logical route. But . . . it was our desire to explore the unknown canyons of the Alaskan Range east of Mt. McKinley. If we could find a pass through the high range from the Susitna River on the south we would explore a magnificent mountain wilderness that otherwise might remain unknown for years [and would further elucidate Dr. Cook's claimed approach route]. While it would be possible . . . during the summer . . . this would require too much time . . . We decided therefore to make a winter trip of it, and to depend for our transportation on the Alaskan dog.*
>
> *"Merl La Voy with his Graflex camera and Arthur Aten of the old party joined us. As we were to enter the Alaska Range our route would lead us up the frozen waterways of the Susitna and Chulitna Rivers. But since Cook Inlet was choked with ice*

during the winter time, we were forced to leave the steamer at Seward during the last days of January . . . A winter trail leads from the end of the incompleted railroad line, through the heart of the Kenai Peninsula, through magnificent mountain scenery to tidewater on Turnagain Arm, and on via Knik Arm to Susitna Station on the Susitna River. Beyond Susitna Station a winter trail now leads over the Alaskan Range at the head of the Kichatna to the Kuskoquim and the gold fields of the Iditarod. At intervals of about ten miles, 'road houses' stand offering food and rest to man and dog. They are one of the most important of Alaskan institutions, and on all the winter trails that cross the great land, one will find these resting places which make rapid travel possible."

In Seward they found:

"The town was stirred by the arrival of the Iditarod gold shipment. The gold was packed in small wooden chests, one hundred pounds to the chest, which were handled with grunts and groans by the bank clerks who took them from the dog sleds. The populace stood packed about, but fully one-half their interest was centered on the two magnificent, perfectly matched dog teams that had pulled the treasure from the banks of the Kuskoquim, four hundred miles to the northwest . . . The teams were hitched in the regulation Alaskan trail manner—two by two with a single leader. Their harness was perfect from the silver bells that jangled so sweetly, to the red pom-poms that bobbed gaily on each furry back . . . We said goodbye to Seward and its hospitable citizens on the first of February, 1912."

Seventeen days later they reached Susitna Station. Here, "everyone showed the greatest interest in our venture. We were invited to a 'civilized dinner' by

McNalley, the Alaska Commercial Co. representative—the last we were to enjoy until five months later we reached the Yukon."

➙ ➙ ➙

Leaving Susitna Station, they turned off the winter trail of comfortable road-houses leading west to the Iditarod country, and swung their dogs up the frozen Susitna river north into the unexplored country east of Mount McKinley, tenting out each night. By March 20 they had made it up the length of the tributary Chulitna, and were crossing the Alaska Range via an unnamed valley and pass. They then proceeded up the West Fork Glacier, over Anderson Pass and down the lower end of the Muldrow Glacier to the timber on the McKinley River, which they reached on April 17, 1912.

Now in excellent game country, they took time off to rest and hunt caribou and mountain sheep for food; and soon came upon one of the Cairns party's recently abandoned camps with tent still standing—in which they found *Fairbanks Daily Times* newspaper clippings carrying speculative stories about themselves and their plans!

Leaving Aten to hold down their tundra base camp and take care of the extra dogs, Browne, Parker and La Voy now proceeded without difficulty to dogsledge their mountain supplies through McGonagall Pass (which in their accounts they refer to as "Glacier Pass") where it emerges onto the mid-Muldrow Glacier. Then they steered directly toward McKinley's twin summits and proceeded up the gently sloping Muldrow, following its miles of turns to near the glacier's steep-walled head at 11,000 feet. Here, immediately on their left, they found the key access ridge leading to the High Basin far above. Near the bottom of this ridge they cached their dog-sled load of food, supplies and mountaineering gear, and returned to leave the dog team with Aten at the base camp.

Spring had arrived during the ten days they had been on the glacier. Back at base camp they found:

> *"Our first sight of grass and flowers and running water in many months, as the lowlands had still been in the grip of*

late winter when we started up the mountain. We took the most extravagant delight in our new life, for living on ice is an unnatural and trying ordeal . . . We now lived largely "off the country" and my days were filled with hunting caribou and mountain sheep, or photographing them and the nesting ptarmigan, or studying the topographical features of the magnificent mountain."

Finally, after weeks of resting in this idyll, they returned in early June for their final attack. On the upper Muldrow Glacier after a three-day snow storm, on June 8, Browne made an unusual and interesting observation:

"The glacier has been very noisy all day; it has groaned and cracked, and at short intervals there have been deep powerful reports, sounding for all the world like the boom of big guns at a distance. We have been talking about the queer noise but are undecided as to its cause. It must be due to the settling of the great ice caverns under the tremendous weight of new snow. It was not until we reached civilization long afterwards that we found the unusual booming sound had not come from the glacial caverns, but that it was made by Katmai in eruption hundreds of miles away—Katmai, the volcano whose eruption buried Kodiak in ashes! Later we found these Katmai ashes in our teapot after we had melted snow, but again we accepted the easiest explanation and decided that the grit in our teacups was merely dust blown from the cliffs."

They reached the base of the northeast (today's Karstens) ridge, without further incident. Then, like the 1910 Sourdough party before them, they found the climb up this access ridge no great technical problem, though very exhausting under the depth of much new snow.

Finally, after back-packing and relaying their supplies to successively higher camps and caches, Parker, Browne, and La Voy on the 27th of June . . . camped between the great North and South peaks, just below the last serac that forms the highest point of the Big Basin.

> *"We arrived with our last loads after the sun had gone down, and I have never felt such savage cold as the ice-fields sent down to us," says Browne. "We were in a frigid hollow at an altitude of 16,615 ft. On the north the great blue ice slopes led up an almost unclimbable pitch between the granite buttresses of the North Peak . . . On the south, frozen snowfields swept gently . . . in an easy grade to the final South summit of the great mountain . . . Our feet and hands were beginning to stiffen as we pitched the tent . . . and we were seriously worried for fear Professor Parker would freeze . . .*
>
> *"The morning of our final climb dawned clear as crystal. As I came out into the stabbing cold to report on the weather, the whole expanse of country to the north-eastward stretched like a deep blue sea to where the rising sun was warming the distant horizon.*
>
> *"We left camp at 6 A.M. At first the snow was hard and required little step chopping . . . We moved quietly and steadily, conserving our strength . . . At regular half hour intervals La Voy and I exchanged places. Between changes both Professor Parker and I checked off our rise in altitude (from the altimeter) and found that although we thought we were making fairly good time, we were in reality climbing only 400 feet an hour.*
>
> *"One thousand feet above our camp we ran into soft snow, and fought against this handicap at frequent intervals during the day. When we reached 18,500 feet we stopped for an instant and congratulated each other joyfully, for we had returned the altitude record of North America to America, by beating the Duke of the Abruzzi's record of 18,000 feet made on St. Elias.*

"*Shortly afterward we reached the top of the big ridge. We had long dreamed of this moment, because, for the first time, we now were able to look down [south] into our battleground of 1910, and see all the glaciers and peaks we had hobnobbed with in the "old days." But the views northeastward along the great wilderness of peaks and glaciers spread out below us like a map. On the northern side of the range there was not one cloud; the icy mountains blended into the rolling foothills which in turn melted into the dim blue of the timbered lowlands, that rolled away to the north, growing bluer and bluer until they were lost at the edge of the world. On the humid south side, a sea of clouds was rolling against the main range like surf on a rocky shore. The clouds rose as we watched.*

"*Now as we advanced up the ridge toward the South summit we felt a shortness of breath and Professor Parker's face was noticeably white, but we made fast time and did not suffer in any other way. At a little less than 19,000 feet, we passed the last rock on the ridge and secured our first clear view of the summit. It rose as innocently as a tilted snow-covered tennis-court and as we looked it over we grinned with relief—we knew the peak was ours! . . .*

"*During our ascent of the ridge and the first swell of the final summit the wind had increased, and the southern sky darkened until at the base of the final peak we were facing a snow-laden gale. As the storm increased we had taken careful bearings, and because the snow slope was only moderately steep all we had to do now was to 'keep going uphill' . . .*

"*As I again stepped ahead to take La Voy's place in the lead I realized for the first time that we were fighting a blizzard, for my companions loomed dimly through the clouds of ice-dust, and the bitter wind stabbed through my parka. Five minutes after I began chopping, my hands began to freeze; and until we returned to 18,000 feet I was engaged in a constant struggle to keep the frost from disabling my extremities. La Voy's gloves and mine became coated with ice in the chopping of steps. The storm now became so severe that I was actually afraid to get new dry mittens out of my rucksack, for I knew my hands would be frozen in the process.*

"Professor Parker's barometer (altimeter) at last registered 20,000 feet . . . As I stepped aside (alternating the lead) to let La Voy pass me, I saw from his face he realized the danger of our position, but I knew too that the summit was near and determined to hold on to the last moment.

"As Professor Parker passed me his lips were dark and his face showed white from cold through his parka hood, but he made no sign of distress and I will always remember his dauntless spirit. The last period of our climb is like the memory of an evil dream. La Voy was completely lost in the ice mist, and Professor Parker's frosted form was an indistinct blur above me. I worked savagely to keep my hands warm . . . when a faint hail from above told me my turn had come again to lead.

"When I reached La Voy I had to chop about twenty feet of steps before coming to the end of the rope. Something indistinct showed through the scud as I felt the rope tauten, and a few steps more brought me to a little crack or bergschrund. Up to this time we had been working in a partial lee, but as I topped the small rise made by the crack I was struck by the full fury of the storm. The breath was driven from my body and I held to my axe with stooped shoulders to stand against the gale; I couldn't go ahead. As I brushed the frost from my glasses and squinted upward through the stinging snow I saw a sight that will haunt me to my dying day. The slope above me was no longer steep! That was all I could see. What it meant I will never know for certain—all I can say is that we were close to the top!

"As the blood congealed in my fingers I went back to La Voy. He was getting the end of the gale's whiplash, and when I yelled

that we couldn't stand the wind he agreed that it was suicide to try. With one accord we fell to chopping a seat in the ice in an attempt to shelter ourselves from the storm, but after sitting in a huddled group for an instant we all arose—we were beginning to freeze!

"I turned to Professor Parker and yelled, 'the game's up; we've got to get down!'

"And he answered, 'Can't we go on? I'll chop if I can.' The memory of those words will always send a wave of admiration through my mind, but I had to answer that it was not a question of chopping, and La Voy pointed out our back steps—or the place where our steps ought to be, for immediately below us everything was wiped out by hissing snow.

"Coming down from the final dome was as heartless a piece of work as any of us had ever done. Every foothold I found with my axe alone, for there was no sign of a step left. It took me nearly two hours to lead down that easy slope of one thousand feet! If my reader is a mountaineer he can complete the picture! We reached camp at 7:35 P.M. after as cruel a day as I trust we will ever experience. On the following day we could not climb [and rested in camp at 16,500 feet].

"Throughout the long day we talked food. We had now given up all thought of eating pemmican. In both our 16,000 and 16,615 foot camps we had tried to eat cooked pemmican without success. We were able to choke down a few mouthfuls of this food, but we were at last forced to realize that our stomachs could not handle the amount of fat it contained. The reader will no doubt wonder why we placed such dependence on one food, and my excuse is that we had put it to every proof except altitude. We were now living, as in fact we had been living since leaving our 15,000 foot camp, on tea, sugar, hardtack and raisins. Our chocolate was finished. We had lost ten days' rations in useless pemmican!

"*We were harassed not only by the thought of the food we had lost, but also by the memory of the* useless weight we had carried. *Moreover we were forced to eat more of our hardtack and raisins in an attempt to gain the nourishment we had been deprived of by the uselessness of our pemmican. This complication reduced us to four meager days' rations, which meant that we could only make one more attempt on the summit of Mount McKinley, and that attempt must be made on the following day. The reader will understand with what breathless interest we now studied the weather conditions . . . We decided to leave at 3 A.M.*

"*The following day, strengthened as far as our insipid food would allow . . . we started on our final attack.*

"*The steps made two days before helped us, and in four hours and a half, or by 7:30 A.M., we had reached an altitude of 19,300 feet at the base of the final dome. From this point we could see our steps made on the first attempt leading up to the edge of the final dome, and from this point we also secured our closest photograph of the summit.*

"*But our progress up the main ridge had been a race with a black cloud bank that was rolling up from the Susitna Valley, and as we started toward our final climb, the clouds wrapped us in dense wind-driven sheets of snow. We stood the exposure for an hour; now chopping a few steps aimlessly upward, now stamping backward and forward on a little ledge we found, and when we had fought the blizzard to the limit of our endurance we turned and without a word stumbled downward. I remember only a feeling of weakness and dumb despair; we had burned up and lived off our own tissue until we didn't care much what happened!*

"*We reached camp at 3 P.M. and after some hot tea we felt a wild longing to leave the desolate spot . . . shouldered our light loads and struck off down the glacier. I turned for a last* look . . . above, the roar of the wind came down from the dark clouds that hid the summit."

[Two nights and a day later] "bare mountain-sides greeted our snow-tired eyes, and at 3 A.M. we . . . laid our tired bodies on soft warm earth. We finally summoned enough energy to eat a little, and pitch our tent, and then we slept like dead men until the afternoon. When we awoke there was a warm breeze blowing up through the pass, and with it came the smell of grass and wild flowers. Never can I forget the flood of emotions that swept over me; Professor Parker and La Voy were equally affected by this first 'smell of the lowland,' and we were wet-eyed and chattered like children as we prepared our packs for the last stage of the journey.

"All our thoughts now centered on Arthur Aten. We had told him we would return in fourteen days and now our absence had stretched to twice that number . . . Our concern for Aten now drove us onward.

"When we came out of the pass into the valley of the Clearwater, we encountered a band of fifty caribou, and while we rested they trotted excitably about until by a concerted flank movement they caught our scent, and floated like a great brown carpet across the mountainside. So it went, in turns of long packs and short rests while the sinking sun flooded the western sky with gold. At last the old rock above our camp came into view, and Professor Parker went ahead.

"Then we saw a figure clear cut against the sky. Was it a man or a wild beast? was the thought that flashed through my mind, until a second smaller shape appeared—a dog! And our joyful yells echoed down the valley.

"Aten came to us, tears of happiness running down his cheeks, and we forgot our stiff-necked ancestry and threw our arms around each other in a wild embrace, while over us, under us, and all around us surged an avalanche of woolly dogs."

One wholly unexpected and startling experience yet awaited them while they rested in their base camp at Cache Creek. On the evening of July 6,

"*the sky was a sickly green color. A deep rumbling came from the Alaska Range, with a deep hollow quality that was terrifying. The earth began to heave and roll, and I forgot everything but the desire to stay upright. In front of me a two-hundred-pound boulder turned, broke loose from the earth, and moved several feet. Then came the crash of falling caches, followed by another muffled crash as the front of our hill slid into the creek, and a lake nearby boiled with stirrings from below. Then suddenly everything was still. We stood up dazed and looked about. Our dogs had fled at the beginning of the quake, and we could hear them whimpering and running about in the willows.*

"*While we were restoring order out of chaos, Aten exclaimed, 'Good God! Look at Mount Brooks!'*

"*The whole extent of the mountain wall that formed its western flank was avalanching. The avalanche seemed to stretch along the range for a distance of several miles, like a huge wave, and like a huge wave it seemed to poise for an instant before it plunged downward onto the icefields thousands of feet below. The mountain was about ten miles away, and we waited breathlessly until the terrific thunder of the falling mass began to boom and rumble among the mountains . . . a great white cloud began to rise and obscure the range as it billowed upward, two—three—four thousand feet, until it hung like a huge opaque wall against the main range.*

"*We knew that the cloud was advancing at a rate close to sixty miles an hour and that we did not have much time to spare. But with boulders to hold the bottom and tautened guy-ropes, we made the tent as solid as possible and got inside before the cloud struck us. The tent held fast, but after the 'wullies' passed, the ground was spangled with ice-dust that only a few minutes*

before had formed the icy covering of a peak ten miles away!
    "My strongest impression immediately after the quake was surprise at the elasticity of the earth. One felt as if the earth's crust was a quivering mass of jelly."

Months later they learned that this devastating earthquake was related to the eruption of Mount Katmai on the Alaska Peninsula, 380 miles away.

"MASTERS OF UNDERSTATEMENT"

FROM
Postcards from the Ledge
BY GREG CHILD

CLIMBER-WRITER GREG CHILD FINDS HIMSELF BEMUSED BY THE differences between the "total disclosure" practices of today's adventure expeditioneers and the "less is more" tradition that originated with the nineteenth-century British explorers. Are there any "understaters" left? Is there anyone who recognizes that the effect of a story can be intensified by telling it with restraint and a trace of irony? Child then spots what he regards as a "masterpiece of restraint" in the 1994 *American Alpine Journal*. Child seeks out its author to discover for himself what he senses to be a compelling account not fully explored on the printed page. What he found was a gripping tale of near-success and incredible pain. This selection is from Child's collection of climbing and adventure essays, *Postcards from the Ledge*, pages 130-136.

R ecently I saw a lecture by the septuagenarian hero of Everest, Sir Edmund Hillary. He stood on the stage, smiling over the crowded auditorium like a friendly old bird of prey, and delivered his life-and-times address, a talk he has probably given more times than there are footsteps up Everest. Clicking through fading images of his youthful climbs in the New Zealand Alps, then dismissing Everest in about six slides, Sir Ed came to his Antarctic climbs and travels.

In 1958 he traveled in a convoy of tractors to the South Pole, a 1,000-mile journey over polar ice. Crevasses lurked beneath their cat-tracks all along the route, and the machines kept breaking through snowbridges spanning holes large enough to absorb a house. To illustrate this point, Sir Ed showed a picture of a Ferguson tractor, nose pointed skyward, its rear end eaten by a crevasse. The tractor, driven by Jim Bates, had been chugging along when the snow beneath it gave way, sending the machine sliding backward toward oblivion. It stopped only when its cabin jammed in the mouth of the slot.

"I walked to the edge of the crevasse and peered in," Sir Ed told the oohing and aahing auditorium, "and I saw Jim looking up through the cabin window."

"'Hello, Jim, how are you down there?' I said."

"'I'm okay,' Jim replied, 'but I don't like the view.'"

The tone in which Sir Ed delivered this punch line was a calm, droll, yet risible monotone. The audience laughed on cue, as he knew they would. Taken at face value, the story suggested that he and his pals were in complete control, that dodging crevasses was all in a subzero day's work, and that nearly losing tractor and driver to the frozen depths was a mere trifle.

Yet a waggish inflection in Sir Ed's voice hinted that there was more to this tale than he was divulging. In fact, there was, no doubt, stress, panic, and drama. But Sir Ed was too stately a gent to run around the stage flapping his arms and gushing about the near-death experiences of his Antarctic tractor boys. He let understatement carry the story instead and left his listeners to imagine the scene for themselves.

Understatement—the knack of intensifying the effect of a story by telling it with restraint and a trace of irony—is a time-honored tradition of the adventure raconteur. It is based on the principle of revealing less in order to tell more.

The origins of the understated adventure narrative go back to the nineteenth-century British explorers. Whether they were dying of thirst in a desert, freezing on a polar quest, or being attacked by headhunters, those upper-crust Brits always downplayed the experience in their accounts. Yes, they were proud, sometimes bombastic imperialists, but the likes of Sir Richard Francis Burton, who in the 1800s roamed uncharted Africa searching for the source of the Nile, or Sir Ernest Shackleton, who at the turn of the century led a rowboat full of men across ocean and ice after their ship was crushed in the southern icepack, had a gift for describing outrageous ordeals and awful privations with comparative humility.

After all, this was Victorian England, and when one stood before the fellows of the Royal Geographical Society to deliver an account of one's expedition, comportment was as compulsory as the top hat and tails that they wore. To be carried away by emotions was unseemly. Understatement was a code of behavior.

The writings of climbers of the early twentieth century—such as Eric Shipton, Bill Tilman, and the American Bradford Washburn—embraced the cult of understatement and the ethos of making light of the most harrowing circumstances. Modern incarnations of alpine understatement include "A

Crawl Down the Ogre," Doug Scott's 1977 article from *Mountain,* about an epic on a Karakoram peak. The following exchange occurs between Scott and Chris Bonington, when Bonington rappels down from the 24,000-foot summit to find Scott has wrecked his legs:

"'What ho!' Chris said cheerily."

"'I've broken my right leg and smashed the left ankle,' I said."

"'We'll just work on getting you down,' he replied airily. 'Don't worry, you're a long way from death.'"

But times change. The 1990s are a decade of total disclosure. It is vogue to wear your heart on your sleeve, to let Geraldo and Oprah squeeze every gruesome detail out of your personal tragedy. In this atmosphere, the understater is an endangered species.

But not extinct. Check out the *American Alpine Journal,* the last refuge of the climbing understater. The 1994 *AAJ* contains a masterpiece of restraint; a story titled "Good Neighbor Peak."

This tightly worded two-page story describes a new route up the south spur of Mount Vancouver, a remote 15,979-foot peak in Alaska's St. Elias Range. The climbers are two Northwesterners, Bill Pilling and Carl Diedrich. Bill's tale begins like any other Alaskan climbing account, but the last three paragraphs betray a *Touching-the-Void*-scale saga when Bill plunges into a crevasse during the descent.

"Ten feet into the fall," he writes, "the frontpoints of my right crampon snagged on the wall of the crevasse, forcing the toes of my right foot upward and hyperextending my knee. Ligaments were torn, a major artery ruptured, and muscles ripped. Forty feet down, the rope checked my fall."

With a miserly economy of words, Bill records his extraction from the crevasse and reveals the severity of his injuries: his leg is purple, swollen horribly, and he is in shock. After a bivouac the escape begins: "On May 19 I was just able to walk with an ice axe and north-wall hammer splinted together into a walking stick. Carl masterminded the 7000-foot descent to the Seward Glacier, carrying an extra-heavy load and lowering me down some 25 pitches. I was in severe pain and moaning and groaning."

The final paragraph tells us that they took nineteen hours to descend the rest of the mountain and three days to walk sixteen miles to base camp. Altogether, they were out for eleven days. During their foodless march along the glacier, Carl carried and dragged both packs while Bill guided them by compass through a white-out. The account ends plainly: "We were picked up by plane on the 26th as planned. It was a month before I walked again without crutches."

This tale of two men in deepest shit was a tale worthy of becoming a talk show tearjerker, a *Reader's Digest* potboiler, but instead the author had presented experience without introspection or anguish. But I couldn't resist—something in me wanted to hear the whole tale—so I persuaded the author to meet me at a Seattle tavern, where I planned to loosen his tongue with a few pints.

As Bill Pilling walked into the pub I detected a slight limp, even though a year and a half had passed since the accident. With gray-flecked, close-cropped hair and thick-rimmed glasses, he looks more like a scholar than the archetypal American wilderness mountaineer that he is; his first ascents include sea-to-summit climbs in the Fairweather and St. Elias Ranges and a big route on Devil's Thumb.

I ask how the leg is doing. "Good enough," he tells me, to plan a return to the mountains in 1995. Yet I sense it will be a long time before those grim days on Mount Vancouver are out of his system, as he says, "For a year after the accident I had dreams of crossing sparkling snowfields and suddenly breaking through."

I tell him that his article in the *AAJ* struck me as the epitome of understatement. He smiles, as if pleased. When I ask why he played down the enormity of his and Carl's ordeal, he replies enigmatically, "Understatement presents the truth by not presenting it."

To Bill, what counts in climbing is not what is written or said, but what the climber actually does in the mountains. Serious climbers who read the *AAJ* can read between the lines and understand what he and Carl experienced. He does not regard climbing tales as "entertainment," and he dismisses the climbing and adventure magazines for shamelessly submerging into the swamp of commercialism. For him, the only climbing publication that matters is the *AAJ*, because it is *not* commercially motivated. All the recognition in the world doesn't amount to a hill of beans to this climber.

Bill expresses his beliefs with conviction, yet he is not strident. Then he lets his guard down and describes what happened on Mount Vancouver.

"It started on the sixth day of the climb, during the descent from the summit plateau. We'd given up the final 400 feet because of bad weather, and because of a cough I suspected was edema. Carl was in front, I was following, when I saw a little crack in the snow. The next instant I broke through into a crevasse. My crampon points snagged right away. The leg bent back. There was so much pain that my mind blanked out. I screamed the whole way down."

The force of the fall dragged Carl backward about twenty feet. When Bill stopped he was forty feet down, flipped over and suffocating under a forty-five-pound pack.

"The pain felt like boiling water was pouring into my leg. That was the internal bleeding, the broken popliteal artery emptying a pint of blood into my leg. Calf muscle torn almost in half. Ligaments ripped. My lower leg swollen to twice its normal size."

I wince at the concept of so much pain in such an austere place. Then Bill goes on.

"I knew that staying alive was going to be so much work that for a few minutes I didn't know if I wanted to bother. I just wanted to go to sleep. But I knew my family would be unhappy if I died, and that Carl would be in a jam, so I told myself, 'Okay, I'm gonna live.'"

Bill swung onto an ice block jammed beside him in the crevasse and stood on his good leg while Carl hauled out his pack.

"Hey, Bill, how're doin' down there?" yelled Carl, peering over the edge.

"Not so good. I've injured my leg."

"Hang tight, I'll get ya out," Carl called back.

"Later he told me he was thinking 'we're totally fucked,'" says Bill, his tone turning serious.

"Carl gave me a tension belay and I climbed out using my ice axes and my good foot. I had to chop through a cornice at the top. He dragged me over the lip. I lay on the snow, writhing, screaming, leg cramping, seeing colors, shivering, verging on shock."

While Bill thrashed around in agony Carl set up the tent; then he took Bill's boot off and got him into his sleeping bag. Every move was agony.

The next morning, their seventh day out, they took inventory of their gear, food, fuel, and painkillers—"to see where the edges of our world were." They figured it would take five days to reach base camp. They had four days of food, five Tylenol per day, and a few codeine pills.

Their radio was at base camp, so rescue was impossible. The weather was bad. They were at 12,000 feet. Carl considered descending to base camp alone to get help, but says Bill, "who gets the stove, who gets the tent?" And the glacier was heavily crevassed. No, splitting up was out. "So I tried moving and found I could walk on my heel. We lashed my ice axes together for a walking stick and set off. Some of the way I walked; some of the way Carl towed me along on the rope and I slid through the snow. I kept hitting my leg and nearly blacking out with pain."

At a steep slope Carl began lowering Bill. Then they did "the Joe Simpson number," and Carl lowered Bill over a cornice and into a big crevasse.

"I was hanging free on the rope, spinning around," says Bill. "Carl couldn't hear me and kept lowering me into the gaping maw. Fifteen feet into the hole I found a false floor and stopped. Carl climbed to the edge and looked in, shouting, 'What are you doing down there? You poor fucker!' I didn't like being pitiable."

On the eighth day they struck steep ice. Carl lowered Bill again, from a metal picket he had hammered into the slope.

Then they traversed, which for Bill was painfully awkward. "I kept hitting my leg. The pain made me somersault backward. I had to self-arrest to stop sliding over a cliff."

Later Bill broke through another crevasse. He screamed, utterly terrified of crevasses.

Composure had now totally gone. "Carl was repeating over and over, 'Gotta get off, gotta get off, gotta get off,'" says Bill. "He was going mad from the stress." Since the accident, he'd been doing everything: making camp, cooking, dressing and undressing Bill, getting Bill's boots on and off, breaking trail, lowering him, dragging him, carrying everything.

They reached the upper Seward Glacier at 1:00 A.M. and camped behind a block of ice that had fallen from a serac. Bill finally took some codeine. He hadn't taken any till then since he needed a clear head. They laughed together for the first time that night.

They slept late that ninth day. Carl shouldered a heavy load, while Bill sat on his pack and was dragged along the glacier on the rope. Their food was down to soup and candy bars now, but Carl was "still strong as an animal. Amazing guy. This was his first trip to Alaska. He's from a German family. Quiet guy, a Deadhead, spent a lot of time hanging out in the Guatemalan jungle in native Indian villages that have since been destroyed by the Guatemalan army."

As the day wore on, they weaved about crevasses and waded through deep, wet snow. Bill was moaning, and, he says, Carl finally shouted, "'Will you shut the fuck up?' Then I stopped whining."

Fog rolled in that afternoon, so they navigated by a compass bearing. They reached base camp on the eleventh day, in perfect weather.

"I felt really unhappy on the walk to base camp because I couldn't appreciate the silent beauty of this glacier. I learned what pain can do to a body: it felt like a hole had been punched in my emotional gas tank. When we radioed the bush pilot for a pickup, we didn't tell him what had happened. Didn't want to alarm him."

Bill finishes his tale and sips his beer. I knew the rest of the story: painful weeks of crawling around his apartment to get from the couch to the kitchen, physical therapy, and then a gradual return to walking and work.

The contrast between his account in the *AAJ* and the story he told me was like night and day. Few climbers—myself included—could resist the temptation to bare their soul and turn such a tale into a personal story. When I suggest this, Bill just shrugs, and, with a smile that tells me the discussion has ended, says, "Modesty becomes a gentleman."

FROM

DEBORAH:
A WILDERNESS
NARRATIVE

BY DAVID ROBERTS

THIS STORY OF AN ATTEMPT ON REMOTE, ICY MOUNT DEBORAH IN Alaska's Hayes Range is called by its author "an account of a long, grinding failure [that] cannot compete with a story of triumph and death." Perhaps so. But Roberts' highly regarded, soul-baring narrative of the profound effects on a close friendship of privation, fear, confinement, and, ultimately, loneliness is unequalled in mountaineering literature.

College students Roberts and his frequent climbing partner Don Jensen had already experienced rewarding adventures in the wilds of Alaska when they determined to tackle Deborah in 1964. It wouldn't be a first ascent if they reached the summit—Fred Beckey and Heinrich Harrer had already been there in 1954. But Roberts and Jensen approached the climb as if it were virgin territory, and indeed for all practical purposes it was. The first-ascent party had described the climb as "the most sensational ice climb any of us had ever undertaken," and no one had been near the peak in ten years. Roberts and Jensen picked the untouched opposite side of Deborah for their climb, pledged to devote two months to the mountain and a nearby peak, and air-dropped supplies in two locations to support their expedition.

As the two climbers ground their way across the untracked wilderness toward the distant Deborah, the differences in their personalities began to show despite their history of successful climbs together. The more impatient Roberts would notice and be infuriated by the most innocuous habit or comment of the slower, more deliberate Jensen. When the famously changeable and mostly awful weather of the Alaska mountains pinned them into their small tent for days, Roberts would find himself "working myself into a silent rage over the sound of Don's chewing as he ate a candy bar."

The climbers alternated spurts of challenging, glorious climbing, when weather breaks allowed, with tentbound stretches that strained communications and tolerance for one another. Roberts and Jensen spent forty-two days alone together before agreeing it was time to pull out and turn toward home. At that point a near-fatal crevasse fall reinforced for the two how dependent they were upon each other for survival.

Roberts started writing *Deborah: A Wilderness Narrative* three years after the climb itself, and says the book "seemed to emerge from a process of slow, incremental brooding." It was published in 1970. In addition to coming at the story from this greater distance, Roberts undoubtedly informed the writing with the perspective gained from his experience on a successful but deadly expedition to Alaska's Mount Huntington in 1965, a trip chronicled in his first published book, *The Mountain of My Fear* (1968).

The following selection is slightly abridged from Chapters 7, 8, 11, and 12 of *Deborah: A Wilderness Narrative.*

Within a matter of hours the sky began to cloud up again. We lost the edge of exhilaration and optimism we had begun to feel. By early afternoon the mist had closed in and it had begun to snow. It snowed for forty hours straight. We wondered whether it was impossible to get more than eight consecutive hours' sunshine here; we had had no more than that for the last ten days. We lay lethargically in the tent, constantly aware, with every meal we ate, that our chances of success were shrinking. We would have been willing to stay until we could climb Deborah or know that we couldn't, but our food supply put an absolute limit on our time.

We had reached the col the morning of July 2. That evening, we decided, we would go despite the weather. But at 9:00 P.M., when we got up to leave, the storm was raging. It was 20°—cold enough to numb us, but warm enough so that we felt the painful sting of wetness in the wind, which ripped furiously across the col. There was almost no visibility; particles of ice flayed our faces when we tried to look into the wind. As we stood there, getting bitterly cold, attempting to pack up and put on crampons, it became obvious that we couldn't accomplish anything that night. Shouting to each other over the wind, we called off the effort. I went back inside the tent; Don, eager for exercise, built a snow wall around the tent. The job took hours; he kept yelling to me to inform me of his progress.

After Don came in, we went to sleep for a little while. The snow wall seemed to divert the wind somewhat. But the storm blew just as hard all day on the 3rd. The storm days fouled up our schedule, because we got too much sleep.

During them there was nothing by which to mark time except Don's watch. We played a few more chess games and read a while. Little things began to get on my nerves; I got angry at Don because he sometimes lost interest in our chess games. At first I hid my annoyance, simply saying, "Your move," to remind him when he forgot. Then I lost my patience and told him the game was no fun unless he paid attention. Don apologized but added that the game wasn't much fun for him anyway. We decided not to play any more. This was unfortunate, because it was one of the few things we could do together during the storms. Our conversations either died insipidly or led to arguments. I felt so frustrated by the weather that I had to get angry at something; Don was the nearest object and the only one capable of response.

The only events during the storm days that we could look forward to were meals. When we had finished one, we would set the time for the next, usually five or six hours later. Lunches we could spread out over the hours as we liked; but breakfasts and dinners had to be cooked. When the time arrived, one of us would curl up or sit up to make room for the stove. To compensate for this inconvenience, the other had to get the food and snow for the pots. When the wind was blowing, this could be a grim job: the fine snow shot inside the tent, and a hand scooping or groping outside would grow painfully numb. At last it got to be such a nuisance that we kept the food box inside all the time, even though it meant that it was hard to find room for our legs. The most comfortable position was to keep our legs slightly bent; but every now and then we had to straighten them. The ends of our sleeping bags were usually touching each other. If one of us felt his legs cramped, he began to think the other was taking up more than his share of space. It took the greatest restraint not to complain about it. When we eventually did, it took the form of aggravating politeness: "Do you have any more room down there?" "Could you move over just a little? My feet are against the wall." Gradually, for me at least—and I think for Don too—the nuisances encouraged a subtle defensiveness. I was always sure Don was more comfortable than I, sometimes at the expense of my own comfort. For instance, a few days earlier I had tried to broach a conversation about food—did we have enough, and did it seem enough, day by day? Don, I thought, had discouraged the talk.

Now I began to look forward to meals inordinately; sometimes I daydreamed about food, simply to pass the time until the next meal, and I read sometimes only for the sake of filling up the same time. I tried not to look at the watch too often but couldn't help doing so eight or nine times a day. But Don seemed unaffected by these problems. Therefore I decided my hunger was only psychological, a function of boredom. So I kept quiet. We played a kind of gamesmanship when eating time neared (though I didn't realize until later that it was also gamesmanship for Don). Typically, our conversation would take this form:

"Don . . . it's about five-twenty."

"Hmm . . . what time did we say for dinner?"

"Five-thirty, I think."

"You hungry?"

"Well, not terribly. I could eat, though."

"That's about how I feel."

"Well, what do you think?"

"Just let me finish this short story first."

In the back of both our minds was the necessity of stretching the three meals over a full twenty-four hours. That was what made sleeping so attractive: the time passed fastest then. I remember waking several mornings, when my first thought was not *How is the weather?* but *Is it time for breakfast yet?. . .*

At last the storm exhausted itself. During the day of July 4, small patches of blue appeared among the clouds. We prepared to go that night. We were surprised to realize that it was already the fourth of July—in our predictions we had thought it possible to have reached the summit by then. Instead, we were three thousand feet below it and had not even begun the real climbing. I recalled last year's Fourth of July, when we had sat in warm, clear weather outside a camp on McKinley, giving each other haircuts and already talking about reaching the summit in another week.

That night we set out. To the north, clouds boiled over the Gillam Glacier, the tops of them just below us. It was cold and crisp underfoot, but the dampness of our clothes and the long, logy hours in the tent made us get cold easily. We moved fast to try to warm up but never really succeeded. Our tracks had completely vanished. We had been counting on this; but we were alarmed when, on the far side of the ridge, we could find no trace of the aluminum stakes either. Everything looked the same, and we had only a vague memory of where we had placed the stakes. It would have been pointless to dig for them; it could have taken a week to find one.

We had counted pitches on the way up; now we counted them backwards, trying to hit the right altitude, always fearful, besides, of the hidden crevasses. The new snow seemed dangerous for avalanches as well.

At last I caught sight of a faint mark in the snow. When we approached, we saw with great relief that it was the upper two or three inches of the lowest aluminum stake. It was the only one left showing at all! I belayed from the stake while Don descended to try to find the highest fixed rope, buried somewhere just above the invisible ice cliff. He could only go to what seemed the top of the cliff, then dig in the snow with his axe. Thanks to his good memory, he found the rope fairly quickly. We descended the ice pitches rapidly, though even there the ropes were completely buried. Fortunately, the ice steps were still solid. Some of the ice-screw anchors had melted loose, but the long daggers were still frozen in.

We found the cache in good shape. We packed up some climbing equipment and three of the precious food boxes, good for twelve days. On the way back up we marked the route again and carefully measured the distance to the ridge. . . .

As we descended to the col, the clouds that had been gathering below rose and engulfed us. In a few moments it was snowing again. The pattern was so familiar that we felt little disappointment; instead, as we crawled back into the comparative warmth of the tent, we felt relieved that we had been able to get the vital food boxes up before a new storm hit.

Until now the wind had been predominantly from the north. This time a strong gale from the south swept over the col, drifting the snow in a whole set of different places. Our protective snow wall did no good: it even seemed to help the drift collect. Our tent was the only object that stuck above the flat crest of the col, so the snow drifted easily around it anyway. At 2:30 P.M. the snow had reached a point halfway up the walls of the tent. Don went outside and thoroughly shoveled away the drift. We were alarmed when, only four hours later, the drift had reached the previous level. This time I went out. It took more than an hour to dig out the tent. As the blinding wind, filled with snow, roared across the ridge, I had the feeling of being lost in a desert. I couldn't even glimpse Deborah. All that existed were the tent, the snow, and the shovel.

Four hours later we had to do the job again. We had never seen snow like this, that could drift so quickly. It was making what should have been a rest day hard work. One of us would have to stay awake now, watching the dark snowline slowly rise on the side of the tent.

At 2:30 A.M. we finished the third shoveling job. We were both tired and sleepy. We settled in again to wait. The monotonous roar of the wind was hypnotic, and it was almost dark inside.

Apparently, we both fell asleep. When I awoke, I was aware of the wail of the tent sagging heavily about an inch from my face. It was almost pitch dark inside and strangely quiet. I tried to force myself to be alert, but I felt a strong desire to fall asleep again. Looking up, I could see only a thin strip of light, just along the ridge pole, at the top of the tent.

Instantly I realized what had happened. "Don!" I said, "Wake up!" The air seemed to be stale and stuffy. I tried to sit up, but the wall got in my way. Eeriest of all was the quiet. Don awoke. "We're almost buried," I said urgently. I managed to reach Don's watch. It was 9:30 A.M., seven hours after our last shoveling.

Don offered to get dressed. Only one of us could move at a time. Awkwardly, he pulled on his pants and boots. Then he slid out of his bag. He started pounding the door of the tent back, at first with his hands, then with his shoulder in lunges, like the football lineman he had been in high school. With intense relief we saw that the snow gave behind the door, though it did not fall away.

At last Don had enough room to open the door. Snow fell in at once when he did, but I grabbed the door behind him as he slithered out. He managed to fight his way up and out of the little trench he had formed. I could barely hear him swear as he got out; later he described to me the frightening sight of a smooth, wind-lashed plain of snow, out of which protruded only an orange, horizontal pole. Had the snow covered that last bit, we might never have awakened. . . .

Before he got the tent completely dug out, Don decided that the only thing to do was to move the tent. I agreed with him and got dressed to go out and help him. The wind was blowing bitterly, but we managed to pull the tent loose. We had left everything inside it, to make it simple to move. We climbed out of the hole we had been in, pulled the tent out, and repitched it nearby. . . .

Before the drifting problem we had had trouble with the radio. It had broadcast all right, but we had had difficulty understanding what Fairbanks was saying. We had assumed it was weather interference because the radio had worked so well on the 2nd. Now, in our new site, we tried the radio again. This time neither the broadcasting nor the receiving worked well. We were quite upset; it couldn't be the battery, for we had a spare one that worked no better. We had been so careful of the damned thing: I had always carried it in the safest, softest spot in my pack; we had kept it absolutely dry, and we had warmed the batteries in our sleeping bags each time before trying the radio. Now it looked as if our only link with the outside world was cut off.

We lay in apathetic discouragement. The hunger was as strong as ever. At last we had admitted to each other that we were hungry. But we could not understand why; we thought we had enough calories and vitamins, especially for the storm days, when we usually did little work. Perhaps, Don suggested, we burned a lot of calories simply trying to keep warm in our soggy sleeping bags. Perhaps, I ventured, it was purely psychological but was affecting both of us. Whatever the cause, we definitely felt hungry. For a short while we sensed a friendly cooperation, partly because we had acknowledged the hunger, partly because of the close escape in the tent.

But it wore off. Our chances on Deborah seemed almost vanished. We had, stretching it, at most fourteen days' food left on the col. Our only hope was good weather and a dash for the summit. But we knew the route was too difficult for dashing. Still, there was always a chance. We developed a defensive feeling of pride. As I had written in my diary as early as the fourth, "We like to think others would have quit by now."

I had been having wish-fulfillment dreams. Typically, I would be a guest at a buffet dinner where every imaginable delicacy was heaped in inexhaustible piles on a huge table. There would be scores of other guests, people to talk to, all my home and Harvard friends, surrounding me. Don, though, was never there. But each time, as I started to eat, someone would interrupt me with a question. . . . Finally I would wake up and see the dull crisscross pattern of the orange tent wall above my face and know that nothing had changed, that it was still three hours until dinner. . . .

The weather improved the evening of July 7. We set out at 9:30 P.M. for the last trip back to the cache. In the northwest, the sun was setting in a purple blaze of clouds. As I stopped to take a picture of it, I dropped a mitten. We watched it roll lazily away; three hundred feet below us, it stopped on a snow ledge. Don wanted to go on, but I insisted on retrieving it. Restraining his annoyance, Don climbed down with me, giving me a belay on the last part so that I could reach the mitten. We wasted forty-five minutes on this delay and much-needed energy.

When we got off the ridge to the south, we found a wind-slab crust everywhere. It looked extremely likely to avalanche. But there was no way to avoid it, and no anchor to place to make it safer. If an avalanche had broken off, we couldn't have stayed out of it, and it would have carried us three thousand feet, certainly to our deaths. Moreover, there was a danger that our line of tracks itself might cut off a slab of snow and start an avalanche. Accordingly, we tried to take big steps and avoided long horizontal traverses as much as possible.

Again the marking stakes were buried. Our careful measurements paid off though; we recognized lumps of snow and subtle contours and found the vicinity of the ice cliff. Then, just as before, we saw a few inches of the lowest stake protruding above the snow. This time the stake marked the top of the fixed rope itself.

Once more we found the ice steps covered with snow but still solid. We went briskly down the pitches, counting the hard part of the job done. But as we rounded the last corner above the cache, we saw no sign of it. When we got to where the cache should have been, we could see that an avalanche had covered everything, even the identifying rocks just below it. For all we knew, our supplies had been swept away.

We tried to reorient, measuring our distance down from the lowest ice screw. There was nothing to do but probe with our ice-axe shafts for the cache. For a long time we had no luck. Here and there our probes hit rock, which meant that the snow wasn't deeper than the length of our axes. But it seemed hopeless. At last, as we were about to give up, I tried farther to the right and hit something soft. It was the last food box. Thanks to the piton, the whole cache had held. Relieved, we dug it out and packed it up.

As we climbed the ice cliff for the last time, we pulled out the fixed ropes. We would need them on the route itself, later. The screws came out easily, but the aluminum daggers were frozen in so solidly that we broke them off trying to get them out.

We dashed across the wind-slab slope, glad to be over it for the last time, and descended wearily to the col.

The inevitable storm arrived. We stayed put all the next day and the next night as well, sleeping and thinking about food. The wind was coming from a new direction, the southwest, but we had less of a drifting problem than before. Our hunger seemed to have increased in the last few days, perhaps because we had talked about it. We had devised a system for dividing the meal into equal halves, at first only for the sake of impartiality. The rule was that the one who divided the portion gave up the choice to the other. To even things out, each of us had to divide different items. But at breakfast, for instance, there were only three things that needed splitting; hence one of us had to split two of them. To make this fair, we exchanged jobs each day. This complicated system would have been absurd normally; but we watched each other distrustfully, and when we had to cut a piece of Logan bread or pour cereal out of a bag, we did so with painstaking care. At first we covered the ritual with nonchalance. Don would finish dividing and say, "O.K., take your pick. Which one looks bigger?"

I would answer, "I can't tell, they look about the same."

"Couldn't be much difference either way."

Reaching for the portion I had in my mind carefully weighed and found heavier, I would say, "I'll just take this one; it looks fine." . . .

The weather cleared at noon on the 9th. By that evening, amazingly enough, it was still clear. Eagerly, we got dressed to go; for the first time we would head toward Deborah, not away from it. We put on our canvas-soled overboots for extra warmth and strapped our crampons beneath them.

As Don led away from the tent, I felt a momentary thrill. It was like starting all over; every inch of ground was new again. As we neared Deborah, the flat platform we were on gradually narrowed, becoming first a broad ridge and finally a knife-edge of snow. As the ridge got narrower and we became increasingly aware of the sheer drop on either side, I had the feeling of walking out on a gangplank. For the last six rope-lengths, we belayed each other. It was not difficult going, but it was certainly spectacular. At places, we had only about a foot's width of safe snow: on the left we could see the cracks where avalanches had broken off and plunged to the floor of the West Fork Glacier; on the right, the tricky cornice overhung empty air and the Gillam Glacier. The belayer vaguely intended, if the leader fell off one side, to jump off the other. It might work as a last resort, though we weren't sure how to get back to the ridge after such a thing might happen. Fortunately, the snow was solid, and we had no troubles. All the same, we had to go slowly; inevitably the belayer got very cold as he stood in his steps, managing the rope.

We had crossed the knife-edge and reached the first rock cliff by midnight. As I hammered the first piton into a crack, I was dismayed to see the rock break away and crumble. It was fully as rotten as the stuff we had found on the way up to the ice cliff. By now we had expected this, but it proved discouraging anyway. We stood together, shivering, on the ledge just below the cliff. The first part of it was steeper than vertical. The rock was clearly difficult enough so that we might have to take off our overboots and, in places, our mittens. Somehow, in the cold, we could not bring ourselves to do it. We realized that if we were going to climb at all, it would have to be during the daytime, bad snow conditions or not. It was simply too cold at night; the cold itself made our climbing dangerous.

We left our supplies hanging from the piton I had hammered in, then returned

to camp. We got back only four hours after we had left, feeling slightly annoyed that we hadn't been able to use more of our clear weather. But we
knew we had made the right decision.

We planned to sleep briefly, then try to climb in the daytime. True to the
familiar pattern, the skies clouded, the wind sprang up from the north, and it
began to snow. We were pleased to have, if ever so slightly, started the route.
But in the backs of our minds we already knew we were probably defeated.
Still, we did not admit it to each other: we talked of "pushing" and of getting
a break in the weather. But I wrote in my diary that morning, "At least we
will be able to say we made a good try.". . .

We slept listlessly. The storm continued without change; by now we were
so accustomed to its sound that we might have felt uneasy in the silence of a
clear day. In the middle of the night, while I was asleep, Don heard a different sound, a deeper rumble, and felt the tent shake. In a few moments it was
over. It was so gentle that I didn't wake up, but Don thought it was probably
an earthquake. After all, it had been only four months since the disastrous
quake in Anchorage. Was this another hazard we were going to have to worry
about? Suppose we were climbing on the rock wall when an earthquake hit—
would it shake us off?

The strain we were feeling was subtle and undermining. We felt physically
relaxed most of the time; so much so, that if the weather showed even a hint
of improving, we began to feel guilty for not climbing. But for all our leisure,
we were undergoing an enervating change. The food was most important;
though we couldn't be sure of it, we were losing weight steadily. We thought
about food even when we thought we were thinking about something else. A
dozen times I told myself what fools we had been not to throw in a huge
sack of oatmeal—it would have cost so little. Had the radio worked, we might
conceivably have been able to call our pilot, Warbelow, asking him to drop
some extra food to us on the col. But that was out of the question now. In
our diaries, both of us began unconsciously to transfer the adjectives of enthusiasm—"wonderful," "beautiful," "great"—from the mountain and the scenery to our meals.

We had partly dropped the habit of arguing; we knew that we would get too angry at each other, regardless of the pretext. We tended to withdraw into ourselves, and our dreams began to use up the supply of imagination that we might once have shared in a good talk. My "banquet" dreams became more frequent and more believable; my "bathroom" dreams, more elaborate and fantastic. Don noticed a tendency in his own dreams away from the mountains, toward the familiar past of his home and friends; but always, he noted in his diary, with "some terrible new element—a combination of the nostalgic and the grotesque."

Outwardly, things were calm between us. But I felt the lack of communication poignantly. I had got into the habit of reacting to Don's mannerisms—to the way he cleaned his knife, or held his book, or even breathed. The temptation was to invent rationalizations: I told myself that I got mad at his deliberate way of spooning up his breakfast cereal because it was indicative of his methodicalness, which was indicative of a mental slowness, which was why he disliked and opposed my impatience. The chain of rationalizations almost always resulted, thus, in a defensive feeling; I was becoming, in the stagnation of our situation, both aggressive and paranoid. So I would try to keep from thinking about it; instead I would daydream about the pleasures of warmer, easier living. But all the while I could be working myself into a silent rage over the sound of Don's chewing as he ate a candy bar.

We had a brief flare-up on the 11th when Don decided to clean the stove at the precise time we had set for breakfast. Though I didn't say so, I suspected that Don had planned the cleaning simply to delay breakfast, which, he might think, would make it easier to wait for lunch. He probably felt indignant, in turn, at the fact that I wouldn't even bother with such things as cleaning the stove unless he suggested it. . . .

On the morning of the 12th, I looked out the tent door to see a pale mist, beneath which ominous clouds billowed in the north. But the wind had almost stopped blowing. We decided to give it a try, and would have been off by 4:00 A.M., except that Don discovered that a trickle of water had rolled off the tent wall and into his boots, where it had frozen to ice. We had to spend an extra two and a half hours thawing the ice over the stove. I was furiously impatient and even suggested, though I knew better, that Don should

put on his boots, ice or no ice, so that we could get off. As in all our out-
bursts, dozens of other hostilities reached the surface; but, as in all our recent
arguments, the bitter words had an important function for us as release. They
allowed us to puncture what Don called the "sound barrier"—the hours of
wordless antagonism when our nerves wound tighter and tighter. By the time
Don's boots were dry, we felt friendly again—painfully friendly, like lovers
after a quarrel. Our situation was, of course, something like that of lovers or
married people, except that, instead of a bond of physical love, our bond
was danger and the mountain. But our relationship was importantly different too. Frustratingly, we could not conciliate like lovers; we had to express
our feelings in self-conscious terms that denied the real affection we felt for
each other, in talk of "getting along" and "climbing well together." Thus, after
all our arguments, a sense of embarrassment lingered with us, a desire to "make
up," for which we could not find the right words.

We got moving by 6:30 A.M. At once, it looked as if the shape of the ridge
had changed drastically: We attributed it at first to a confusion of memory,
since our previous steps had been covered by snow. But Don thought of the
possibility that the earthquake in the night had shifted the ridge slightly or
broken off sections of it. A few days later our old steps miraculously reappeared, and we saw them lead right off the present edge of the ridge into
space, rejoining the ridge a few hundred yards farther on. What would an
airplane pilot flying over have made of that line of steps! It was an idle specu-
lation: we had not seen an airplane since the first day of the expedition.

We reached the first rock cliff by 8:15 A.M. Though we had been going less
than two hours, we decided to eat half our lunch there. At least there was a
small platform of snow to sit on, and the cliff gave us some shelter. We each
ate a candy bar, a few bites of dried sausage, and a lemon candy or two. The
air felt warm, although a light, wet snow was falling. We took off our crampons
and overboots so that the rubber soles of our boots could touch the rock.
After lunch I started the first pitch as Don belayed me from our little platform. Rounding a corner to the left, I entered a steep chute of snow. Out of
sight of Don, I soon found myself shoveling piles of snow away to get to the
rock underneath. How absurd it seemed to be burrowing in the snow like a

gopher, on the side of this mountain, which no one but us had ever really seen, much less cared about; to go short on food and patience simply to be allowed to paw through the snow in search of rock! But I was excited and happy; at last we were back to real climbing. With a foot on either side of the chute, gradually I could work my way up it. After a long time I was standing directly above Don, at the top of the little overhang that protected him. I shouted, and we flipped the rope out of the chute so that it ran straight up to me. I moved up for sixty feet more, hammering an almost worthless piton for "safety" at the hardest point and two more pitons for an anchor above. Don came up; he had been getting cold, standing there—now it was my turn to shiver. The rock above was even more rotten than what I had found on my lead—almost like frozen, chunky mud. But Don slowly and carefully worked his way up the last thirty feet. At last he was at the top of the cliff. He found an anchor and brought me up. We complimented each other for two and a half hours of work that had got us up a paltry 140 feet of the mountain. Still, it was as hard as anything we had done on McKinley the year before, and our fingers were still tingling with the feel of the rock. We ate the rest of our lunches. It was almost noon; we kept thinking about the knife-edged snow ridge softening in the warmth of the day. We had to go back. We stretched a single fixed rope all the way down to the snow platform. As we hurried back over the sharp ridge, we saw to the south, all along the massive wall of Deborah, little avalanches shooting downward, one or two each minute. By the time we got back to the tent we were tired and famished. Dinner was a bland "glop" of powdered egg and rice—but it had become our favorite because it was the largest.

The weather seemed to be getting steadily nicer. By now we knew better than to count on anything lasting, but we looked forward to whatever chance of working on the route we might get. There was still a faint hope for the summit. One rope-length for a day's work—it didn't seem much at all. But in good weather we would go much farther. Still, we had been tired when we got back, very tired. Perhaps it was all those days of inactivity; perhaps it was the lack of food. One thing was clear: we would soon need a new camp site on the ridge. It took too long to retrace all the old steps each day, and the farther we got, the more there would be to retrace. So far, however, we had hardly found a place where we could sit down, much less pitch a tent.

But we went to bed happy and slept soundly that night.

At 1:30 A.M. Don woke up to go outside. The mist had cleared completely; the crisp, startling blue of clear sky surrounded us. In the northeast the sun was just rising. It looked like the best day we had had in weeks. Don photographed the sunrise, trying to shake off the aura of a nightmare he had been having. In it someone, some close friend of his, had died or been in a violent accident; it was all fuzzy, elusive, disturbing.

We got started by 5:00 A.M. This time we attached our crampons directly to our boots, leaving off the overboots. The snow was in fine shape, frozen and crunchy. We moved together, without belaying, and nearly flew across the knife-edge. Exuberantly, we knew that we were working together as well as was possible. The fixed rope helped immensely on the rock cliff. In only an hour and a half we were as high as we had got the day before. Quickly we climbed three pitches of steep and somewhat treacherous snow, warily staying below the cornices. Twice we hammered the aluminum daggers that Don had made into the soft slope for protection; even they seemed not to hold very well, but they gave us some psychological security. To belay, we would stamp down a little pocket of snow, thrust the axe as far in as possible, then feed the rope around the head of the axe. Often we could sit down, which made the belaying much more comfortable. Still, there were no level spots, or even gentle ones, and certainly no places to pitch a tent. . . .

At the top of the third pitch I reached an isolated block of rock. Curiously, it was far more solid than any of the rock below; the piton rang in the cold air as I hammered it in. On the next pitch, while Don climbed out of sight above, I felt wonderfully secure. Again the route grew difficult. Don had to scramble up patches of rock and snow until he reached a prong of rock, on the north side of which he swung around. As he did so, he was dizzily hanging over the vertical drop above the Gillam, which we had never been able to look down before on account of the cornices. After this, he climbed over a tower that was topped with a froth of snow, like whipped cream, through which he dug a kind of canal. On the tower's far side he had to drop into a deep gap spanned by unstable snow, from which he clambered onto rock. I yelled that he was out of rope. He went a little farther and hammered in a mediocre piton. This was exciting stuff! Nothing on McKinley had been so spectacular. Don's pitch had been the hardest yet, and it was still early in the day.

I climbed above, finishing the short, tricky cliff and forging up a smooth snow slope to a big rock. When Don came up, we stopped for lunch. For once we didn't mind the meager amount of food. We were full of optimism and spoke almost breathlessly about our progress. It looked easier above. As we ate, we craned our necks back to try to gauge how high we were on the mountain. We knew the steepest part of the ridge was yet to come, a frightening, nearly vertical 600-foot wall of rotten black rock. And above that was a thousand feet of steep ridge, festooned with the unbelievable curls, loops, and blossoms of ice we had seen from our tent. But it looked easier just above us, and our hearts leaped. For once we hurried through the lunch instead of trying to make it last. The sun was warm enough for comfort. This was what we had come to Alaska for!

Above, we had to go carefully, for the snow thinned in places to a bare skin over the ice beneath. Long sections of steps had to be chopped with the ice axe. The higher we got, the more empty space seemed to yawn below us. So far there had not been a single spot on the whole route where, had we fallen, we should have had a chance of stopping before the floor of the glacier, three thousand feet below. But to prevent that was what the rope, the pitons, the ice daggers, and all our skill were for.

Alternating leads, we climbed three quick pitches. At the top of a fourth, I reached rock again. We were tempted to go on but knew it was time to return; it was past noon, and the snow was melting. On the way down we were forced to go slowly, often having to improve the sun-weakened steps. We hadn't carried enough rope with us to string over all the route, but we placed fixed lines on the lowest five pitches.

As we neared the bottom we grew extremely tired. The snow on the knife-edge was very dangerous; much as we wanted to hurry over it, we had to go slowly, with gingerly steps. At last, at 5:00 P.M., we stumbled back to the tent, near exhaustion after twelve hours of hard climbing. Our throats were parched for lack of water, but we were tremendously happy. True, we had found no reasonable camp site yet, but the weather seemed to be getting even better; indeed, this was the first entirely clear day of the whole expedition. And we had done nine new pitches in a single day!

In the tent, we were overjoyed to find our sleeping bags drier than they had been in weeks. Lying down seemed a luxury again. We talked about whether or not we could keep up such a pace and whether such a pace might make the summit possible. Despite our enthusiasm, we really knew how unlikely success was. We had only about a week's food left on the col; with any safety margin at all, we could afford to climb, at most, three or four more days. We needed at least a day's food to get down to base camp, and a storm might besiege us at any time. But it wasn't in our hearts to waste such good weather.

From the best picture we had had, months before, we had hypothesized a camp site on a short, apparently level gap of ridge at 10,400 feet. We guessed that we had got almost that high already. Perhaps in the next effort we could reach the gap. If a camp could be placed there, then the following day we might move the tent, or Don's tiny bivouac tent, up there. And then, the day after, dash for the summit? But a "dash" over the hardest two thousand feet of the climb was out of the question. Still, with some unforeseeable break . . .

But the effort was hard on us. We fell asleep right after dinner, knowing that all too soon it would be morning again and that we would *have* to get an early start for the sake of good snow conditions. We almost wished for a storm, simply to rest. Best of all, though, with the good weather there had been hardly an ill word between us. That night we slept as sound as rocks—sounder, in fact, than the rocks on Deborah.

July 14 dawned even clearer than the day before. We got started at 6:10 A.M., impatient but still tired from the day before. When we reached the first cliff we decided, for the sake of speed, not to take off our crampons. This worked surprisingly well: the spikes held on the crumbly, wet rock at least as well as the rubber soles of our boots had. Above the cliff, we found the snow in splendid shape; in places our steps were like plaster casts. The cold nights, without precipitation, had allowed the snow to freeze hard. Don suggested that we climb continuously, a rope-length apart, without belaying. It was pretty difficult climbing not to belay, but we tried it. It worked perfectly; our instinctive understanding of each other, even when we were out of sight, paid off now. We were making remarkable speed. I felt a piercing joy—Don was the only one in the world with whom I could have climbed like this; in fact, there were few people anywhere who could do this as capably as we. If we did no more climbing the whole trip, we could remember this day with gratitude.

In the astonishingly short time of one hour and forty minutes from the tent, we had reached our previous high point. I led on. The little rock cliff was no trouble, but the snow above it suddenly changed in character from the solid stuff below. On a very steep, wrinkled slope, I traversed to the left. I had to climb almost on the cornice, and I prayed that it would hold. A powdery surface layer of snow brushed off at the touch; underneath, instead of firm snow or hard ice, I found a pocked and brittle lacework of ice, like a hideous honeycomb, that seemed limitlessly deep. The whole ridge was made more out of air than anything else. I placed an ice screw that seemed to offer a little security; when Don followed later, though, he picked it out of the slope with his fingers. The farther I got above Don, the more I felt as if I were walking on a kind of cloud that might suddenly collapse. Finally I put in a dagger, which, though it wouldn't have held a long fall, seemed better than nothing. If not the most difficult, this was the scariest pitch yet. When Don came up, we were suddenly isolated from the rock, with nothing but the honeycomb holding us to the mountain. But there was rock about forty feet above us; with infinite caution, Don led beyond me. For a little while the slope got very steep. I think I was holding my breath as I belayed. At last Don reached the rock where, after some searching, he could hammer in a piton. At once I felt better. Don found an ample, but narrow and downsloping, ledge from which to belay me. There we had half a lunch, a few minutes after 10:00 A.M. We were less than a pitch below the sharp plume that hid the level gap—our hoped-for camp site.

After we had eaten, I led on. Don had a fairly good rock piton for anchor. As I climbed the plume, it got steeper and steeper and smaller and smaller. Halfway up, I stuck my axe through the cornice into blank air on the right side. A few minutes later I did the same on the left side. This was appalling; the plume was corniced on both sides! I tried to hug the middle and ended up virtually crawling up it, almost like shinnying up a pole of horrible, empty, airy ice. Still, I was dying with curiosity to see over the top: A long stake I tried to place for protection went in and out like a toothpick in butter. Clumsily, but carefully, I inched to the top, then looked over.

In a glance that lasted a few moments, the expedition seemed to end. I stood silent, not quite able to believe what I saw. Both Don and I had thought about the little gap often, and it must have taken on in our imaginations something of the quality of a heavenly oasis. Perhaps we had even begun to think of it as a reward in itself, like the summit, an isle of safety in the middle of a vertical sea of danger. At best it would be a broad, flat platform, as big as a tennis court; if things went badly, perhaps only the size of a large mattress. But we could pitch a tent on a mattress.

What I saw, instead, was a serpentine wisp of snow, like the curl of a ribbon on edge. This time I could see the double cornice—the whole of the little bridge was undercut incredibly on both sides, so that it looked as if a strong wind might topple it. It was only ten feet below me and thirty feet long. The last ten feet of it were impossibly thin. Next, I saw the face of the mountain beyond. The crumbly brown rock towered, flat and crackless, a few degrees less than vertical. A thin, splotchy coating of ice overlay most of the rock. Where the rock overhung, great icicles grew. A few vertical columns of plastered snow, like frozen snakes, stuck to the coating of ice. And above, blocking out half the sky, was the terrible black cliff, the six-hundred-foot wall that we had once blithely, back in Cambridge, allowed three days to climb. At its upper rim, nearly a thousand feet above me, hovered monstrous chunks of ice, like aimed cannons at the top of a castle wall. As I watched, one broke off, fell most of the six hundred feet without touching anything, then smashed violently on a ledge to my left and bounced out of sight down the precipice.

I had never seen a mountain sight so numbing, so haunted with impossibility and danger. Don yelled up, "How does it look?" I almost laughed. I shouted back something inane, like "Not so good." Then I told Don that I would climb just over the plume to try to find a spot from which to bring him up. I pivoted over the top and started kicking steps down the back side of the little tower. Bizarrely, I felt safer at once, because the rope passed over the plume; if I fell, it might conceivably act like a piton. My feet broke through the steps, and I half slid down to the bridge, I walked out a few feet on it, just short of the point where it grew impossibly narrow. Then I tried to stand in the middle of the little gap, as I delicately stamped the snow down under my feet. It gave and gave; soon I was nearly shoulder deep in it. I could imagine myself imbedded in the ice-cream cone as the whole thing toppled off its pedestal. There was something desperately ludicrous about it. My axe could find nothing that gave any resistance. But it was safer than being on the other side of the plume when Don came up.

I yelled, "Off belay!" Don had trouble hearing me and yelled back something indistinguishable. His voice seemed infinitely remote. At last we communicated by rope tuggings; then, as I gradually pulled in the rope, I could tell he was slowly climbing.

Don's head poked over the top of the plume. "Don't come any farther," I said. "It isn't safe." Don stood there, as transfixed as I had been; perhaps more so, for he saw me sitting like a pilot in a plunging airplane, in the cockpit of the bridge of snow. As he looked, the inevitable decision, without a word, passed between us. We could go no farther; Deborah's summit was unattainable. With another twenty days' food and some kind of equipment not yet invented and brazen skill, perhaps we could have gone on. With a handful of days left, a few puny fixed ropes, a few pitons made for rock that stayed in one piece, and some vestiges of sanity, we had to give up.

Of course we were sad. But as we turned to head down, we were almost lighthearted, too. The mountain had been fair to us; it had unequivocally said *Stop,* instead of leading us seductively on and on, forcing the decision of failure on us, so that we might suspect and blame only our weaknesses. The mountain had allowed us pride. . . .

⋆   ⋆   ⋆

We woke comfortably late the next morning and dawdled over breakfast. When we looked out, we saw that a beautiful day had dawned on the Gillam Glacier; it was virtually windless, and a strong sun warmed us and dried the tent and sleeping bags. We were packed up by 12:30 P.M. As soon as we had put on our snowshoes and hefted our packs, we looked over all the glacier, which was blindingly white with sun. The snow looked perfectly smooth, but here and there we could see pale, diagonal hollows that suggested crevasses. Don led off. Only fifty yards from camp he stuck his foot into a crevasse. He yelled back to me, "Give me a belay." I put my axe in the snow and knelt, as he gingerly stepped across. Then we were both moving again.

Perhaps sixty yards farther, Don suddenly plunged into a crevasse and stuck, shoulder-deep. Immediately I thrust my axe into the snow and took in slack. Then I waited for Don to crawl out. I was not terribly worried: I had belayed a few crevasse plunges like this on McKinley, and Don had belayed me in one near the summit of our 11,780-foot peak. I even grew slightly impatient as Don seemed to thrash around helplessly.

But then he yelled, "I'm choking!" I was alarmed; I imagined the pack strap or the edge of the crevasse cutting off Don's wind.

I waited a few more seconds, but it was obvious Don couldn't get out. Perhaps rashly, I took off my pack, untied myself from the rope, tied the rope to my axe, and thrust it in again for an anchor. It didn't seem solid enough, so I quickly took our spare ice axe from my pack and tied the rope to that too. Then I walked quickly up to Don. I could not really see the crevasse at all, but I could see that Don was wedged pretty deeply in it. His hands clawed at the snow, but he said that his snowshoed feet were dangling loose. He was not actually choking, but he was in a cramped situation. The heavy pack seemed to be the obvious problem: its straps were constricting his arms and upper body. I reached out and carefully tried to pull the pack up and back. Don screamed, "Stop! It's the only thing holding me up!" His voice was full of panic. My pulling had made him slip a little farther into the crevasse so that all but his head was below the surface. Don sensed, as his feet waved in space, that the crevasse was huge. He warned me that I was too close to the edge. I backed up about five feet. For a moment I stood there, unable to do anything.

Suddenly Don plunged into the hole. The anchoring axes ripped loose and were dragged across the snow as Don fell within the crevasse. I grabbed the rope, but it was wet and whipped violently through my hands. I heard Don's yell, sharp and loud at first, trail away and fade into the frightening depth. All at once the rope stopped. About sixty feet of it had disappeared into the hole.

An excruciating silence surrounded me. With a kind of dread, I yelled Don's name. There was no answer. I yelled twice more, waiting in the silence, and then I heard a weak, thin shout: "I . . . I'm alive." The words were a great relief, but a scare as well: how badly was he hurt? I yelled, "Are you all right?" After another pause, his voice trickled back: "I think my right thumb is broken! I hit my head and it's bleeding and my right leg is hurt!"

I ran back to reanchor the rope. From my pack I got our snow shovel, dug a pit in the wet snow, tied one of the axes to the rope again, and buried the axe in the pit, stamping down the snow on top. Perhaps in a little while the snow would freeze, making the anchor solid. Through my mind flashed all kinds of thoughts, reminders of warnings before the expedition about the dangers of going with only two men, fears of never getting Don out, the thought of his blood spilling, a curse for the worthless radio.

When the snow had broken around him, Don's first impressions had been of bouncing against ice and of breaking through ice: he was not aware of screaming. He expected to feel the jerk of the rope at any moment, but it had not come. Then suddenly he had been falling fast, free; he somehow supposed that I was falling with him, and he instinctively anticipated death. Once before, in an ice-gully avalanche in New Hampshire, Don had fallen eight hundred feet—but he had been knocked out that time and had remembered only the beginning. This time he stayed conscious throughout the terrible fall.

At last there was a crushing stop, followed by piles of ice and snow falling on top of him in the darkness. Then it was still. The fear of being buried was foremost. He fought his way loose from the ice; some of the blocks were heavy, but he was able to move them and scramble out. He realized that, miraculously, he had landed on his back, wedged between two walls of ice, with the heavy pack under him to break his fall. His hands hurt, his leg felt sharply painful, and his head rang from a blow. He became aware of my shouting, the sound weak and distant, and yelled an answer upwards. As his eyes grew used to the dark, he could see where he was.

The inside of the crevasse was like a huge cavern. The only light came from the small hole, appallingly far above, and from a dim seam in the ceiling that ran in a straight line through the hole: the continuation of the thinly covered crevasse. The bottom was narrow, and the walls pressed in on him, but about thirty feet above him the space bulged to the incredible width of a large room. Above that, the walls narrowed again, arching over him like a gothic roof. Don began to glimpse huge chunks of ice, like the ones that had fallen and shattered with him on the way down, stuck to the ceiling like wasps' nests.

When I had got the anchor buried, I returned to the edge of the crevasse and shouted again to Don. With great presence of mind, he realized how possible it would be for me to fall in too, and shouted, "Dave! Be careful! Don't come near!"

His voice was so urgent that I immediately backed up to a distance of twenty feet from the little hole. But it was much harder to hear each other now. We were shouting at the tops of our lungs; had there been any wind, we could never have heard each other.

Fortunately, Don's bleeding had stopped. Struggling loose from the debris had reassured him that he wasn't seriously hurt; in fact, the thumb seemed only badly sprained instead of broken. Industriously, he got his crampons loose from his pack and put them on in place of his snowshoes. He still had his axe; chopping steps and wedging upward between the walls, he got to a place where he could see better. At once, he discovered the real nature of the subsurface glacier: corridors and chambers, at all depths, shot off in every direction. The whole thing was hideously hollow. At first Don had thought he might climb out; now he realized it would be impossible. But he had a furious desire to get out. He had put on his mittens but was getting cold anyway. Around him, on all sides, water was dripping and trickling: it was impossible to stay dry. . . .

We both realized Don's pack had to come out first. We could not afford to leave it there. He could not wear it on the way out; I would have to haul it up. It would not be safe at all for Don to untie from the rope; I might never be able to feed the end back down to him. But it was the only rope we had. I racked my brain for an alternative. There was some nylon cord in the repair kit, which was in my pack. I ran back and got it out—it was not nearly long enough. Then I remembered our slings and stirrups, nylon loops and ladders we had brought for the technical climbing on Deborah. I dug them out, untied all the knots, found some spare boot laces, and finally tied everything together in one long strand. When it was done, I threw the end into the hole and lowered it. Don yelled that it reached.

He had taken his pack apart. Now he tied his sleeping bag onto the end of the line, and I pulled it up. But as the load neared the top, the line cut into the bad snow at the edge of the crevasse. Just below the top, the load caught under the edge. I jerked and flipped the line, to no avail. Don saw the problem but could think of no solution.

It became obvious that I had somehow to knock loose the rotten snow from the edge. But I didn't dare get near the hole, and Don would be standing beneath all the debris I might knock down. I could imagine only one way to do it.

I checked the rope's buried anchor again: it seemed solidly frozen in. I pulled and jerked on the rope, but it wouldn't budge. With one of the nylon slings I had left, I tied a loop around my waist, then tied a sliding knot to the main rope with it. When I pulled, the knot would hold tight; but when I let up, the knot would slide. Don, meanwhile, had found a relatively shielded place to hide. I inched toward the hole, carrying an axe and the shovel. If the edge broke, I should fall in only a few feet: then I might be able to scramble back out. I got no closer than I had to, but finally I was within two feet of the dangerous edge. The rope was stretched tight behind me. I squatted and reached out with my axe. The stuff broke loose easily and plunged noisily into the crevasse. As the hole enlarged, I slipped the knot tighter and waddled back a foot or so. Some of the snow had to be dug loose; some fell at the blow of the axe. It was awkward work but it was profitable. At last I had dug back to bare, hard ice. The rope would not cut into it. Leaning over, I peered into the awesome cavern. At first I could see only darkness; moments later, I glimpsed the faint outline of Don below, much more distant than I had even imagined.

I retreated from the hole and resumed hauling Don's sleeping bag; this time it came easily. One by one, I fished out the pieces of Don's load. With each, we grew more optimistic. The pack frame itself was hardest—its sharp corners caught on the ice; but at last I shook it loose and jerked it out.

Now there was only Don himself to get out. There was no possibility of hauling him. He would have to use the sliding knots on stirrups, which would support his feet, to climb the rope itself. I dangled some stirrups into the hole for him. He yelled when he got them. Then I retreated to the anchor, added my weight to the solidity of the frozen snow, and waited.

Slowly, painfully, Don ascended the rope. Everything was wet, so he had to tie an extra, tighter loop in the knots. This made them tend to jam, and he had to claw them loose several times. He was shivering now, soaking wet, and tired; in addition, his sprained fingers made handling the knots clumsy and painful. But from time to time he shouted his progress, and each time his voice sounded stronger and closer. . . .

At last Don's head poked out of the hole. I cheered him on, but I was struck by the shaky tiredness I could see in his face. He crawled out of the hole and sat gasping on the edge. I came up to him, full of a strong impulse of loyalty, and put my arm around his shoulders, telling him he had done a good job. We ate a few bites of lunch—the minute the emergency was over, it seemed, our appetites returned.

We decided simply to backtrack the hundred yards to the camp site and pitch the tent again. I gathered the pieces of Don's pack and loaded it up. We staggered back to the fresh platform, very careful as we recrossed the first crevasse. In the subtle light of afternoon, looking back eastward toward the mountains we had been trying to reach, we could see faint blue line after faint blue line intersecting our potential path, parallel marks indicating a dozen farther crevasses like the one Don had fallen into.

I repitched the tent while Don rested. Inside, we looked at his injuries. He was badly bruised, especially on the right thigh; his head was bruised, with a small cut showing through blood-matted hair; half his fingers were sprained, the thumb badly. But it was a blessing there was no injury worse than that. Gradually, Don warmed up as his clothes dried out. We cooked dinner and ate, with a sense of peace and reprieve. Afterward, as it grew dark, we each took a sleeping pill; within a few minutes we were deep in slumber.

❯   ❯   ❯

In the morning, when we awoke, we found the watch had stopped. We set it arbitrarily and started breakfast. Don was stiff and sore from his injuries, but the sleep had done him good. In my mind there was no question now but that we had to hike out to civilization. I was pretty sure Don would agree; even so, I was reluctant to bring up the matter. Finally I did. To my surprise, Don was set on going on.

We argued for more than an hour. I listed all the reasons for my decision. First, we were down to five days' food (perhaps seven, if we stretched it), and the hike out, we thought, would take about five days. If we went two days farther toward the airdrop basin, we might be forced into a seven-day hike out on only three days' food. And we had encountered only one of the obviously many hideous crevasses on this glacier. I argued that we had been very lucky to get Don out alive and that nothing would keep us from falling into another crevasse. The snow conditions, as we had found, were no better at night. Moreover, part of the hike-out route, to the south down the Susitna Glacier and River, was off our maps, since we hadn't anticipated it: who could say what obstacles we might run into? The radio was worthless, we were constantly hungry, and Don was bruised all over.

Despite all this, Don was determined to push on. He did not want it to be his accident and his injuries that stopped us. We could hike up the glacier on its southern edge, he argued, where the crevasses would be small enough to be safe. He was as eager as ever to climb the peaks ahead, and he was willing to go without food a few days, if need be, so long as we could definitely ascertain whether or not our airdrop was buried.

Don's stand put me in a strange situation. I was torn between admiration for and fear of him: at once he seemed terribly brave and terribly foolish. I remembered his insistence, early on the expedition, on going ahead the night he had been feeling dizzy and losing his balance. I wondered now if he wasn't expressing the same kind of overreaction: if so, it seemed a kind of madness. My inner voice, with its calculation of risks and complications, seemed to be speaking pure common sense, while Don's was fanatic. At the same time I could not help wondering if I was quitting on him, panicking prematurely. After all, before the accident I had been the one who was anxious for the trip to be over. I remembered the urge toward the safe south I had felt that dreary night, a week before, hauling loads across the West Fork Glacier. Perhaps I was "crumping"; perhaps I was not good enough for Don.

Our argument was uncommonly restrained, and for once we seemed objective and frank, as if a residue of respect for each other had settled out of the recent accident. I admitted that I was afraid of the glacier; Don granted that he didn't look forward to getting back to California. But I was possessed with a feeling that Don had gone slightly crazy, or that the crevasse fall had done something to him. I even fancied that the blow on his head had distorted his reason. At one point, as we were arguing about food, he said, "I'd almost rather starve here than go out now." Each symptom of fanaticism, like this one, made me look at Don in a more curious light. Yet I could not bear to attack his motives, as I had before, so soon after his ordeal in the crevasse. Don interpreted my reluctance to force the decision as a cowardice about taking the responsibility for it, which it may partly have been; all the same, I wanted the decision to be both of ours, so that we could not recriminate later.

Gradually, with heavy heart, Don saw that I was firmly set on hiking out. He could not be as staunchly in favor of going ahead—he naturally recoiled at the thought of falling into another crevasse. At last he gave in and agreed with me. I tried not to gloat over the relief I felt, and Don concealed his bitterness. We got dressed and packed up the camp in a marvelous spirit of reconciliation, a spell of grace over our life of antagonism. When we were ready to leave, we called it 2:00 P.M. With wistful glances back at the mountains we would never reach, still holding out their clean arms to us under a warm sun, we started trudging back up the pass to the Susitna Glacier. . . .

At the top of the pass, we stopped to rest and gathered our last look to the north. Our marks on the snow eloquently told our story. Below us was a flat rectangular patch, where the tent had been pitched. From it a short track led straight east until it abruptly ended in a little hole. There were stray marks around the hole, but the snow lay untouched beyond.

We turned and headed down the Susitna Glacier. For a mile I led, here and there picking out our tracks from two days before, where they still showed under an inch of new snow. At the corner, the tracks turned west toward the pass we had crossed from the West Fork Glacier. We continued straight down the Susitna. We had only about a thousand feet of altitude still to drop before we would reach the névé line, below which all the snow had melted, leaving bare ice, with the crevasses exposed and safe. But there were still quite a few crevasses to cross. I led for another half mile, through what seemed to be the worst of it. I was nervous about the hidden cracks and stuck my foot through a couple of snow bridges. However, the crevasses didn't look as big as the ones on the Gillam. Still, Don belayed me over any stretch that looked dubious, and we carefully skirted the obvious crevasses. It was slow going. As we seemed to enter a comparatively safe plateau, Don took the lead. The snow was soft and wet, scalloped with confusing sun cups. At about 4:00 P.M. he stopped to ponder an apparent pair of crevasses that nearly touched end to end. At the other end of the rope, I kept the line almost taut between us. Don started to cross what he thought was a little island of snow between the crevasses. Suddenly the island collapsed. I saw Don disappear and plunged the axe in immediately, crouching for the shock. A little pull came but it didn't budge me. I supposed Don had fallen about five feet and waited for him to scramble out. But there was no sign of him. Without getting up, I yelled, "Are you all right?" After a moment I heard his weak, distant voice, tinged with something like hysteria: "I've stopped bleeding, I think!"

With a gust of weariness and fear, I thought, "Not again!" I shouted, "How far in are you?"

Don's voice came back, "Thirty feet . . . there's blood all over in here. I've got to get out of here quick!" He sounded beaten, as if a vital string in him had broken.

When the island had collapsed, he had fallen slightly backward into the crevasse. The nylon rope had stretched and cut back into the near bank, allowing Don to fall as far as thirty feet. But this time the walls were only three or four feet apart. He had smashed his face brutally on a shelf of ice halfway down.

Outside, I imagined having to go through all the emergency procedure of evacuation again and hurriedly got out our hauling line. But Don, seeing that he could climb out by himself, took off his pack and snowshoes and put on his crampons. This was difficult, wedged as he was between the close walls. The crevasse, at a lower altitude than the one on the Gillam, was dripping and running with water. With the energy of panic, Don forced his way up and out of the crevasse, chimneying between the icy walls. As soon as I realized what he was doing, I pulled the rope in to try to aid him. Within a few minutes he had reached the surface.

I hurried over to help him. He looked scared and exhausted, on the verge of tears. His lower face was covered with blood; I winced at the sight of it. He was in an agony of pain. I made him sit down and got some codeine from the medical kit, which he managed to swallow. We got the bleeding mostly stopped. It was fairly warm, but Don was shivering uncontrollably in his soaked clothes. I helped him take off his shirt and put my own jacket on him. Don apologized for getting blood on it; I told him not to be silly, but I felt suddenly defenseless before his pathetic concern.

I changed to crampons; as Don gave me a nominal belay with one hand, I slithered down into the crevasse to get his pack. The ice on which Don had cut his face was actually sharp to the touch. The wetness was oppressive, and as I got farther into the crevasse, the darkness added to a sense of claustrophobia. I found Don's pack at a place where the walls were not much wider than my body, and tied the rope to it. Don's blood was visible on both walls of the crevasse; I felt an irrational fear of getting it on me. There was a rank smell of stale air and blood in the gloomy, wet cavern. I felt the same panicky urge to get out that Don must have felt. Quickly I chimneyed back to the top of the crevasse; then I sat, wedged feet and back, between the walls of ice, and tried to pull the pack up in one piece. It took an extreme effort, but at last I got the thing up and shoved it over the edge onto the snow. Then I crawled out of the hole myself.

Don was obviously in some kind of shock. The bleeding had essentially stopped, but his chin was a raw, ragged mess, and he could hardly talk. Despite the down jacket, he was shivering miserably. We decided to set up camp on the spot. I pitched the tent and got the stove and food out of our packs. Still, it was 7:30 P.M. before we were settled inside. The codeine had helped numb the pain, but Don was still in great suffering. He had sprained all the fingers on his left hand, so that he could barely use them. The knuckles were scraped raw. At last he could get into his sleeping bag and begin to warm up. I started the stove, which helped warm the tent, and melted snow for hot water with which to bathe Don's cuts. I daubed at the lacerations on his face with some wet cotton, but it only made the blood flow again. With pained words, Don complained of cuts inside his mouth too. I tried to look, and saw gouges on the inside of his lower cheek. Blood was getting all over the tent.

Just when we seemed to be getting the cuts clean, Don closed his mouth, and we heard a soft hissing sound as he breathed. "What's that?" he asked. With alarm, I saw bubbles of air in the blood on his chin. Checking his mouth, I found that the cut went all the way through the cheek below the lip. We both felt nauseated, but I tried to cheer him up by telling him that such things happened all the time. Finally Don settled into his bag, where he could hold a piece of cotton to his mouth to clot the blood. I cooked dinner. When it was ready, Don tried to eat, at my insistence. He found that by cutting the food into small pieces he could feed them into his mouth, chew them delicately, and swallow. This was crucial, even if it took him an hour and a half to finish a meal.

He took another pill for the pain. He seemed numb and sluggish, but he was taking the injury bravely. We divided a sleeping pill between us, Don taking three quarters and I a quarter. We would have taken more, but we felt we had to get up in the early morning, just on the chance that it might be colder and safer then. Ideally, we would have rested there the next day. But we did not have enough food and would have to push on. We had only made about two miles that day, much less than we had planned. We were down to four days' food, and we still had a mile of this treacherous glacier to cross and forty-five miles of wilderness beyond.

As I lay awake in the gathering dark, I heard Don's breathing grow deep and even. It was a blessing that he was able to sleep. Since the moment he had apologized for getting blood on my jacket, I had felt an inarticulate impulse of love for him. He had been so courageous; already he was showing signs of taking this accident, too, in stride. But I could not sleep. I imagined the morning's trek through the last of the crevasses. They were fiendish; there was no way to find them or tell how big they were: the axe could not probe far enough. And there was no way to belay across them safely. Even now, as we camped between a pair of them, I sensed the others crowding around our tent, like wolves in the night, waiting for us. . . .

FROM

THE LAND
THAT SLEPT LATE

BY ROBERT L. WOOD

DESPITE ITS MODEST HEIGHT, 7,965 FEET, WASHINGTON'S MOUNT Olympus was shrouded in mystery for many years until the late nineteenth century. Easily seen from Seattle and other Puget Sound cities on clear days, the prominent peaks of the Olympic Mountains formed what long seemed to be just a thin row of mountains. Not until several major expeditions beat their way through the rugged wilderness of the Olympic Peninsula was it known that this "range" was instead a huge, squarish jumble of peaks arranged protectively around Mount Olympus, the crown jewel.

An expedition sponsored by the *Seattle Press* crossed through the mountains in 1889–90 but made no attempt to explore Olympus itself. A larger expedition in 1890 led by Army Lt. Joseph P. O'Neil included some "civilians" from the Oregon Alpine Club, and a contingent was detailed to conquer the peak. The party planted a copper box on what they thought was the summit of Mount Olympus, but wasn't. In 1899, Jack McGlone broke off from a USGS survey team and, overnight, made a solo ascent of the East Peak of this multi-summited mountain. Things got serious in 1907 when a newly formed climbing club, The Mountaineers of Seattle, announced the peak as the target of their summer outing.

Hearing the news, Professor Herschel Parker and Belmore Browne of the Explorers Club in New York hastily made up a small party to grab off the peak before the large and ponderous Mountaineers group could get there. The Mountaineers, in advance of their outing, had arranged for a trail to be carved out of the wilderness to ease their passage. Nipping up this handy trail ahead of The Mountaineers, Parker and Browne proclaimed their first-ascent success on Olympus, only to learn later that they were on the wrong summit!

This selection on the Parker-Browne ascent is taken from Chapter 7 of *The Land That Slept Late* by Robert L. Wood, pages 126-130.

As a note of historical interest, this was the same Parker and Browne who worked to disprove Dr. Frederick Cook's 1906 claim of success on Alaska's Mount McKinley, and who in 1912 came within a few hundred feet of achieving the first ascent of McKinley themselves.

Olympus slept again, but not for long. Fate intervened shortly afterward in the form of two mountaineering clubs that focused on the peak simultaneously. One of them, The Mountaineers, was new; the other, the Explorers Club of New York, was an old, established institution.

The formation of The Mountaineers came about as follows. On November 6, 1906, a volunteer committee, consisting of members of the Mazamas Club of Portland, Oregon, and other climbers living in Seattle, Washington, met to welcome Dr. Frederick Cook's party when it returned from an alleged successful ascent of Mount McKinley. This committee drafted a resolution calling for the appointment of another committee that would confer with the Mazamas and the Sierra Club in order to ascertain what form of local club could be established "to best promote the interests of the parent clubs." This committee was further directed to arrange for a meeting, at an early date, of Seattle residents interested in mountain climbing, to discuss the formation of a club.

Additional meetings were held later, and bylaws drafted and adopted, officers elected, and a permanent organization effected. The new club held its first meeting on January 18, 1907. The Mountaineers had 151 charter members, and it held its first local outing when members and their guests visited the West Point Lighthouse in Seattle.

The members decided to schedule an annual "summer outing," complete with packers and cooks, that would last from two to three weeks. The purpose of the outing was to climb, on each trip, one of the major peaks in Washington State. The Olympic Mountains were chosen to be the site of the first outing—to be held in the summer of 1907—with the object in view of making the initial ascent of Mount Olympus. This would be the first large party attempting to "conquer" Olympus, but the outing's organizers never suspected they would spark a race between two competing teams of alpinists. Thus was the stage set for a tug of war between The Mountaineers of Seattle and the Explorers Club of New York.

Several Explorers Club members recognized a rare opportunity when they were apprised of The Mountaineers' plan to make the first ascent of Mount Olympus during the club's 1907 outing. A trio from the New York club quickly organized an expedition and rushed in to climb Olympus before The Mountaineers did. The elite climbers composing this little party were Herschel C. Parker, Professor of Physics at Columbia University; Walter G. Clark, an engineer; and Belmore H. Browne, artist and writer. The men were members of the American Geographical Society, Washington, D.C., and of the Explorers Club, New York. Parker had also been one of the founders, in 1902, of the American Alpine Club, and he had made numerous ascents—of Mount Blanc and the Matterhorn in the Alps; of Shasta, Hood, and Rainier in the western United States; and six first ascents in the Canadian Rockies. He and Browne had been with Dr. Frederick Cook's expedition to Mount McKinley in 1906, and in 1912 they would attempt to climb that mountain again. The guides hired for the Olympic adventure were Will E. Humes, who lived on the lower Elwha, and DeWitt C. Sisson (according to Clark), or Henry Sisson (according to Browne) of Port Angeles.

The party left Port Angeles on July 9—Parker's fortieth birthday—with supplies for five weeks, and "full equipment for cutting a trail." Sisson was in charge of the pack train; Humes joined the party later—either at Geyser Valley (according to Browne) or Elwha Basin (according to Clark). Because trail builders sent out by Port Angeles citizens at the instance of The Mountaineers had preceded them, the Explorers Club party contributed to them the amount of money they had expected to spend on the work, "and joined forces with them to complete the trail." When it was finished, the party made its base camp in the Elwha Basin, close to the snow line.

Everyone then struck out for Olympus, by first climbing the Elwha Snowfinger. The snow was broken by crevasses and dotted with deep potholes, so they roped together for safety. They climbed to the gap in the divide between the Elwha and the Queets, and gave to it the name Dodwell-Rixon Pass because they believed, erroneously, that the surveyors were "the first to cross over the pass for scientific geographical work."

The men then descended into Queets Basin to below the snow line and established Cloud Camp. At times they had glimpses of the Pacific Ocean beyond the cloud cover lying over the land. After reconnoitering, they decided

they were camping too far from Olympus, and therefore moved to a new lo-
cation they called Camp Olympus. This site was close to the terminus of an
icefield that they named Humes Glacier for one of their guides. Here they
prepared for the climb. They would take with them canned pemmican, a nour-
ishing mixture of beef, beef suet, sugar, and currants, melted and run together.
They also had crackers, chocolate, raisins, and tea.

The men began the climb at an early hour the next morning, and they were
soon plodding up Humes Glacier, which was broken by numerous fissures
that they were compelled to jump. They ascended at a fair speed toward a
pass at the glacier's head, and upon reaching it they could look down onto
another, larger glacier that appeared to be the source of the Hoh River, whereas
the Humes Glacier lay at the head of the Queets. The men named the gap
Explorers Pass for their club, but shortly afterward The Mountaineers renamed
it Blizzard Pass for a very good reason.

The glacier to the north and below the climbers "stretched in one vast snow-
field up to the foot of Mount Olympus," and from the pass the men had their
first truly unobstructed view of the mountain. They descended steep snow
slopes to the glacier. Although it was badly broken by crevasses, they were
able to work their way forward by jumping the crevasses at narrow places.
Because they were roped together, they did not hesitate to jump. "The day
was hot, and the bright sun on the snow burned through the previously acquired coat of tan, and produced blisters." After a long walk up the glacier,
they reached a "ridge of exposed rock at the base of the final peak." Here
they stopped to brew tea over an alcohol lamp, and the hot liquid "instilled
new life for the final climb."

After a bit of steep snow and loose boulders, the men reached the top of the
mountain, and the scene, they thought, surpassed the view from most peaks
having a much greater altitude. Glaciers descended from every side, and hundreds of snow-clad peaks and snowfields were in view, reaching down into the
forest-filled ravines. The men were so impressed, in fact, that they thought the
Olympics were "surely entitled to be christened the Alps of America."

The climbers stood atop Middle Peak, second highest pinnacle of Mount
Olympus. The date was Wednesday, July 17, 1907. They searched the summit rocks, but could find no trace of anyone having preceded them. They

marked their visit by building a cairn, and they left an American flag, and a note with the date. They had scaled the peak in advance of The Mountaineers and won the race. Or so they thought. But their elation was tempered by a little doubt, and they expressed the thought that a pinnacle west of them might be slightly higher than the point upon which they stood. But they had run out of time; they could not go over and climb it.

The men from the Explorers Club gave names to a number of natural features in the Mount Olympus area—to nineteen of them, in fact—but only two of the names (Humes Glacier and Dodwell-Rixon Pass) have endured to this day and are still used. Most of the names they gave were replaced, later, by names suggested by other people. The climbers also prepared a map of the Mount Olympus district.

Once they had climbed the mountain, the men didn't linger. They descended to Queets Basin, broke camp, and quickly packed out over the trail. When they reached Port Angeles, they announced to the world that Mount Olympus had been climbed, and they saw to it that accounts of the "first ascent" were hastily published. The stories appeared in the newspapers just as The Mountaineers were beginning their own outing to Olympus, and therein lies a tale.

"LIVING DANGEROUSLY"

FROM
This Game of Ghosts
BY JOE SIMPSON

IS HE ACCIDENT-PRONE? CURSED? OVERREACHING? BLESSED WITH overwhelming luck? However one looks at it, British climber and writer Joe Simpson has used up far more than the normal allotment of second chances in the mountains. Readers in more than a dozen countries and in as many different languages thrilled to the gripping story of his fall, injuries, and agonizing self-rescue on Siula Grande in the Andes, recounted in his best-selling book *Touching the Void*. Sometimes Simpson has been successful in achieving the challenging summits or the sharp end of the new route, and sometimes he has failed, but adventure always accompanies him. And, even as he muses in his writings about why he has survived where fellow climbers have not, Simpson always compels the reader to ponder the effects of the choices we all make in our lives, both on and off the mountains.

In this selection, Simpson has gone to the Alps for a ten-day course to be an apprentice guide, in order to "look good" when later trying a stringent series of tests set by the Association of British Mountain Guides to qualify as a guide. Simpson already had a fine Alpine record behind him, but the guiding experience itself, involving as it did clients of wildly varying ability, quickly proved in his mind to be unacceptably dangerous.

So Joe found a kindred spirit and the two set off to attempt the Bonatti Pillar on the Petit Dru, one of the Alps' more exciting climbs. And the two nearly made it up the route, but true to Joe's usual luck, things went horribly, crazily wrong . . .

This selection is taken from Chapter 11 of *This Game of Ghosts* by Joe Simpson, pages 159-174.

teamed up with a Lancashire climber called Ian Whitaker, also known as Bolton because of his almost unintelligible accent. He was a short cheerful young man, with a mop of dark curly hair and a ready smile. After a while, I found I could generally understand him if we were talking face to face, but once we were more than fifty feet apart I couldn't make out a word he was saying.

We had decided to attempt the Bonatti Pillar on the Petit Dru. Walter Bonatti had made the first ascent of this stunning route alone over five days in 1955. I had read Bonatti's account of it in his autobiography, *On the Heights,* in which he speaks of his fear and exhilaration while fighting his way up the 2,000-foot golden granite pillar. It was a legendary mountaineering story, perhaps one of the greatest exploits in the history of Alpinism to rank alongside the first ascents of the north faces of the Eiger and the Grandes Jorasses.

Ian and I decided to climb the south face of the Dru to reach a gap on the Flammes de Pierre, the rock of flames, a jagged, crenellated rock ridge abutting the summit spire. It derived its name from the way in which it blazed with fiery explosions as lightning blasted up its shattered crest. Our plan was to abseil from the gap down 800 feet to the foot of the pillar. At the bottom of the abseil we had to rush across a shadowed and icy couloir. Bonatti first pioneered this approach in a successful attempt to avoid having to climb up the couloir which had a reputation for ferocious avalanches and almost constant rockfalls.

Only after completing two irreversible abseils did we realise that we had taken the wrong line. We should have been descending a series of loose walls and broken chimneys. Instead we found ourselves swinging in space due to the rock walls leaning out from vertical and overhanging. I was alarmed to find myself dangling twelve feet away from the rock. As I neared the ends of the ropes I cursed myself for being so stupid as to forget to tie a knot in them. One rope was longer than the other and I could see that it almost reached a small ledge. There was no alternative but to try to swing into the wall and look for some sort of anchor point.

Burdened by a heavy rucksack, I found the attempt to get up some momentum exhausting. I threw my axe back and forth on its lanyard and, curling my feet around the slack rope, eventually managed to swing close enough to the rock to grab at hollow flake. With no other anchor points, I reluctantly threaded a tape sling behind the flake and gingerly lowered my weight on to it. There was a creaking sound and a hollow thumping echo, but it held. Ian quickly joined me and then abseiled down into the bed of the couloir. It was a frightening place. The huge sunlit pillar of the south-west face towered above us, beckoning us away from the high-walled cold shadows of the couloir.

As Ian crossed the hard black water ice that was crusted with granular snow I heard the first stomach-clenching sounds of rockfall. I screamed a warning to Ian, who was over halfway across the ice, and saw him hunch his shoulders. He began a frantic sideways scuttle towards the shelter of a rock buttress. There was no cover on my side. I decided to keep looking up. If I could see the rocks coming I might be able to avoid them. The air around me exploded with black spinning shrapnel. There was a peculiar knock-knock-knocking sound as well as the familiar thrum and whistle. The stones were all flying far above me, perhaps as much as forty feet up, as they ricocheted from side to side off the walls of the couloir and the pillar. The hollow flake where we had hung half an hour earlier was strafed by a handful of rocks. It was over almost as soon as it had started. Silence crept back, broken only by the muted echoes of the stones cracking their way down the thousands of feet of couloir below me. The air had a charged electric feel to it and there was a smell like cordite and sulphur from the explosive impact of the rocks.

"Are you okay?" Ian shouted.

"What?" I yelled back, not understanding him.

He waved me across and I teetered out across the black marble shine of the ice, tip-tapping my axes and crampons as fast as I could without falling off and feeling the tingle and spinal shudder of hairs rising on the nape of my neck. I shivered with the anticipation of being caught in the open by more enfiladed stone bombardments.

As Ian led up the first pitch on the pillar I spotted a butterfly lying motionless on a patch of snow by my feet. I leant down and touched it gently with my finger. It was dead. This was a harsh and hostile place for a creature of such delicate and exquisite beauty to meet its end. It must have been caught in an upwelling turmoil of heated valley air and spun helplessly up into these high cold regions to die at the first touch of night's black chill. Bonatti wrote of finding a dying butterfly at the start of his solo ascent of the pillar with a poignancy and philosophy typical of his approach to the mountains.

> *I saw a poor butterfly, lured there by the day's warmth, which*
> *fell helplessly to the snow a few feet away from me with a last*

beat of its wings. Poor living thing, what bad luck you had to find yourself about to die in this cruel world, whose existence you never suspected! In that last beat of its wings I saw before me an almost human drama. Who knows, I thought to myself, with what terror your little eyes watched the last rays of the setting sun, the unexpected metamorphoses of their colors? Who knows with what horror your senses warned you of the fateful bite of the frost, the atrocious certainty of death and, like me, the same infinite regrets? Wretched insect, my brother in misfortune in this place of death, how much I feel for you and with you. Your tragedy is mine too; what I am searching for in the conquest of the Dru is similar to the intoxication which brought you here. The Dru which I was about to challenge was nothing else for me than that last ray of sunlight which only a few minutes ago you saw set for ever. If tomorrow I do not succeed in mastering myself, I will share your end.

I could see how climbing was never a death wish for him, more an intoxication with life. I felt ashamed that my butterfly had not moved me at all. Later, high on the intimidatingly Red Walls, I was showered with tiny silver insects—silver fish they were called—which came tumbling down the golden red granite and across my bare arms, making me pull back in fear. Where had they come from? Two Alpine choughs cawed and spun acrobatically in the thermals below us, feeding swiftly on the sudden falling bounty. Those that they missed fell softly into the icy couloir below to die of cold.

We climbed fast in glorious sunshine on the slabs, corners and cracks of the rough granite. The Dru is a truly extraordinary pinnacle of rock. It sports an icy north face, one of the six classic Alpine north faces, a phenomenal 3,000-foot west face of slabs, smooth vertical walls and overhangs, the spectacular south-west pillar, and a superb modern mixed route up the north-east couloir between the Petit Dru and the Grand. Few mountains offer such a variety of magnificent lines on them or appear so hypnotically arresting. Crusted with a winter lacework of ice and gilded in the golden pink of Alpen-glow, it is one of the most beautiful sights in the Alps.

The Bonatti Pillar rises in a series of steep columns, presenting fissures, overhangs and, here and there, flat-topped pedestal ledges. Slightly off vertical at first, it gradually rears up towards the massive capping overhangs just below the summit. We quickly dispensed with the lower slabs and climbed the diedre known as the Lizard. Bonatti had given it the name because, from the valley, it appears as if a huge green lizard is trying to slither up the Dru. There was little shade from the hot sun on the exposed pillar. By late afternoon we had reached 300 feet on intimidatingly blank granite wall, split by a thin hairline crack that bristled with old pitons. We were tempted to bivouac on a series of terraces and ledges at the top of the walls, but confidence got the better of us and we decided to climb past the huge roofs looming above us and then settle down, knowing that the main difficulties were all below. We knew, if we got that far and the weather began to break up, we could escape from the pillar via an airy traverse to the right towards the spot where the Flammes de Pierre abutted the summit ridge of the mountain.

As darkness began to close around us we found ourselves in forbidding territory, with no sign of any ledges. The dark shadow of the roofs blackened the early night sky above and tendrils of mist began swirling up from the depths, thousands of feet below. I stood uncomfortably on a small stance, dancing from foot to foot, trying to revive the circulation and peering anxiously into the dark shadows of the corner above me. I heard the distant jangle of hardware and shouted up to Ian, asking if he had found a ledge. The reply was as unintelligible as they had been all day. The rope moved up uncertainly and then dribbled slackly down again, a sure sign that the climbing was hard. After what seemed an age I felt the rope tighten and there was a muffled call from above.

The rope tugged three times and I began to follow stiffly, clutching in the darkness at unseen holds and shouting anxiously for Ian to keep a tight hold. After about forty feet the vertical corner seemed to pinch out into a smooth wall. Groping my fingers to the left, they slipped into a reassuringly sharp-edged crack, and with help from Ian I struggled up twenty feet until I saw the dark shadows of his legs hanging in space above me. He was sitting on a narrow ledge about four feet wide and six feet long.

"Well, this looks all right," I said.

"Yeah. We can just about lie foot to head with a squeeze."

"It's an odd looking ledge, don't you think?" I asked when I had got my torch out and glanced around me. "It looks detached to me?"

"It is," Ian said. "It's a sort of pedestal on top of that last corner. We used the crack on its left side."

I shone my torch down between my legs which dangled over the edge. Our ropes hung down in two huge coils that swung gently in the slight breeze. I could just make out the top of the corner appearing through gray spectral streamers of mist. The ropes vanished into the dark chasm below. I clipped myself to a handrail rope that Ian had fixed above the ledge. It had been knotted into an old ring peg and stretched across to the far end of the ledge where he had tied it to a small flake of protruding granite.

"Do you think it's safe?"

"Sure, solid as rock," Ian said confidently. "I gave it a good few kicks and it didn't move."

"Suppose you're right." I could see nothing suspicious about the pedestal. We had climbed past dozens of them all day.

An hour later, as Ian was preparing to do something smelly off his end of the ledge and I was zipped into my bivouac bag, there was a sickening lurch accompanied by the grinding sound of splintered granite plunging into the abyss. I had my arms outside the bivy bag as I fell and flailed blindly, trying to grab something. The drop must have taken only a fraction of a second but it seemed to last forever.

I heard a cry of alarm and pain above the roar as tons of granite went thundering down the pillar, echoed and then died to silence. The rope brushed my arms and I clamped them down by my sides as the falling stopped and I bounced on the springy stretch of the rope. The handrail had held and for a confused moment I desperately tried to remember whether I had clipped myself on to it. I was momentarily disorientated. Where was Ian? I remembered that sudden yelp during the fall. Had he gone with it?

"By 'eck!" I heard close by in gruff Lancastrian. I struggled to get out of the tightly squeezed bag. Close beside me Ian's head lolled down on to his shoulder and his torch reflected a sodium yellow light off the surrounding rock walls. There was blood on his neck.

"Are you okay?" I asked

"Banged me 'ead." He groaned and then lifted his head.

"It's okay," I said, inspecting his matted hair. "It's only a small hole."

It took a while to realize that the whole pedestal had detached itself and dropped straight off the mountain face. There was a good deal of swearing before we became aware of the seriousness of our position. We hung side by side on the tightly stretched V of the handrail rope. Shining our torches down, we were horrified to see the remains of our two ropes, cut to pieces by the falling rocks. All our equipment, including our boots, had gone with the ledge.

We looked at each other and giggled nervously. *No ropes. Two thousand feet up and no ropes!*

The handrail shifted suddenly, causing us both to squeak with fright, hearts hammering at the thought of falling again. I turned and shone my torch on it. There was something wrong. I twisted round, grabbed the rope and hauled myself up towards the ring peg. The rope shifted again and the ring peg moved. I lowered myself gingerly back on to the rope.

"Oh my God," I whispered.

"What?"

"The peg's knackered. It's coming out."

"Christ! Where's the gear, let's put something in."

"It's gone. The hardware, boots, everything. We can't do anything."

Ian was silent. I looked at the flake above him to which the handrail had been tied off. Tiny pebbles trickled from the sheared off base of the flake where it had been attached to the pedestal. We were suspended against a smooth vertical rockwall. There were no handholds or small foot ledges and both attachment points could break at any moment. If either one went we would be hurled into the abyss.

"I think we had better stay very, very still."

"Aye," Ian muttered, taking a last swig from his water bottle and then flicking it into space. The tinny clangs of the metal bottle rang up from below in decreasing volume. There was nothing we could do.

To attempt to climb up or down would be suicidal. Fifty feet above us loomed the huge roofs and 200 feet below lay some ledges. We couldn't hope to climb down in our socks and there was too little rope to make an abseil. There was no chance of making the fragile safety line that was keeping us alive more secure.

We hung there for twelve interminable hours. It was an endless night. Fear rose and fell between bouts of hysterical giggling and a hollow dread. It was not long before we were suffering agonizing cramps from where our sit harnesses cut deeply into our thighs and waists. Inevitably one of us would shift position to try and relieve the painful pressure, the handrail would shudder, and for a heart-stopping second we would be convinced that we were about to fall into the abyss. We hardly spoke. The tension would not allow it. We silently endured the waiting, unable even to comfort one another. There was no escape from it. If you were standing at the very edge of a high cliff and a friend gave a slight push, then immediately pulled you back, you would gasp with shock and your heart would beat furiously and it would not be very funny. Each time our handrail rope moved we felt this exquisite shock of fear. The wire tightrope transmitted the faintest of movements and our fevered imagination did the rest—Was the peg pulling out? Did I hear the flake move? Like condemned men shackled and strapped, awaiting the drop of the trap, we waited for someone, anyone, to help us.

          ⋟   ⋟   ⋟

The helicopter hovered directly in front of us, its rotors edging nearer, we flinching back in fear. The pilot gave us a thumbs-up signal, and then the machine rose effortlessly above our lonely stance. We watched in awe as the tiny figure of a man was lowered on a silk thin wire from the belly of the helicopter. Four more figures followed. They had deposited the rescue team on to the summit two hundred feet above the roofs.

Yves, the last to descend, spun crazily on the silver thread of wire. Looking down, he saw his four colleagues crouched over the Troyes winch. The black wrought iron Madonna on the summit of the Petit Dru flashed past his eyes as the wire lowered him towards the four guides. Glancing up at the red belly of the helicopter he noted how thin the wire now looked. Swaged wire cable six millimeters in diameter appears as thin as a silver silk thread when a man hangs from the end of sixty feet of it. Yves pushed from his mind any thought of it snapping. He knew the breaking strain of the wire, he knew it wouldn't snap, but even so it was best not to look at it. The prospect of a 3,500-foot freefall was hard to ignore.

Earlier Yves had relayed instructions from the helicopter as it had hovered mid-way between the guides and the climbers. The two men had looked pathetically small, hanging on the vast walls of the pillar. The pilot had inched the helicopter in towards them until Yves could plainly see the expressions on their taut, hopeful faces. Their arms were outstretched, and one climber was pointing to his feet. Both had socks but no boots, and two short lengths of rope hung below them. He could see where the white core had been exposed by the shearing force of the rockfall. A fresh rock scar began above the climbers and extended to just below where they hung on what appeared to be a fragile handrail.

"I've tried to get them off directly," the pilot had said through Yves' headphones. "It's not possible. Those roofs are too close." He pointed to the huge stepped overhangs fifty feet above where the climbers were hanging, and 250 feet below the summit. "The winch is the only way." He turned and grinned at Yves, who glanced back at the roofs.

The fall line of the pillar drew Yves' eyes inexorably downwards. The shadowed couloir lay far below, a thin dirty ribbon of ice snaking between dark rock walls. He spotted the chimneys on the far side where they had worked all morning.

During the night the climbers stranded under the roofs had alerted the rescue team by flashing their torches at the Charpoura Hut, but when the first helicopter had gone to investigate they discovered two more severely injured climbers three-quarters of the way down the abseil descent from the Flammes de Pierre. After a long complicated rescue the two victims, a guide and his client, had been hauled to safety. One was paralyzed from the neck down, the other from the waist. They had inadvertently pulled rocks down on to themselves while retrieving their abseil ropes. It had been lucky for them that the two hanging climbers had needed help. In the dark depths of the couloir, with no line of sight to any huts or places of possible help, the two paralyzed climbers would never have been able to attract the attention of the rescue teams.

"At least these two are not badly hurt," Yves said as he dragged his eyes away from the hypnotic sweeping fall of the pillar.

"Still wouldn't like to go down over those overhangs." The pilot smiled at some private joke as he eased the aircraft into a climbing turn towards the summit and Yves prepared to be lowered down to his colleagues who had already been ferried to the summit.

"Bon chance," the winchman said, clapping him on the shoulder.

I hope it doesn't come to that, Yves thought as he was lowered beneath the helicopter. Once safely on the summit he moved quickly over to his four colleagues by the Troyes winch. They had sited the winch with care so that the wire would run directly over the overhangs down towards the two stranded climbers. The leader of the team issued a few curt orders, nothing that Yves hadn't already gone over endlessly in his mind. The winch was hand operated. Two guides on each side of it controlled the speed of descent and kept in touch with him by radio. When the time came they would winch him back by turning two handles on each side of the machine.

"Okay. I'm ready. Let's do it," Yves said standing up and leaning back on the thin wire.

His team mates smiled encouragingly and began to release the brake on the cable. Yves stepped back and over the edge of the first wall below the summit. The cable ground noisily on the edge of the rock, setting Yves' nerves on edge.

Ignore it. It is nothing. It will not snap. I have done this many times. It will not snap. He repeated it like a mantra, vocalizing it in his head, pushing the fearful thoughts away, convincing himself. While he descended short broken walls, the true verticality of the pillar did not affect him. He kept glancing up the wire cable and then down below him in an attempt to visualize his position on the face as he had seen it from the helicopter.

"Slow down, slow down." He spoke calmly into his radio. The reply crackled back in his headset. "Okay. Approaching the roofs now, wall is steepening, keep it steady." He found that relaying the instructions back with a non-stop commentary on the geography helped him to forget his fear.

The last smooth vertical slab of granite led him to the lip of the roofs.

"Stop." He said it too sharply. The abrupt view of the abyss between his legs had made his heart lurch into a sickeningly fast rhythm.

"What's the problem?"

"Uh . . . wait . . . one minute, please?" He tried to gather his thoughts and his courage. The thin streak of the couloir was visible nearly 2,000 feet below. Nothing obstructed his view. *Oh my Lord! And to think I had ambitions to climb this route!* He squeezed his eyes shut and took several deep controlled breaths. Gradually he calmed.

"Okay," he said quietly, "let's go again."

The wire crunched horrifically as he stepped down into space and hung suspended. It grated over the sharp granite edge of the roof. The sound, like that of fingernails scratching a blackboard, shivered down his spine. He glanced down. Two pale faces stared up at him. "I see them," he said into his mike with a note of triumph. "Bang on line. Keep going slowly."

He watched the two men carefully. There was blood on the neck of the one without a helmet. The other appeared to be uninjured and was watching him with catlike intensity. Yves saw the ring peg with the handrail attached to it but could not make out the other anchor. He was being lowered in line with the peg. He had already decided to clip it when there was an abrupt shout of alarm.

The uninjured man was shouting something in French but he couldn't understand the words because his companion was yelling in English. Something had alarmed the men but he did not understand what it could be. He continued to descend towards the peg. As his left boot came towards it the uninjured man hit out at his foot.

"Touche pas, touche pas, il est très mal. *MAL!*" he screamed.

Yves glanced at him and realised that only utter terror could produce an expression of such intense ferocity.

"Stop," he ordered into his radio. The man visibly relaxed, his shoulders slumping.

"It is about to break. There is no strength," the hanging climber said in poor French, pointing to the ring peg. Yves glanced at the far end of the rope. The shattered flake with the rope looped over it appeared to be on the point of detaching.

"Merde!" he swore in a whisper. So that was why they were so scared. He felt a momentary pang of guilt at the thought of how long they had left these two men hanging on such a fragile thread. The rescue of the paralyzed climbers below had taken nearly seven hours. It was at midnight, twelve hours ago, that the alert had come through. He shook his head.

"Qui est blessé?" he asked, despite knowing which was the injured man.

The climber nearest him answered in appalling French. "Er . . . he is, but it's nothing really. Not bad, just a little hole." He reverted to English. "It's nothing to worry about. I'd take me first since I'm nearest, and heaviest."

The talkative man grinned hopefully at Yves who couldn't help but laugh, admiring the humor under such stress.

"No, I must take your injured friend first. It is a rule."

He shrugged eloquently.

"Ah . . . A rule, you say, eh? Can't break it then? Just this once . . . "

"No." Yves laughed as he swung across the wall towards the injured man. "I would lose my job if the injury turns out to be serious." He bent forward to examine the man's head. It was a superficial scalp wound.

"You see. It's nothing. Come on, let's toss a coin for it."

Yves ignored the noisy one as he prepared to clip the injured man to his harness. He spoke quickly into his radio.

"Okay, okay. Listen." The uninjured man was no longer joking and Yves turned towards him. "This rope is no good, right? So when you suddenly lift his weight off it I will drop down. I don't know if it will hold the sudden jerk. Do you understand?"

"Yes. I understand. I will move him slowly, softly. Do not worry."

"That's easy for you to say." The man muttered and looked pointedly down at the couloir far below. Two choughs wheeled across the thermals, spinning extravagant acrobatics through the air.

"Up. Slow and smooth." Yves spoke into his radio and at once he heard the harsh crunch of the cable on the overhang, his harness tightened and he began to rise. He braced his feet against the granite and swung the climber awkwardly round so that he hung below his back.

"Return soon," he called, glancing at the remaining climber. "Do not worry, my friend. I will come back soon." Judging by the man's expression, he clearly wasn't convinced. His eyes were wide in a white face, staring fixedly at the ring peg. Alone now, he looked vulnerable and scared, like a child.

Once over the roofs Yves swung across the granite wall above to a small ledge perched above the awesome fall of the west face. He lowered the injured climber on to the ledge and clipped him to two pitons.

"What is your name?" he asked, looking into the man's eyes and checking to see that he was stable. Suddenly he appeared very tired, drained by the abrupt release from his hanging.

"Ian." He said it quietly.

"Okay, Ian . . . " Yves faltered, trying to remember his English. "I leave you here. I go for your friend. You are safe, yes?"

"Yes," Ian said, shaking his head as if trying to clear it of confusing shadows.

"You are safe, okay? Stay here and do not move, understand?"

"Yes, okay. I'm not going anywhere." He smiled at Yves.

"Good, good."

Yves spoke once more into his radio and the cable tightened and swung across the wall. "Au revoir, Ian." He called as he went back down over the roofs.

When he returned to the ledge with the second climber they began an animated laughing conversation while Yves called the helicopter. It curved round from the direction of the Grandes Montets with a clattering of rotor blades. The silver cable extended slowly towards him. At first it swung tantalizingly out of reach, forcing Yves to lurch out from the ledge in an attempt to grab it. He caught the shackle on his third attempt. The shackle was a simple and very small snaplink attached to the cable. A metal ring fixed two feet above it allowed a handgrip to prevent toppling over backwards. Turning to Ian, he unclipped him from the pitons, keeping his body between Ian and the drop. Once he had secured the shackle to Ian's harness, he lifted his arm and made a turning motion with his hand. As soon as he felt the cable tighten and begin to lift he twisted round and, with a violent swinging movement, hurled Ian out into space. There was a yelp of fear as the man launched away, riding up, and fast, as the helicopter climbed swiftly clear of the mountain to escape the danger of rocks falling into the rotors.

"Was that necessary?" the remaining climber asked anxiously, staring at Ian spinning crazily above the void, with his woollen mitts still covering his stockinged feet. The climber raised his camera and took a photograph.

"I suppose you were worried that he might panic, which of course I completely understand. And with a head injury you never know of course." Yves knew what was coming. "I assure you that I am very calm. Rock solid, I promise you, and there won't be any need for throwing me off the ledge. Just let them lift me off, nice and steady. You know?"

"Yes. Do not worry. I will not push you."

"I wish you would stop telling me not to worry . . . Aaaahh!"

"Salut!" Yves yelled, as he hurled the protesting climber off the ledge and grinned as a stream of obscenities came back to him. He watched, shading his eyes from the sun, as the helicopter rose up far above the summit. *That must be some view,* he chuckled to himself.

↗   ↗   ↗

After two attempts I abandoned trying to climb up on to the metal ring in the wire. The Nant Blanc glacier spun giddily below my feet. There was a fall of some four thousand feet beneath me. I stared up the wire. *Oh Jeez, it's gonna snap, I know it'll snap.* I shut my eyes and didn't open them until I was sprawled on the floor of the helicopter and staring at an utterly deranged-looking man huddled on a small metal bench. It took a while to realize it was Ian. I scrambled over to the seat, reaching it as the aircraft curved round in a sickening, dropping turn. The centrifugal force seemed to be dragging me towards the open door. I felt Ian's body slide against mine, pushing me closer to the exit. We both grabbed at the seatbelts but in our panic got the wrong ends. In desperation I tied a granny knot in the two buckled tapes and braced myself against a ridge on the floor.

We met Yves two days later. He shook our hands and laughed when we presented two crates of beer to him and the rest of the guides. He said that no one had ever brought them a present after a rescue and seemed genuinely enchanted with the gift. We decided not to tell him that since we were penniless we had employed cunning logic and borrowed it from the local supermarket—disguised as Spaniards, just in case we were caught. It's the thought that counts.

A few days later Ian left for home. He was deeply disturbed by how close we had come to a painful end. I too felt unnerved by the accident.

A fortnight after our ledge had collapsed I witnessed a massive rockfall on the Dru. I had taken a temporary job washing dishes at the Montenvers Hotel, which was perched 6,000 feet above the Mer de Glace had a spectacular view of the West Face of the Dru. I heard a commotion on the balcony and, poking my head out of the window, saw everyone pointing up at huge blocks that were tumbling down from the summit. They were bigger than helicopters, plunging straight into the white snow-filled Niche on the north face and then catapulting out into space again. I shuddered to think of anyone on the mountain, knowing that I would be witnessing their deaths. A dust cloud gradually formed, rising a thousand feet up the face and extending for half a mile on each side. Fortunately only two climbers were caught in the rockfall and miraculously they escaped with only minor injuries. The summit of the Dru had changed shape forever.

"JUNE 14, 1943 FLEISCHBANK EAST FACE, WILDER KAISER"

AND

"FIRST WINTER ASCENT OF THE WEST FACE OF THE MARMOLATA"

FROM
Hermann Buhl: Climbing Without Compromise
BY REINHOLD MESSNER AND HORST HÖFLER

THE FAMED AUSTRIAN CLIMBER HERMANN BUHL (1924–1957) WAS a man extraordinarily in love with mountains. He was seemingly driven to exceed at ever harder, more challenging climbs—not in any sense of competition with other climbers, but rather in some way pushing himself for his own inner purposes. His climbing achievements on the rock and ice of the Alps and Dolomites are unparalleled. It was Buhl's iron will and incredible stamina that won him the first ascent—solo—in 1953 of Nanga Parbat, the high Karakoram peak that had thwarted numerous expeditions and that was the death scene for many of the world's most illustrious mountaineers.

Buhl was also one of the first-ascent party on 26,402-foot Broad Peak in Pakistan, a triumph that turned to tragedy a few days later when he stepped through a cornice on Chogolisa and fell thousands of feet to his death. Before this tragic failure on Chogolisa, Buhl had almost never known anything less than complete success in the mountains. Thus it is something of a relief to learn from his diaries and journals that earlier in his career there *were* times when Buhl failed to summit—the man *was* mortal after all! The two short selections included here recount times when Buhl didn't make it—at least not the first time. In typical Buhl fashion, he returned later to complete the ascents.

The first section is a diary entry from 1943 where, climbing with Waldemar Gruber, the nineteen-year-old Buhl takes a 50-meter leader fall down a rock chimney and survives. In his insouciance he worries more about his new climbing pants than the bleeding hole in his head. In the second section, a more mature Buhl writes of the 1950 climb on the Southwest Face of the Marmolata in winter, an ascent that took him three tries to complete.

Extracted from *Hermann Buhl: Climbing Without Compromise,* by Reinhold Messner and Horst Höfler, pages 53-55 and 69-72.

JUNE 14, 1943
FLEISCHBANK EAST FACE,
WILDER KAISER

A new route up the East Face of the Fleischbank, first climbed by Aschenbrenner and Lucke in 1930. Four ascents to date. Weather fine. We wanted to go straight up to the start of the West Face of the Middle Summit [of the Predigtstuhl], but at the "Tor" I caught sight of the Asch-Lucke; it was looking back at me, too. So we did that. We went up to the overhang unroped. The overhang itself was still wet and what a sight it was. 45 m high and leaning out about 5 m; every meter overhangs. So it is all peg-pulling. You could not have free climbed it but neither could we see many pitons and usually there are almost 50 of them in place. As luck would have it, I had plenty, and plenty of long ones. The constant rope drag and having to place pegs all the time made me dog-tired. Then, from my scanty little belay ledge, I had to give Waldemar a tight rope since he had to knock the pegs out again. I had rarely been as exhausted as I was up there.

After a pitch with a real pig of an overhang I came to a chimney; a few pitches up this landed us a hundred meters below the North Ridge. Now, a smooth, overhanging chimney blocked further progress. No pegs, no peg holes. I realized immediately that it was a blind alley. 20 m above the stance there was a little shelf in the chimney. The whole world seemed to be nailed shut and barred. I bridged up onto the pulpit but hardly was I standing on it than it broke off underneath me. I could not hold on any more, had the presence of mind to jump backward away from the wall and fell—down into the chimney. A 50-meter fall. I was fully conscious. Felt everything. Bounced four or five times in the chimney, hitting it head first. Suddenly there was a tug as I was dragged upright again, but the fall went on. I did not think of much at all, just that the flight seemed a long one.

Soon I came to a halt, standing upright on a tiny little ledge in the chimney, 30 m below Waldemar. In the first few moments I felt nothing and was even in quite a good mood. I felt myself all over. Blood on my head; that meant a hole. The fine new velvet breeches were torn, and that was the thing I was most sorry about, since I had always looked after them. Knees and hands ripped to pieces, waist badly chafed by the rope.

I was about to climb up to Waldi. No strength in my left hand. The metacarpal bone was broken. Waldi was just amazed that I was still alive. His belay peg had ripped out, he had been pulled off with it and just as he was dragged to the furthermost edge of the rubble ledge—he could picture both of us taking the big fall—I came to a stop in the chimney. In actual fact neither of us had been frightened, it all went so quickly. Quite calmly, Waldemar said we had to carry on up. But he could not get beyond my stance.

⹀   ⹀   ⹀

We now rappelled off. We were soon at the big overhang. With no protection we stood there, two of us on a tiny belay ledge. Or rather, I stood with one foot in the foothold and the other in mid-air and he sat on my knee. We both clipped in to the same peg and tried to pull the ropes down. Then I set off with no protection, abseiling into the wild blue yonder. The rock soon curved inwards and I was hanging free; first one, then two, three, four, five meters out from the cliff. I was spinning around in circles. The seam of my anorak split and I had the rope running over my neck. The weight of the two ropes, hanging free in mid-air, almost pulled me over backward.

I was soon level with the belay, there was no more rope left and I was still hanging in space. It was now or never, I started to pendulum, swinging farther and farther but still spinning, just at the right moment I lashed out, got my feet on the belay ledge, swung my upper body after them and stood up. Waldi now followed me down; he had it easier, I simply pulled him in to me. I would not have been able to hold out much longer in that position; my hands were hurting from hanging on and I had a nice rope burn on my neck.

Just to cap it all, a thunderstorm now came in. The rope was wet and could not be pulled through. It was as if we were stuck in a mousetrap. We could not go up and without a rope we could not go down either. We tried every trick in the book to get the rope back. He swung on it, while I pulled in as much as I could. . . . Slowly at first, as it fought against its own weight, then faster and faster, the rope came down. Then it flew down in a great arc. We were happy when we had it in our hands. Another 40-meter abseil and we were in the Steinerne Rinne, just as the storm really broke. But what did we care? We were happy just to have got down off that wall at all.

It was now that I really noticed the bruises on my feet and waist for the first time; everything hurt when I walked. Since I could make only slow progress I went ahead, while Waldi coiled the ropes and had something to eat. When our companions saw me coming back down alone and so unusually slowly, they knew there was something wrong and came up to meet me. When they saw my blood-encrusted face they feared the worst and asked if Waldi was dead. They soon calmed down when I told them everything and they saw that things were not quite so bad. First I got tons of food to eat and a bed to sleep in. The next morning my feet were so painful I could hardly get up. Our company doctor prescribed four weeks rest confined to barracks.

FIRST WINTER ASCENT OF THE SOUTH WEST FACE OF THE MARMOLATA

March 4, 1950. The mountains lie under a cloak of new snow but a steel blue sky stretches out above them. A foursome, we flash up the Brenner Pass road in the car of a fellow club member. Our companions are Theo Plattner and Rudl Seiwald. From the wintry Brenner the road drops down into the green and sunny Etschtal. In Bozen we take a break. We call in at an acquaintance's to make careful inquiries about the conditions on the Marmolata, but he advises us against it. There is too much avalanche danger and we ought to leave it be. Naturally, we do not mention anything about our true plans.

A wonderful car journey through the Fleimstal to Predazzo leads us back into winter again. To the right and left of the road walls of snow several meters high obstruct our view. After a punctured tire we arrive at four o'clock in the afternoon at Canazei, the starting point for the walk to the Contrinhaus. We inquire after the guardian and are directed to the Hotel Maria. Herr Dezulian receives us with a most friendly welcome. He was once a mountaineer, too, and so he understands. When we announce our request for a key to the Contrinhaus he is at first not very enthusiastic. The hut belongs to the Milan section of the C.A.I. and he says he does not have permission to hand over the key. After a few impractical suggestions we find a way round it: a mountain guide will accompany us and entrust us with the key up at the hut. After heartfelt well-wishes we leave that hospitable house. The skis sink deep into the virgin powder snow and the rucksacks press heavy. At seven o'clock in the evening we reach the hut.

During the night, I look out of the window. Above the Marmolata the mists hang heavy and a violent wind shakes the hut. But at eight o'clock in the morning it is fine again. Now, for the first time, we see the South Wall of the Marmolata. She looks impressive in her winter dress; we had not imagined her to be so terrible. Nevertheless, we want to attempt her just the once. The climbing rucksacks are packed, and then Kuno Rainer and I haul the heavy sacks the three hours to the start of the Face. A violent north-easterly drives the loose powder snow from the North Side over the ridge to us, where it trickles down the Face like silver snakes.

It is bitingly cold. The double ropes link us together, each of us has an extra 30-meter length of rope and the ironmongery draped about him, plus a 10 kg climbing sack. And so Kuno starts climbing. The rock is coated in ice, every hold covered with spindrift, and our fingers are soon without feeling. The way forward is a 40-meter-long, left-ward-leaning chimney. It, too, is partially full of snow and farther up it becomes narrow and smooth in places. With the utmost care, I climb this impeding chimney. Moves that are given IV and V in the route description demand everything we have got. Of course, IV and V on this Face would mean maybe grade VI anywhere else. We arrive at a series of snow-covered slabs. With no protection at all I set off up them and climb 30 meters up to a stance. Hands rummage around in vain in the powder, searching for holds, feet perched on the icy slabs. I hardly dare to breathe. If the snow had not held, it would have been impossible to climb.

And then this, the worst part of the route so far, is also behind me. Kuno leads on through and soon disappears into a crack over to the left. Snow trickles down toward me uninterrupted. The crack continues for 30 meters to below a zone of overhanging, smooth plates of rock. Despite the tremendous steepness we are up to our chests in snow. When we look down into the abyss we see nothing but snow. The start of the route lies invisible beneath the overhanging sections of the wall. Black roofs and slabs of rock look down on us from above. It is five o'clock in the evening. In the previous six hours we have managed only 150 meters, hardly a quarter of the wall. We calculate that we will possibly get as far as the second terrace, maybe even the overhanging corner, but the subsequent traverses, which count among the hardest pitches—

these three rope-lengths of holdless, snow-covered slabs—we will, in all probability, not have time to do. To say nothing of the summit gully. And so we decide to retreat. We leave the greater part of the ironware here. Since the rock overhangs so severely in the direct fall-line from where we are, we have to dispense with an abseil and down-climb the route. Darkness has fallen by the time we feel our way down the last pitches.

We intend to wait a few days until most of the new snow has melted from the wall and then make a new attempt. . . . While Kuno waits for me at the Contrinhaus I drive back with our friends to Innsbruck to stock up on provisions for a longer siege. On March 9 I go south again. The eye infection I picked up on the Marmolata makes its unpleasant presence felt. Every ray of light is like a stab with a needle. Wearing the darkest glasses I can find, I arrive at the Sellajoch, where an icy west wind greets me. On the south side of the Pass the snow is rotten right down to the ground; keeping to the side of the road it takes me a full two hours to get down to Canazei. Just before the sun goes down I set off for the hut. Kuno has been expecting me and soon busies himself making something for my stomach. We set the alarm clock for four o'clock and soon go off to sleep.

The next morning my eyes are considerably better, thanks to the household remedy prescribed by Frau Dezulian; namely, stiffened egg white applied to the eyes overnight. The inflammation has gone. At half past four we leave the hut. The sky is covered in a light veil of clouds, but these soon disperse. At eight o'clock we lay hands on the rock. The wall looks much different today. Although there is still enough snow cloaking the rocks at least the cold new snow has gone. Instead an icy west wind is blowing directly onto the Face. After two hours we are already back at the point from which we retreated. We divide up the ironware we had left behind, then I attack the first extreme pitch of the wall. Above a roof I reach an overhanging crack which leads in 20 meters to a little projecting ledge. The rock is wonderfully sound. A vertical crack follows. Kuno has a hard job on the crack, which goes up for 40 meters interrupted at intervals by overhanging bulges. We meet up again on the top of a pillar, where we study the route description: "Descend a few meters and traverse ten meters left to a hidden crack." With a little tension from the rope I push myself leftward across the holdless slabs. We encounter the first piton on this wall, but it does not look very trustworthy. Moving down and around a bulge, I get to the start of the thin crack, which soon loses itself among smooth, overhanging bulges. Ten meters above me I can see a peg. With my hands in the crack and feet bridging out wide, I slowly move up toward the peg. Meanwhile the warming rays of the sun have now reached us. Again and again, overhangs block the way. Several pegs help me gain a little height but soon the crack becomes just a crease, will not accept pegs, and is quite holdless. "No more rope," comes the call from below, and I can just about stand and make an emergency belay. When I'm hauling the rucksack up, the whole side of it rips open and only the tent sack inside prevents the entire contents from making a break for the freedom of the ground below. Strapped up like a parcel, it goes back on my shoulders. . . .

At two o'clock in the afternoon we are standing on the roomy snow ledges of the second terrace, amid holdless, overhanging sweeps of rock. To the west, heavy clouds have formed and are drifting threateningly toward the Etschtal. We take only a short rest, since the huge yellow corner at the left-hand end of the terrace awakens our curiosity. We traverse across snow to get to it. It is only in the Dolomites that one can find such impressive bits of climbing. The right-hand section of this corner is a huge slab of rock, as if cast in a single piece, while on the left tremendous roofs overhang the corner. Another 200 meters higher and 20 meters out from the terrace we can make out the exit from the gully. In between, the cliff lies back a little—that must be where the traverses are. We decide to carry on up. The corner pushes me violently outward. I feel like a spider; hands and feet almost level, bridging out wide, I feel my way up on friction alone. Holds are scarce. Back-and-footing against the slab, then bridging once more, I drag myself up 30 meters. At a little knob of rock I prepare to bring Kuno up but he urges a retreat. The wall of cloud has got nearer, he says, and, for sure, the weather is about to change for the worse. I drape a rope sling around the knob and lower myself back down, while Kuno uses the second rope to pull me into the rock. Meanwhile, over in the Rosengarten, it has already begun to snow. Over the Pala, a serious storm is brewing. A dense gray bank of cloud comes out of the west, heading straight for us. Hurricane cloud. As we are getting ready to continue our descent, the mist is racing over the Ombretta Pass. It is six o'clock in the evening.

We tie the two 40-meter ropes together, belay ourselves with the extra 30-meter lengths and start off down. It is mostly a mid-air trip. Again, I glide down on a carabiner brake. I cannot see the ends of the rope, but I do know that the rope will not reach the next stance. I am at the traverse. Like a pendulum I swing to and fro until I reach the top of the pillar. While Kuno pulls down the ropes, I am already hammering in the next abseil piton. The straight-down abseils are finished now. On the very next abseil we have to descend the face by the same route we climbed it. And meanwhile the wind has risen; it has started snowing, and the ropes arc out from the wall in a sweeping curve. At eight o'clock in the evening we are standing back at the foot of the route with our skis. . . .

FROM

SUMMITS AND SECRETS

BY KURT DIEMBERGER

THE GREATEST JOY, FOLLOWED SWIFTLY BY THE GREATEST SORROW, described by a master mountain storyteller . . . Kurt Diemberger, the Austrian climber, filmmaker, and writer, tells of the death in 1957 of his climbing companion and mountain legend Hermann Buhl on Chogolisa, in the Karakoram of Pakistan.

Only days before, Buhl and Diemberger had been part of the triumphant Austrian Alpine Club party that completed the first ascent of nearby Broad Peak, one of the world's fourteen eight-thousanders. Then the party split up in smaller groups to explore the many seven-thousanders in the Baltoro region. Buhl and Diemberger settled on the lovely Chogolisa, also called "Bride Peak" for its perpetual snowy covering.

The two were only about 1,500 feet from the summit when a little cloud ballooned into a horrific storm that finally turned them around at 24,000 feet. Almost blinded by the whirling snow, they were feeling their way back through steep avalanche slopes and corniced areas, unroped, when suddenly things shook—and Buhl simply disappeared.

In this look backward at one of the saddest days of his climbing career—and one of the most tragic days in the history of mountaineering—Diemberger tells movingly of his shock and disbelief and his search for his fallen partner, always thinking of the "what-if . . ."

This selection is taken from Diemberger's book *Summits and Secrets*, as republished in *The Kurt Diemberger Omnibus*, pages 120-129.

Chogolisa: It was by now mid-June. There was a fly sitting on the tent-roof and a spider mountaineering on a boulder. The ice had melted steadily and our base-camp tents were perched on lofty plinths. We were slowly recovering from our exertions and spent the time writing reports and letters: "All four members of the expedition reached the summit of Broad Peak on June 9th by the shortest and best route, employing neither high-altitude porters nor oxygen equipment . . ." The sun was beating down on the roof of our tent. We were surrounded by the white glitter of high peaks. "We intend to stay here a little longer and do a few gentle climbs—maybe one or other of the six- or seven-thousanders . . . "

Down there in the valleys it must be high summer. It even makes itself felt a little up here. I lay in my sun-warmed tent and, while the melting ice-streams gurgled away outside, I kept on picking out from among my home mail (we were so much at world's end that the latest the mail-runners had brought up the glacier were six weeks' old) a picture post-card, with a meadow, a tree and, in the background, a little lake on it. On the back was written: "I am here on a little walking-tour. Tchau!" The card was from Busle, and the tree was a real tree. (How long since I saw a real tree?) Then I re-read her last letter, which came from Norway. "I have come to the far north," she wrote, "I can't describe to you how big that world is—something that I can't explain." She could not describe that great world of the north, which I had never seen. An odd idea occurred to me. Hadn't I, too, penetrated a great world which I could not describe to anyone, not even to her? Up there on the summit-ridge of an eight-thousander? When I got home would I be the same person I was before I came out here? I took another thoughtful look at that tree. Oh, I should like to be going home this very minute! I looked up and saw the great peaks that ringed us, Chogolisa's heavenly roof-tree, the seracs of the Baltoro glacier. Here I was, once in a lifetime. I wrote her a letter from one remote world to another.

Chogolisa is a magic mountain.

It is so lovely that the statistic of its height, 25,110 feet, seems irrelevant. The British had long ago christened it "Bride Peak," because it is always entirely clad in white. A white rhombus, an icy roof, high up in the heavens. Dyhrenfurth, when he wrote his book about the Baltoro, remarked: "Its classic beauty of form and the repose of its outlines stamp it as the ideal ice-mountain." Only when seen from a distance of some twenty miles does it reveal, at the left-hand end of its great pitched-roof, a minute dark tooth, the small rock-turret of its summit. The mighty south-east ridge, sweeping up for something like three miles, catches the full sun from early morning onwards—a great advantage—and it was as long ago as 1909 that the Duke of the Abruzzi's expedition attempted to reach the summit by it. At 24,600 feet, only 500 below the top of that immense roof, they were forced by a storm to retreat; and, for a long, long time that remained the greatest height achieved by man. Nor had anyone reached the summit since.

On our ascent of Broad Peak we had all marveled at that beautiful mountain to the south of us; but much nearer, to the west, there had been splendid peaks in the Savoia group which had caught our eye as possible secondary objectives. In the end Hermann, who like the rest of us had made a good recovery while resting at base camp, was especially attracted by Mitre Peak and the Trango Tower; besides which we also wanted to visit the Gasherbrum glacier and reconnoiter Gasherbrum IV—or at least take a close look at it from there.

However, the first consideration was to evacuate the Broad Peak camps. Markus and Fritz, taking Captain Quader with them, cleared camp I; and while Hermann and I went all the way up again to deal with II and III, Markus and Fritz, on short skis, went over to the Savoia glacier and climbed the group's highest peak, a fine summit over 23,000 feet high. This lightning foray came as a great surprise to Hermann and myself, who had no idea they had such a venture in mind. We turned our eyes southwards: we would make Chogolisa and the Gasherbrum glacier our program. And we, too, would carry it out as a two-man expedition.

❧   ❧   ❧

Chogolisa would demand several high camps, that was obvious. Yet we could not carry more than one tent. The solution was daring: a single transportable high camp—a ladder of camps consisting of a single tent. Herbert Tichy and his Sherpa had worked their way up Gurla Mandhata in Tibet that way. So our single tent should serve as our base camp and all succeeding camps, I, II and III, as necessary; a single rung in a ladder which we would push up the mountain day by day.

After Hermann and I had decided, during the course of June 20th, exactly what we should need for our attempt on the peak, I went on ahead that evening towards Concordia, carrying about 80 lbs. Hermann who still had some things to fetch from the foot of Broad Peak, followed me early next morning, humping a similar load. Thanks to the marker-pennants I had planted, there was no difficulty about rejoining one another, and we were able to push on together, late in the afternoon, over the endless humps of the Battoro's central moraine. By evening we had found a marvelous site for our base camp close to the enormous ice-falls at the bottom of Chogolisa, and there we pitched our tent. High overhead soared the mountain's fantastic roof; wherever we looked, we saw nothing but ice and snow.

In spite of that, Hermann thought our climb would only take a few days; after it, we might still turn our attentions to Mitre Peak. The Gasherbrum glacier and more especially Gasherbrum IV were perhaps rather too far to contemplate.

On the 22nd we were already halfway up Chogolisa's ice-falls and laid a depot down on a ridge of hard snow we found there. The next day, the weather was bad; we decided not to wait too long, but to push on as far as we could get.

"June 24th: 4.30 A.M. off with tent; snowing gently; weather nothing special; going very well; 7.30 A.M. depot at 18,000 feet; rucksack, with depot material, about 55 lbs.; on up the Spur in knee-deep snow; trail broken all the way to the Kaberi Saddle; about 5 P.M., pitched camp at 20,900 feet; whole route marked with pennants."

What was the story behind these cryptic entries of Hermann's? First of all, that he was in splendid condition. In spite of the deep snow, he broke the trail all the way up to the Kaberi Saddle and would not hear of my relieving him in the lead. Secondly, that on that first day of ours we climbed 4,600 feet. (These facts should, I hope, convince anyone who imagines that it was an enfeebled Hermann Buhl who tackled Chogolisa, beyond any doubt, that the contrary was the case. Certainly every mountaineer will recognize it.) Moreover we were carrying anything up to 65 lbs. on our backs and, in view of our rapid progress in spite of poor weather, our spirits were very high. After heating a drink on our hissing cooker with great difficulty, we went happily to sleep in our first Chogolisa camp.

Next day, Tuesday the 25th the weather was bad again. We stayed in our sleeping-bags till 10 o'clock, cooked a meal and, at 1 P.M. struck our tent and, in spite of knee-deep snow, climbed to the shoulder in Chogolisa's South-east Ridge, at a height of 22,000 feet. There we erected our tent again, this time as camp II. We were now high enough to warrant a direct attempt on the summit. All we had to do was to wait for fine weather . . .

Towards dawn on the 26th a furious storm blew up. It leaned against the outside of the tent and we against its inside. Luckily we had anchored it well. A few feet higher up, bedlam had broken loose. The wind was screaming over the shoulder with unremitting fury. When at last, after several hours, the walls of the tent stopped flapping, we went out, intending to go up a little way towards the crest we called "Ridge Peak" and stretch our legs. It was only then that we realized how sheltered our tent-site was. Up on the shoulder we were almost blown away. The rope curved out in a wide festoon, parallel with the ground, weightless, airborne. Ridge Peak looked down on us through clouds of blown snow, flecked here and there by the sun, and the air was full of the howling of the storm, a mighty symphony.

We were soon back in our sleeping-bags, hatching out future plans. In the autumn, Hermann wanted me to come with him on a double-traverse of Mont Blanc, by all its great ridges. Then, the following year, perhaps, we would have a go at Rakaposhi . . .

Towards evening the barometer began to rise again and we cheerfully fell to packing our things for the morrow. Then it suddenly cleared, and through the entrance to the tent we saw Baltoro Kangri, sublime in the light of the evening sun . . . we might climb it after Chogolisa . . .

       ➤   ➤   ➤

June 27th dawned clear, fine and calm, a veritable gift of the Gods. We were happy beyond words. Our rest-day had done us good, and we felt brimming over with fitness, and a burning zeal to bag the summit.

We were off at about a quarter to five. It was still very cold, but we knew it couldn't be for very long. The sky grew lighter and lighter above Baltoro Kangri. To the south lay a sea of summits, peaks about 20,000 to 23,000 feet high, and hardly even explored. To the north the sun was already touching K2.

Between us and it, Broad Peak displayed only its main summit, masking the other two.

Almost as soon as we had got our legs moving, the warmth of the sun reached us. We tramped happily up over the glittering snow. Free of our loads, we made unbelievably easy progress. The going was excellent on the very crest of the ridge, but the snow was deep and trying on either side; besides which, the wind had formed dangerous wind-slabs on the slope. One of them broke away quite close to us and went thundering down in a fair-sized avalanche to the level plateau of the Kaberi Saddle below. It made quite an impression on us and we stuck carefully to the crest of the ridge, which was so far uncorniced. But how would things go up there on Ridge Peak, where we could see cornices several yards wide projecting unpleasantly in a continuous hem? No doubt the storm of the previous day had notably increased their size.

At 23,000 feet we left the ridge, by now corniced, and traversed a little way across a smooth ice-slope to reach a projection farther up. There were actually a few rocks here, quite a curiosity on this mountain. And what about the route above? Ye Gods! There was the summit, just over there! It couldn't be any great distance and it certainly didn't look difficult. We ought to be up on it by midday, we thought.

Indeed, the next bit was easy; the slope flattened out appreciably and all we had to do was to keep along it to the deep notch beyond Ridge Peak. We made light of turning the huge cornices which towered over us to the right. Chogolisa's immense roof drew rapidly nearer, but after a quarter of an hour we had to admit it wasn't going to be easy. The slope grew steeper and the sector of ridge rising behind it had a distinctly airy look. Then suddenly we could see the whole route, and there was nothing about it to be lightly dismissed. The ridge down to the notch was as sharp as a knife-blade, its left-hand side a giddily steep precipice of rock and ice, to its right great cornices hanging far out over the North Face. We should have to be very careful there. The rock precipices below us kept on forcing us farther up towards the jagged white crest. We belayed carefully with the rope, watching for avalanches. A small wind-slab did in fact break away and went sliding away into the abyss. The snow conditions were really a curse. Just as we got to the rocks, Hermann went through to his waist, and hardly had he scrambled out when he was sitting in another hole. Damn it, the slope was a positive honey-comb! Hermann balanced his way forward as if walking on eggshells—lucky man, he didn't weigh much. He reached ice-plastered rocks and moved from foot-hold to foot-hold with incredible delicacy of balance, hardly touching the holds as he moved. A moment later he disappeared over a rib. "Up you come!" I could hear him calling.

Rope's length by rope's length, we worked our way along the ridge, sometimes on the slope, sometimes right up at the edge of the cornices. Steadily, the wind passed over the crest; glittering snow rose towards the deep blue dome of the sky. Down in the south there were huge clouds now. But they did not move.

We had made good time in spite of the unexpected difficulties. It was only 9 o'clock when we reached the saddle at 23,000 feet. And there, only 2,000 feet above us, was the sharp tip of the turret on the long crest of the summit-ridge. A steep, but for the most part broad, ridge of snow led up to it.

We sat down in a sheltered hollow, in glorious warm sunshine, and took off the rope. We were ravenous; what about a drop of tea and those delicacies we had saved up for our trip to the top? "This is the best day for me since I came out with the expedition," mused Hermann. How well I understood him. Climbing a seven-thousander in three days . . . not in three weeks! This was just his pigeon—very different from what he went through on Broad Peak. I shared his obvious delight.

We didn't move on for a whole long hour. When we did, we took alternate leads in deep snow. We were unroped now. It was enough to carry the rope with us in the rucksack, Hermann said, so I did not think much about it. A steep pitch with a short ice-cliff called for work with the axe; after that it was easy again. Occasional cracks in the slope spelled avalanche-danger. They pushed us out farther on to the brink of the precipice than we had intended.

Ridge Peak was gradually sinking below and behind us. To the south, the great mountainous banks of cloud were moving very slowly nearer. The sky was calm and of a deep, deep blue. The banner of snow blowing from Ridge Peak seemed to have grown a little. To the north lay a tremendous prospect:

all the giants of the Baltoro lined up in a row, a whole chain of peaks 26,000 feet high or only just less. We let our gaze range in wonderment from K2 to Hidden Peak. We took photographs and then moved on again.

How quickly the clouds were coming towards us now! We hoped they wouldn't interfere with our view from the top. We quickened our pace. The last steep pitch began a little way up there, and close above it we could see the tower that was the summit—1,500 feet at the most—*that* couldn't take so very long.

Presently a little cloud came climbing up the slope below us. It grew larger, enveloping us, enveloping the peak. Without any warning, all hell broke loose. Grey veils of mist scurried across the ridge. Unnatural darkness swamped us. We fought our way forward through clouds of blown snow, bending double to meet the fury of the gale. On the crest of the ridge it flung itself upon us in full blast, snatching at our clothes, trying to claw us from our footing. It was terribly cold and the needles of ice blowing down into our faces hurt savagely. We could only see the next yard or two ahead. We kept on changing the lead, struggling grimly upwards.

It didn't seem possible. I thought of the blue sky such a short time back. It had all been so quick. I had an uncanny feeling—hadn't exactly the same thing happened to the Duke of the Abruzzi, quite close to the summit? Were we going to be robbed, too? Away with such stupid thoughts; it was only a few hundred feet, and we had *got* to do it.

It grew lighter for a moment, as the wind parted the driving clouds. We stood rooted, looking up to where the summit must be. There it was, near enough to touch, looming darkly above us. An instant later the wrack had swallowed it up again.

The storm continued its horrific din. Laboriously we moved up, with a steep, bottomless precipice below us, keeping close to the ridge crest. Everything was white now and we could hardly see.

We were at about 24,000 feet. Only another thousand to the summit-tower. Suddenly Hermann spoke: "We've got to turn back at once, or the wind will cover our tracks up, and then we shall stray out on to the cornices!" He was quite right. We hadn't given a thought to it; and now visibility was almost nil.

We should have to hurry. We turned then and there. Hermann had been leading, so I was in front now. He followed at a safe distance of ten to fifteen yards, which was all that visibility would permit.

Bent double, I felt my way downwards. It was incredible—only 150 feet down, there was no trace to be seen of our upward trail, except the deep holes made by our axes. Very soon there wouldn't be very many of *them*. And still the tempest kept up its infernal din.

I reckoned we must be at about 23,600 feet, and that we must be near the steep avalanche slope which had pushed us so close to the cornices. If only one could see a bit more! I turned and saw Hermann coming after me, keeping the distance unaltered, following in my actual steps. As I moved down, I kept on looking across to the left, trying to see through the mist. All I could see was that it was getting a bit darker overhead and a bit lighter below. That must be the edge of the cornices. It seemed a safe distance away, but in mist distances can be deceptive. Perhaps it would be better to keep a bit to the right, but then I should have to look out for the precipice. It ought to be here by now. Ah, there's another axe-hole . . .

I looked anxiously to the left and then down to the surface at my feet. I was at a loss; it was almost impossible to see anything at all. *Crack!* Something shot through me like a shock. Everything shook, and for a second the surface of the snow seemed to shrink. Blindly, I jumped sideways to the right—an instantaneous reflex action—two, three great strides, and followed the steep slope downwards a little way, shattered by what I had seen at my feet—the rim of the cornice, with little jagged bits breaking away from it. My luck had been in, all right! I had been clean out on the cornice. What would Hermann have to say about that, I wondered? I stopped and turned, but the curve of the slope prevented my seeing over the crest as I looked up. The light was improving a little. Hermann must bob up any moment up there. I still couldn't fathom that extraordinary shaking sensation; had the snow really settled under my weight?

Still no Hermann. "Hermann!" I shouted. "For God's sake, what's up? Hermann!" I rushed, gasping up the slope. There it was, the crest . . . and beyond it, smooth snow . . . and it was empty . . . Hermann . . . You! . . .

Done for . . .

I dragged myself up a little farther. I could see his last footmarks in the snow, then the jagged edge of the broken cornice, yawning. Then the black depths.

The broken cornice—that had been the quaking beneath my feet, then.

I couldn't get a sight of the North Face from anywhere near. I should have to get down to Ridge Peak for that. As I went down, the storm gradually abated, and the mists lifted from time to time. I was utterly stunned. How could that have happened just behind me? I had the greatest difficulty in getting up the short rise to Ridge Peak, but even before I got there it had cleared up. I hurried out to the farthest edge of the cliffs.

The storm was hunting the clouds high into the heavens. Above the veils of mist and through them a ridge loomed up—a tower—a great roof with tremendous banners of blown snow streaming from it. Chogolisa, the horrible. I could see the spot where we had turned at about 24,000 feet. Our trail down the broad snow-field below was crystal clear. Then that fearsome drop to the north—into the clouds. And there, even closer to our tracks as they ran straight downwards, the encroaching precipice. And then I could see it all with stark and terrible clarity. Just at that point, Hermann had left my tracks at a slight bend, where I was hugging the rim of the precipice, and gone straight on ahead, only three or four yards—straight out on to the tottering rim of the cornice—straight out into nothingness. Of the foot of the wall I could see nothing. Stupidly, I stared upwards again.

If we had been roped . . .

I looked down along the face, shuddering . . .

No, I should never have been able to hold him there; at the moment of his fall I myself was too far out on the overhanging snow.*

At last I could see clearly down below, where the broad snow-masses of an avalanche fanned out. The crashing cornice had set it off and it had swept the face clean. Hermann was nowhere to be seen. He must have fallen at least 1,000,

---

*Though, perhaps, the pull of the rope would have kept him in my tracks, and he might never have strayed from the right line of descent.—K.D.

A similar thought was expressed by Othmar Gurtner, commenting on the author's account in *The Mountain World*, 1958-59.—Translator's note.

maybe 2,000 feet and was lying there buried under the piled-up snow. Could he have survived that? There was no answer to my shouts and I had no way of getting down there. I should have to fetch the others and we should have to come from below. That was the only faint possibility. I strained my eyes, searching every cranny, searching for a rucksack, a ski-stick, a dark blob. But there was nothing to be seen—absolutely nothing. Only our tracks—up there . . .

Clouds blotted the mountain out again. I was alone.

    ➤   ➤   ➤

Mists and a high wind were sweeping the corniced ridge as I tried to find the way down. At times I could see nothing at all and could only tell from rifts in the snow that I had strayed too far down the slope. After what seemed an age, I found our tent. It was a horror of emptiness. I took the absolute essentials for the descent and went on down. At the Kaberi Saddle there was knee-deep fresh snow, through which only a tiny corner of the marker-pennants showed. I probed with my feet under that smooth expanse of white to find out from which side our ascent-route had come, then went straight on into the whiteness . . . to the next pennant. I wandered vaguely down endless hollows, over crevasses, through fog, then into the darkness of night. For long, indescribable hours of horror—during which I at times had a feeling that Hermann was still with me—I managed, by some miracle, to find my way, onwards, downwards. Then, just before the great ice-falls, my pocket-lamp failed; so I had to bivouac at 18,000 feet. In the first pale light of dawn I made my way down the ice-falls. On and on . . . endlessly on . . . till, 27 hours after Hermann's fall, I tottered into base camp.

The search which followed found absolutely nothing.

    ➤   ➤   ➤

Once again, the monstrous rubble-covered river of ice lay freed of all human presence. The sun burned down on it with scorching intensity. The snow was rapidly vanishing, melting into the waters of gurgling glacier-streams. Chogolisa's white roof-tree seemed to lift into the very sky itself. The great peaks stood silently all around. Were they, too, mourning? Or was this only the great healing silence which eternally enfolds all living and dying?

⋗   ⋗   ⋗

The engines droned as we flew down the Indus Valley, with mountains close on either hand, sharp spires past which we floated. Steep ridges thrusting up; an occasional glimpse back to the giant Baltoro peaks . . . K2, Broad Peak . . . already distant, as the minutes sundered us from the months. We should soon be seeing Nanga Parbat.

My thoughts went back to our inward flight, when the weather had been bad. I could see Hermann's face, as his eyes bored into the gray clouds for a sight of *his* mountain. At last he had spoken. "We'll only fly back on a fine day," he said.

Today was a fine day.

The savage peaks ahead parted, and only then did we realize that they were only low wing-pieces to that great stage-setting. High above them there was a shimmer of white; snow banners rose to the heavens. There it stood, the mountain—immutable, immense, imperishable—Nanga Parbat.

We could see its dazzling glaciers, and the summit crowning them. Above it the sky stretched blue-black and deep—as if yet another sky were climbing, incessantly, over and up it—up to an infinity of heights and depths.

Hermann Buhl.

Silver banners, ever-growing up into that dark vault.

"DISASTER ON NANGA PARBAT"

BY ERWIN SCHNEIDER

FROM
Peaks, Passes, and Glaciers
BY WALT UNSWORTH

EWHERE OVER TIME, IN THE LORE OF INTERNATIONAL MOUN-
eering, many of the major peaks of the Himalaya came to be associated
h the various countries that most often sent people to climb them. Thus
Everest became informally known as "belonging to the British," K2 was "the
American peak," and Nanga Parbat in the Punjab Himalaya was for many
years the province of the Germans. Unfortunately for the German climbers,
Nanga Parbat, also known as the "Naked Mountain," has a frightening history
of fatalities on its slopes.

Throughout the 1930s many Europeans and Sherpas died during attempts
on Nanga Parbat, through bad weather, objective dangers, and accidents. The
summit was finally reached in 1953 via the Rakhiot Face—on a German expedition, by the Austrian climber Hermann Buhl, who continued on, solo, when
his last companion gave up 700 meters below the summit. Even once climbed,
the Naked Mountain refused to give quarter: in 1970 the brothers Reinhold
and Gunther Messner climbed the Rupal Face as part of a German expedition, and Gunther was killed on the descent via the Diamir Face.

The 1934 attempt by a German party led by Willy Merkl, described in
this journal article by expedition member Erwin Schneider, was particularly
tragic. The lead climbers had reached a point only about 200 meters from
the summit when a violent storm lasting several days forced a retreat. Despite further attempts by the climbers at regaining their high point, storms
and avalanches took a severe toll: in all, six porters and four Germans died
on the expedition, including leader Merkl and Willy Welzenbach, the greatest German climber between the two world wars.

A surviving Sherpa, Angtsering, adds a final word to these selections from
The German Assault on Nanga Parbat (1934), vols. XLVI and XLVII, as republished in *Peaks, Passes, and Glaciers* by Walt Unsworth, pages 195-203.

 anga Parbat, the western corner-stone of the Himalaya and
probably the tenth highest peak of the world, has a comparatively ancient history. In 1895 Mummery's party, composed
of some of the best and most active mountaineers of the time,

made the first attempt—an attack worthy of the party's reputation. Mummery, coming from the Rupal Nullah over the Mazeno Pass to the Diamirai Glacier with two Gurkhas, attained a height of over 20,000 ft. on the W. flank of the mountain. But passing over the Diama Pass to the N. face of the mountain, he disappeared there with his two companions.

Willy Welzenbach first, then Willy Merkl, began preparations for another assault many years later. In 1932 Merkl led a party of prominent German mountaineers to the peak. He tried to find a way over the N. flank from the Rakhiot Glacier. With his companions he succeeded, after overcoming great difficulties, in reaching a height of nearly 23,000 ft., the expedition failing through snowstorms and porter troubles. The party was nevertheless certain that Nanga Parbat was definitely accessible by this—in all probability the *sole*—route. In 1934 Merkl wished to complete his unfinished task, but fate was once more against him; the mountain has prevailed again.

The Sports Clubs of the German State Railways provided the necessary funds. Towards the scientific aims of the expedition the *Notgemeinschaft* of German science and the D. u. Œ2.A–V. contributed generously. After months of intensive labor Merkl completed the necessary preparations. The members of the expedition started for India in two parties at the end of March and beginning of April respectively. Merkl was, of course, the leader: as members of the climbing party came Peter Aschenbrenner, who on off-days in the Base Camp was able to supply us with ibex, thanks to his skill with the rifle; Fritz Bechtold was the official photographer; Alfred Drexel was in charge of the wireless for quick transmission of reports between the different high camps as far as Camp IV; Peter Müllritter was another photographer, while Willy Welzenbach was second in command of the party; Ulrich Wieland, together with myself, looked after the high-altitude porters. Dr. W. Bernard was medical officer and Hans Hieronimus commanded the Base. The two transport officers, Captain Frier—who had been in charge of the same in 1932—and Captain Sangster, gave us great assistance, as did the Swiss, Kuhn, who with the German Consul, Kapp, joined the Base Camp a month later, coming from Rawal Pindi. The scientific side, to study topographical, geological, and geographical questions concerning the region, was composed of Doctors

Finsterwalder, Misch and Raechl. One of their most important functions was to produce a good map on photogrammetrical methods to illustrate the terrain traversed by the expedition. The map, moreover, should prove a basis for scientific study of the vast mountain range and the solution of all sorts of further problems. We trust that the far-reaching results in these respects—results obtained with great labor—will prove of scientific value.

Thanks to the co-operation and help of the British and Indian officials, as well as that of many friends, our work in India was completed speedily and, by May 2, a start with 500 loads could be made from Srinagar. Accompanying us were thirty-five of the best Sherpa and Bhutia porters, together with their *sirdar*, Lewa, from Darjeeling. These men had all proved their worth on many previous expeditions on difficult ground and at great heights.

Our route from Srinagar to the Base Camp in the Rakhiot glen was well over 100 miles in length. It leads over the Tragbal and Burzil Passes of 11,580 ft. and 13,775 ft. respectively. Both these passes at this season of the year were still lying deep under winter snow. It was not altogether easy, with our large party and in bad weather, to cross them without loss of time. After Astor, one of the smaller resorts on the way to Gilgit, we did not take, as in 1932, the weary route *via* the ridges, but, having the necessary permits, proceeded by the Indus valley to the Rakhiot. At Rakhiot bridge the Indus flows at a height of only 1,100 m; 7,000 meters of sheer height separated us from the summit of Nanga Parbat. Nowhere else in the world is there a similar difference of altitude. At the bridge we took in the Indus our last bath for a long time, reached Taro after a long and steep climb, and attained our former camp in the high forest two days later; seventeen days after our departure from Srinagar we pitched our tents there. At this high altitude the thick snow carpet began; to reach the Base Camp, situated at the same spot as in 1932, we had to break a trail. We sent our Darjeeling and Balti porters, of whom we had collected twenty, up and down in succession with our kit and stores from the above-mentioned camp to the permanent Base. The latter, situated at 3,850 m, was now—middle of May—still buried under 7 ft. of snow, its appearance being anything but prepossessing. Camp was pitched in a scooped-out hollow in the snow; the luggage was piled alongside in sorted heaps. Later, on the snow melting, it was a wonderful experience to rest here on off-days; the camp gave the impression of a Middle-Ages town in the midst of modernity.

The first advance to the upper camps was made by Bechtold, Müllritter and Wieland, accompanied by some porters. Camp I was pitched behind the top of the great moraine at the base of Nanga Parbat's N. face, at a height of 4,200 m. The object of this reconnaissance was to ascertain snow conditions for a further advance and to enable Bechtold to film the great ice avalanches falling continuously day and night and sweeping the entire 13,000 ft. face. The party returned with the cheering information that snow conditions were very good. One day later Aschenbrenner, Drexel, Welzenbach and I, with sixteen porters, left the Base Camp with the intention of pushing on to Camp IV and inaugurating it. Our route was the same as in 1932, the weather being changeable and mostly bad. With intensive labor we forced our way up to Camp II, but on the first day had to pitch an intermediate camp in the icefall owing to deep snow and difficult terrain. Camp II was in the most magnificent situation amidst the wildest icefalls that we had ever seen. In the evening especially, the view towards the W. over the immeasurable chain of the Hindu Kush was of surpassing splendor. The quick movements of the glacier in this part made, however, life anything but pleasant in Camp II. As time went on, great crevasses formed under the tents, while during the night avalanches thundered and the ice burst all round in the vicinity. Finally the site was abandoned after some thousands of tons of ice had fallen one night just in front of the tents. The farther route towards Camp III led also through icefalls; we were again compelled to pitch an intermediate camp owing to the difficulties. From this spot we tried vainly for half a day to find a route through the great, sheer walls of ice. Camp III was inaugurated on a névé ridge at the end of the difficulties: from this spot more or less gentle snow slopes led towards the watershed between the E. peak (of Nanga Parbat), the Rakhiot, and the Chongra peaks.

We had short light skis with us fitted with skins. They proved useful, and we had already employed them in the approach march over the snowy passes. On the mountain we took them to Camp IV, whence they lightened the labor of an ascent of the western Chongra peak. From Camp IV to the Base we accomplished most of the journey, even portions of the icefalls, with their aid. Quick descents were often possible with decent snow. Thus we once accomplished the 3,000 ft. descent from Camp IV to Camp II in ten minutes. The "slalom" through the icefalls and over the narrow snow-bridges below Camp III was quite unique. Moreover, the employment of skis was justified since in the final stage they provided admirable fuel for camp fires!

Bechtold and Müllritter had arrived at Camp II and assured the upwards transport of kits. We were in wireless communication with the Base and could quickly transmit our observations and wishes. The small apparatus communicated only at short distances, while later on connection failed between Camp IV and the Base. Nevertheless, one afternoon Captain Sangster got into touch with a military instrument which informed him that various unknown British officers of the Indian Army had been granted leave. But what was the use of that when we could not even "get" our own operator in the Base Camp? . . .

. . . Drexel was usually in charge of the wireless. In Camp III a violent storm was raging that day and Drexel's usually clear voice was difficult to understand in the Base camp. He seemed to have caught a chill. We called to him (by wireless) to descend to the base to recover his health there. Drexel went down with his porter Angtensin to Camp II. We three others went up higher to Camp IV. On the following morning a porter arrived with a letter from Bechtold in Camp II, saying that Drexel had arrived there in a collapsed condition and that Müllritter had left at once for the Base to fetch the doctor and help. During the day and night the condition of Drexel had grown so rapidly worse that he was incapable of descending farther. Dr. Bernard arrived in the afternoon with Müllritter, but Drexel died at 9 P.M. from pneumonia. During the night Wieland arrived through the savage icefall with two porters and oxygen, but it was now too late. We all returned to the Base camp and buried our comrade on a moraine pinnacle with his head facing the north wall of Nanga Parbat. This was our first great blow and the fourth victim that the mountain has claimed since Mummery and his two companions.

During the following days Camp IV was fitted out with equipment and food, Captain Frier making the arrangements. On June 22 Merkl, Bechtold, Müllritter, Welzenbach, Aschenbrenner and I went as the advance party to

Camp IV. Captain Sangster, Wieland and Bernard followed three days later. From Camp IV nearly everyone climbed the Western Chongra peak. This camp, at it height of 5,950 m, served as a kind of advanced base and from it we went up and down twice with porters to Camp V conveying stores. The route is steep but can be accomplished with good snow and tracks in 3 hrs.; a long climb still separated us from the summit. Our intention was, from Camp V at the foot of the Rakhiot peak, to make our way to the great upper névé plateau by passing *over* this peak and the connecting ridge to the *Silbersattel* lying between the two eastern peaks: this rises gently from a height of 7,600 m over a distance of nearly 3 kilometers to the little lower top, whence the route continues, *via* a descent into the last depression and a steep shoulder in the ridge, upwards towards the summit. The route is mostly difficult and especially very long as it lies at an average height of 7,000 m (23,000 ft.). This constitutes the main difficulty and the solution to the attainment of the top. We considered our best plan was to overcome these troubles by a rapid assault and short pauses, thus not meeting with hindrances from lack of (atmospheric) oxygen. We wished to preserve our strength and powers for the final assault on the summit.

Camp V was situated at 6,700 m, just in front of the abrupt final step leading to the Rakhiot peak. This step we rendered secure by fixed ropes and the hewing of big footholds for the porters—a two days' job. On July 4 Merkl, Bechtold, Welzenbach, Wieland, Aschenbrenner and I, with eighteen porters, arrived at Camp VI. Camp V was the true take-off for the real assault on the summit of Nanga Parbat, for in this place it was possible to construct a "strong point" fitted with sleeping-sacks, food and fuel. Müllritter returned from this point to Camp IV with a sick porter. His orders were to return later to Camps VI and VII and equip these in case of need with fuel and food, thus covering our retreat (from the top) to these camps.

From the jutting ridge-shoulder of the Rakhiot peak we turned on to the W. slope and avoided the summit. Afterwards, once more on the crest, we attained our Camp VI at a height of 6,900 m. It stood in the same place where Camp VII of the 1932 Expedition had been erected. In that year the party had attained the locality by the great hollow followed by a steep and fatiguing snow and ice gully. On this occasion, however, that route was blocked by an ice wall at the base of the gully, consequently we took the ridge route.

During this period, below at Camp IV, the weather was mostly bad. Higher up progress was *above* the clouds; these latter rising only towards nightfall and smothering the ridge. The wind, although violent, was not disagreeable. Progress along the snowy ridge was marvellous since everything below us was concealed by a sea of cloud from which Nanga Parbat—like an island—alone emerged. Below us fell the immense wall towards the Rupal Nulla; often the wind scooped a clearing in the clouds and we saw, 14,000 ft. below us, the level, débris-strewn glacier with its neighboring green meadows. For us who had lived for so many weeks in snow and ice, it was like a vision of another world.

We dug out a camp site for our tents in a notch in the ridge just below the steep rise to the *Silbersattel*—Camp VII, 7,100 m. The clouds had met on the ridge, causing a snowstorm and making our labor severe, in the evening, however, it cleared, and once more on the following day we became inhabitants of a lonely isle far above the clouds. In this place we could still eat, but it consisted mostly of soup, in which we dumped a great mass of butter for increased nourishment. We slept in two tents with two in each sleeping-bag. Bechtold left us here in Camp VII with two sick porters; he had been taking films up to this spot. His instructions also were to follow up with Müllritter later and keep Camps VI and VII open. At Camp VI four porters had had to fall out sick, so on July 6 we set out with eleven porters to Camp VIII—the last before the summit. We got away early, all were in good form, and progress was at the rate of 200 m (650 ft.) per hour. On the steep slopes leading to the *Silbersattel* we cut a series of steps for the porters. Above, sitting on the rocks of the E. peak, Aschenbrenner and I waited for the others following up with the porters, smoking cigarettes we had borrowed from the latter. The doctor had forbidden smoking for the party, consequently tobacco in Camp IV was very scarce. On the head of the column attaining the *Silbersattel* we proceeded, skirting the upper névés, as far as the first top (*Vorgipfel*). We then turned back, since we saw that the porters could not go farther, and Camp VIII, 7,600 m, was pitched close to the *Silbersattel*. It was still early when we turned back, the height was about 7,900 m, 50 m below the measured first top (25,800 ft.). A ridge some 900 m long and 240 m in height *(ca.* 800 ft.) still lay between us and the summit (26,620 ft.). We were full of confidence and never doubted about attaining the top next day.

That evening we were able to eat some soup and were quite carefree concerning the following day which was to consummate our victory. Fate, however, was against us. The night was still clear, but the wind raged—probably always the case. In the morning a tremendous snowstorm burst over the tents. The blizzard was so violent that it was almost impossible to breathe in the open; the driving snow was blown horizontally in broad sheets, while perpetual darkness seemed to gather about us. During the preceding night a pole of the larger tent was smashed, while a second went the same way on the following. It was impossible to dig out a cave in the level névé; the surface of the latter was wind-blown into an iron substance which even on the first night had but barely allowed us to scrape out a hollow for the tents. The small tent occupied by Aschenbrenner and myself was no longer sufficiently wind-proof against the elements; during the first night we lay in our sack amidst driving snow, but had managed to become almost accustomed to it. In spite of everything we decided to wait one more day, since according to the observations of 1932, a storm of this nature on Nanga Parbat hardly ever lasted more than a day. On this day we took nothing at all beyond half a cup of tea apiece. Food and fuel we possessed in sufficiency, but in the howling storm it proved impossible to melt snow or prepare any warm nourishment.

The second night was almost worse than the first. Yet another tent-pole broke during a squall, while at daybreak there was still no improvement. It was useless to wait yet another day and night; accordingly we decided to descend. Aschenbrenner and I led with three porters to break the trail, our companions intending to follow at once with the remaining natives. None of us was in bad condition and there were no complaints as to ailments. Our only sorrow was the thought of the long grind upwards again from Camp IV to VIII and of the valuable time lost. We thought ourselves certain to return in a few days when the weather had cleared.

On the *Silbersattel* an india-rubber mattress was torn off the back of a porter; this was immediately followed by a heavy sleeping-bag. The storm blew these horizontally and bodily into space—they vanished round a corner. The sleeping-bag was ours, the porters still possessed their own. On the steep traverse below the ridge we cut steps, while on the crest itself we forced our way through the snow masses. The storm drove countless snow particles into our eyes, so that we could see nothing; in fact, Aschenbrenner, 10 or 15 ft. away from me, became nothing but a greyish shadow.

We lost sight of our three porters near the tent of Camp VII. On the Rakhiot peak we followed the ridge over the top, turning down at the ropes towards Camp V. We dug the tents out of the snow and ate something. In the late afternoon we reached Camp IV, where Bechtold, Müllritter and Bernard were waiting. They had attempted vainly to mount on the preceding day, but were held up by masses of snow before reaching Camp V. We were of the opinion that the porters and our companions would soon follow us; when no one appeared we thought they had spent the night in Camp V. On the following day the storm continued, as it had in fact done in this spot for nearly a week. During the evening of the following day it cleared with a raging gale that swept the billowing clouds off the ridge. We perceived figures descending the Rakhiot peak and made towards them. They were four porters, Pasang, Kitar, Kikuli and Da Thondu; all were frost-bitten and completely exhausted. We rubbed them with snow and sent them down to the Base camp with Bernard on the following day. We attempted to go up and give help, but it proved impossible. Once we attained Camp V, three climbers and six porters, literally buried in bottomless snow up to our shoulders. Here another storm caught us; not a porter could move. We ourselves were too weak to go higher alone. On another occasion we even failed to reach Camp V; no porter then accompanied us—even they were exhausted utterly by the long high-altitude sojourn. On July 15 came the porter Angtsering from somewhere above Camp VI. From him we learnt of the tragedy above. Wieland had died near Camp VII; he appears to have sat down for a short rest and went to sleep without waking. Welzenbach died in Camp VII, while two porters, Nima Nurbu and Dakshi, perished higher up still. Merkl proceeded with Gay Lay and Angtsering some way towards Camp VI. About this place he sent on Angtsering to bring help; had it not been for this (? *i.e.* the previous presence of Merkl and his porter), the latter could hardly have possessed the strength to force his way down alone through the storm [sic]. Three porters, Nima Tashi, Pintzo Nurbu, and Nima Dorji, died shortly before Camp V. Gay Lay stayed with his Sahib—to die with him. May his memory be honoured for ever.

Meanwhile we sat almost within shouting distance and could do nothing. Always we tried to force our way up and ever we failed. Raechl and Misch came up to Camp IV to help; they failed equally to reach Camp V. It was dreadful, this continued effort, worse still to know that it was always vain and useless.

On July 18 we evacuated Camp IV and descended. The way was difficult, harder than on the way up, as we sorrowfully tracked through deep snow and the torn icefalls. Halfway down, between Camp II and III, we met Bechtold and Müllritter who had once more come up to help. It was far too late: our last hopes of being able to bury our dead friends and porters were extinguished in the drifts of new snow and continuous storms. Weary and worn out, we descended over the moraine pinnacles to the tents of the Base camp. Hieronimus and Kuhn came to meet us. Everything had been arranged at the Base, the sick porters looked after and much labor accomplished. The frost-bites of the porters healed well under the doctor's care . . .

▸   ▸   ▸

Shall we be lucky enough to fight another round with Nanga Parbat? And shall we once more return there?

A SHERPA'S STORY BY ANGTSERING

> "On the morning of the 9th, after sleeping between Camps VIII
> and VII—on the descent—the party left: myself, Gay Lay and
> Dakshi. I was snowblind and the other two weak. We three spent
> a further two nights without moving, after which my eyes im-
> proved. Dakshi was alive, but too weak to move, and so with

Gay Lay I proceeded down, leaving Dakshi. Before reaching Camp VII we saw Wieland's body. At Camp VII we met Merkl and Welzenbach. Merkl said, "Stay with us until food and help arrive." The Europeans had no sleeping-bags and sheltered in the only two-man tent. We two porters had sleeping bags and no tent. We all stayed at this camp for another two nights. On the second night Welzenbach died, after which I said to Merkl, "We must go down, as no help will come up to us." So myself, carrying two sleeping-bags and Merkl's rucksack and ground-sheet, made the track down, Gay Lay and Merkl following. After covering three quarters of the distance to Camp VI Merkl could not go on, and at this point we spent the night. The next morning, from our position above Camp VI, I saw three Europeans and four porters coming up from Camp III to Camp IV, but no movement was made upwards from Camp IV. I pressed the Sahib to continue on down. His hands and feet were very badly frost-bitten, also his face, and he was absolutely helpless. He then ordered Gay Lay down to Camp IV with orders to the Sahibs to bring up brandy, food and every assistance. Gay Lay was unable to proceed, and I undertook to go down carrying my ice-axe only and leaving at 5 A.M. As my hands and feet were frost-bitten, progress was very slow. Below Camp V I called out for assistance to Camp IV. It was a long time before anyone heard me. At last Pasang Dorji and Nurbu Sonam came out with tea laced with brandy, and assisted me in to Camp IV. I told Lewa that Merkl (and Gay Lay) were above in Camp VI and wanted immediate help in the way of stimulants, food and porters to carry them down. A rescue party was fixed for the following day. This party was unable to venture upwards, as conditions were too bad. I had not eaten from the day we left Camp VIII. In Camp IV there were six Europeans and four porters, the former fit, but the latter unfit for further work."

"MUZTAGH ATA"

FROM
Two Mountains and a River
in *The Seven Mountain-Travel Books*
BY H. W. TILMAN

ARGUABLY THE MOST GIFTED MOUNTAIN-TRAVEL EXPLORER AND writer of all time, H. W. "Bill" Tilman loved climbing mountains, but he loved even more exploring new territory. Tilman climbed and explored all over Africa and Asia, often with his frequent expedition partner Eric Shipton. He recounted his land-based adventures in a series of lushly detailed, masterfully written books that are benchmarks in the field. Then when he deemed himself too old to climb mountains, he took up bluewater sailing—and produced a series of books on his high-seas adventures. Born in 1898, Tilman responded to surviving the horrors of soldiering in World War I by taking off to explore the natural world. He had a home in Britain but spent much of his time in foreign lands, always looking for what lay in the next valley or over the next ridge, always enjoying his meetings with native peoples who found their visitor equally fascinating. Tilman's adventurous life came to an end in an appropriate fashion: he was on a boat that disappeared in the South Atlantic in 1977, his eightieth year.

Tilman's most serious climbs took place in the 1930s, during which he made first ascents on Mount Kenya and in the Ruwenzori, twice attempted Mount Everest, and made the first ascent of Nanda Devi in 1936. By 1947, the year in which the Muztagh Ata expedition took place, he was more interested in the journey through remote territories than in bagging the peak. Tilman and Shipton, with Gyalgen Sherpa, came within 500 feet of a first ascent on this 24,788-foot peak in the Kunlun Range of China. They approached the peak by an easy but long route and were surprised by extreme cold near their high point. The retreat came when Shipton experienced frostbite on both feet and all three were exhausted.

This chapter on the Muztagh Ata attempt represents some of the best examples of Tilman's self-mocking, ironic style and the dry humor with which he approached human foibles, including his own. The reader is treated to some vivid portraits, including Mrs. Shipton's attempt at entertaining a "posse" of Chinese officials who cannot even get themselves through the door, and a discussion on the proper way to ride a yak (which goes unrewarded, as the party's yak is a model of unreliability).

This selection is Chapter 11 from *Two Mountains and a River* by H. W. Tilman, first published in 1949 by Cambridge University Press, and republished in *H.W. Tilman: The Seven Mountain-Travel Books*, pages 597-605.

I n a tent in the garden of the Postal Superintendent (a Hunza man) I found the Consul and his wife. They were on an extended tour and had arrived the previous evening. In most countries I associate consuls with long flights of stairs at the top of which is an office with a locked door and a small printed card bearing the legend "Consulate of Utopia—Office hours, Saturdays only, 10-12," and it struck me that in Kashgar a consul must be an even rarer bird of passage. The answer is, however, that here the British Consul being no mere parochial stamper of passports is expected to travel about and, like the sun, to shed his beneficent rays over the whole of Kashgaria. Tashkurghan, the capital of Sarikol, is also a receiving and dispatching center on the mail route to India and is therefore important enough to deserve official attention. If then by any chance his return journey were to lie in the direction of Muztagh Ata the Chinese of all people would be the last to demur; for did not Confucius say: "The wise find pleasure in waters, the virtuous in mountains": and again the epigrams of Chang Ch'ao tell us: "If there are no famous hills then nothing need be said, but since there are, they must be visited."

In former days Tashkurghan must have been a town of some importance, for it lies on one of the two ancient routes from China to Western Asia and the Persian Gulf. Two very great travelers, Marco Polo and the Chinese Buddhist pilgrim Hsuan-tsang (c. A.D. 600) must have visited it. Nowadays it is only of secondary importance, for the bulk of what trade there is with India goes by the Leh route. A lifeless bazaar, some serais usually empty, the modern Chinese fort and magistracy, and the ruins of the walled town of earlier days, are all it can boast. But its proximity to the Russian frontier, across which there is a pass less then twenty miles south-west of the town, make it of some interest to the Chinese, who have installed a small garrison. In 1946 the local "nationalists," with assistance from over the border, took and held Tashkurghan for some time.

Before we could start for Muztagh Ata the duties of hospitality had to be discharged. The Amban and the officers of the garrison invited us to lunch and, since we were in haste to be off, the Consul insisted that they should give us our revenge by dining with us the same day. The Chinese custom of multiplying the courses of a meal almost to infinity is well known, and though the resources of Tashkurghan did not give our hosts the scope they would have wished they did their best and we had to deal seriatim with the following: by way of limbering up there was tea with brandy butter in it, cake and apples; then meat patties, meat balls, fried eggs and radishes, roast mutton, liver, duck, local fish, soup, and rice, the last being the accepted way of delivering the *coup de grâce* at these feasts. Chopsticks, knives, spoons, forks, and fingers, were all brought into play according to the toughness of the opposition, and the whole was eased down with "kumiss," fermented mare's milk—colorless, slightly alcoholic, sour, and reminiscent of cider. The uncultured yahoo when he gives a feast (and I prefer it his way) merely increases the amount of the ordinary meal. Instead of a few scraggy bones, one or two sheep are dished up, instead of a bowl of rice or pilau, a bucket of it; but civilized people like the Romans, the Chinese, and to a lesser extent ourselves, like to measure their social status by the number and variety of the courses, which I consider a barbaric habit, destructive to the stomach and inimical to good cooking.

One of the principal difficulties in entertaining a posse of Chinese officials (Mrs. Shipton had fourteen to cope with) is to get them inside the room. Questions of precedence lead to what threatens to be an interminable contest of polite diffidence until it is cut short by the pressure from behind of those whose claims are too lowly to be worth disputing and whose hunger is too sharp to be any longer denied. The posse surges forward, and when the less nimble have picked themselves up from the floor the contest is renewed over the question of seating. It was a pretty motley assortment that eventually got themselves sat down—one which was difficult to weld into a convivial whole, aided though it was by Russian brandy and Shipton's manful sallies into the uncharted intricacies of Chinese, of which he had enough to excite my admiration and to fascinate the Chinese. Most Chinese are abstemious

to a fault. Only the Amban and a man who claimed to have accompanied Sir
Aurel Stein on some of his journeys (in the capacity of coolie I judged from
his appearance) willingly submitted themselves to the mellowing influence
of the brandy.

Next morning, August 8, we got off at the surprisingly early hour of 9:30,
accompanied by two camels carrying the baggage and a Mongolian horde to
speed us on our way—the Amban himself, all the officers, and Sir Aurel Stein's
coolie, whom I only recognized with difficulty, as he was now wearing a
Homburg hat, silver-rimmed sun goggles, and knickerbockers, looking like a
great explorer in his own right. At the first village the cavalcade dismounted
and after a long bout of grinning and handshaking the Lesser Horde took its
departure and we headed for the north.

At this point the Tashkurghan river is deflected eastwards and a low ridge,
pierced by the narrow gorge of the Tagharma river, separates its wide valley
from the even more extensive Tagharma plain. This extends to the north for
about twelve miles, until it meets another ridge upon which lies the Ulugh
Rabat pass (14,000 ft.). The pass leads into another almost equally wide valley
running north between the Sarikol range on the west and the Muztagh Ata
and Kungur groups to the east. The Tagharma plain abounds in villages and
cultivation, while the higher valley beyond is the happy home of many Kirghiz,
their herds and their flocks.

Emerging from the bare yellow rock gorge we were delighted by the sight
of the green Tagharma vale, its scattered villages, the tall poplars, the browsing
herds, and waving wheat-fields. Our guides, vaguely aware that the consular
mind was intent on mountains, took us too far to the east in the direction of
the most southerly foothills of the Muztagh Ata group, until we finally came
to rest in a village at the foot of a nallah, which undoubtedly led directly to
the heart of the mountains. With some difficulty we resisted the insistent invitation of this interesting unknown nallah, and next morning we sheered
away to the north-west in the direction of the Ulugh Rabat pass. The transport—ponies now instead of camels—passed us going at the rate of knots
and Naiad Shah was instructed to tell the men to halt for the night at a graz-
ing ground this side of the pass. But he apparently failed to select from his

repertoire the correct language in which to give the order, for when we reached the place—all of us fully ripe for stopping—there was no sign of the ponies. Shipton, the two mounted infantrymen whom we had been obliged to accept as escort, and anyone else whose beast was capable of it, galloped off in pursuit but without success. By 7 P.M. we were on top of the Ulugh Rabat and in extremely bad tempers. There was a noble prospect to the dark plain below and the white dome of Muztagh Ata above, now rapidly dissolving in the dusk. But the noblest prospect is improved by the sight of an inn, and though our inn was now in sight on the plain below, it was rapidly receding across it. How we reviled that man of many tongues. Water arrested the march of the flying column and by 8 P.M. we and our transport were united by some muddy pools. Stragglers were still coming in an hour later. Most high uplands are made unpleasant by constant wind, but that night we were spared the usual gale which makes cooking in the open impossible. While supper was preparing we had leisure to reflect on the truth of Cromwell's remark that "no man goes further than he who does not know where he is going."

We were now fairly under the western slopes of Muztagh Ata, and although we were not yet within striking distance we were well able to appreciate its enormous bulk. The south side of this so-called "Father of Ice Mountains" is defended by two outlying peaks each over 22,000 ft.; the north side is steep and broken and the east side is unexplored. (On my return journey I passed round by the east side, but bad weather shut out any view of the mountain.) The west side is a huge gently curving sweep of snow, the lower part split by three almost parallel glaciers. Originating at about 20,000 ft. in deep narrow clefts these glaciers, when they reach the snow line at about 17,000 ft., spill and spread over the slopes of brown scree like streams of white lava, descending in a cascade of ice pinnacles to as low as 14,000 ft. That one aspect alone of a mountain can contain three such glaciers is an indication of its breadth, for the lower parts of the glaciers are separated by two or even three miles of scree slope.

Two names famous in Central Asian exploration are connected with Muztagh Ata. In 1894 the great Swedish explorer Sven Hedin, in addition to making a rough survey of the mountain, made four attempts to climb it. Rough survey is the word, for he ascribed to it a height of 25,600 ft., and "the un-challenged pre-eminence over the peaks which cluster round, which is proved by its name 'Father of Ice Mountains.'" The Kungur group, less than twenty-five miles north-east, he either ignored or else did not see, for the unaided eye can appreciate that one at least of its peaks is higher than Muztagh Ata. As for the name, the story is that the reply to the question about its name was simply "Muztagh, Ata" or "Ice Mountain, O Father." In 1900 the late Sir Aurel Stein made a survey of the Sarikol valley and his surveyor, Ram Singh of the Indian Survey, carried out the triangulation of the Muztagh Ata and Kungur groups, discovering that the highest peak of Kungur is 25,146 ft. against 24,388 ft. for Muztagh Ata.

Having studied both the ground and Sven Hedin's account of his attempts we decided that the best line of approach was that between the two largest of these western glaciers, the Yam Bulak and the Tergam Bulak. Some Kirghiz yorts were reported to be in a valley north of the Yam Bulak glacier about two hours away and there we thought we would have our base. In these parts of Sinkiang yorts exert a powerful attraction which the wise traveler should on no account resist. Such a thought never occurred to us for a moment—we merely crawled from one yort to the next, drinking tea, eating yogurt, and studying nomadic life, though we ourselves were much more nomadic than our hosts, whose lives seemed to be remarkably static, even sedentary. Since travelers are rare they are usually welcome; food, fire, and shelter are auto-matically put at their disposal by the kindly Kirghiz.

When we reached the little valley under the slopes of the mountain where we had proposed harboring, we were disturbed to find only one yort. All the families but one had just moved down to Subashi a few miles away and the principal place of the Sarikol plain. The remaining one, too, was about to go but they readily postponed their departure when they heard that Mrs. Shipton would be alone for a few days while we were on the mountain. In the afternoon we sorted out food for our expedition and in the evening we walked up towards the Yam Bulak glacier to reconnoiter a route for the morrow. On the moraine two herds of what looked like wild goats were playing about.

Sven Hedin was a great explorer, but he made no claim to be a mountaineer.

As he therefore had no false pride to maintain he made full use of the local aids to progress in his attempts on the mountain. Of the four his most successful was the second, when, carried on the back of a yak, he claimed to have reached a height of 20,600 ft. As he justly observes, the secret of freedom from the troubles of altitude (a secret which so far has eluded research) "is the avoidance of bodily exertion."

He employed yaks for all his attempts and from his free use of them on the mountain we may deduce several things; the absence of any technical difficulties on the west side, at any rate for a great part of the way up; the absence of man-power in Sinkiang, where no Turki who can afford an ass and no Kirghiz who owns a yak or a pony ever walks, much less carries anything; and finally the all-round supremacy of yaks over donkeys, mules, horses, camels, or even elephants, though Hannibal might dispute the last. As a load-carrier the yak's powers are well known, but his virtues as a hack are unrecognized. Although Central Asia is the ancestral home of the horse, one may travel there a long time without becoming aware of it, or if already aware of it one may conclude that he has remained at home too long. No doubt there are some good horses, but the locals very wisely keep them for themselves, mounting the innocent stranger on their sorriest screws, so that if it should happen to fall down with him no harm is done except, perhaps, to the stranger.

A good riding yak is much to be preferred to the sort of beast one is commonly invited to put one's leg over. He will do his three miles an hour without the incessant kicking and flogging which is essential in keeping the local jade up to the bit (the yak, by the way, has no bit, only a rope through the nose), while his short legs and quick step give the rider the comfortable if illusory impression that he is covering the ground at a great rate. On going uphill there is no need for the rider to dismount to spare his yak. On going downhill there is no need for him to dismount to spare his own neck, for the yak takes everything as it comes, uphill or downhill, rough or smooth. In fording rivers, despite those short legs, he is as steady as a rock, for his great weight keeps him well anchored to the bottom. And, of course, at heights of 16,000 ft. or more, when the horse like the rest of us is beginning to suffer from the effects of height, the yak is just beginning to feel at home; he may blow like a grampus but his tremendous girth ensures that there is plenty of air in the bellows. And finally, if the snow is reached, he is sent ahead to break a trail for the floundering men and horses behind him; and should his fortunate rider need a pair of sun glasses all he has to do is to turn round and yank a length of hair from his copious tail.*

Profiting by Sven Hedin's example Shipton and I determined that though we ourselves might condescend to walk we should have a yak to carry our camp to the snow-line at about 17,000 ft. Not wishing to retract much of what I have just written I must assume that our yak was the exception that proves the rule, or that like all other mountaineers yaks have their off days. He was, indeed, a total failure.

With stores for six days three of us started on August 11 accompanied by a Sherpa (Gyalgen, a former Everest porter and one of Shipton's servants), a Turki lad, a yak and his driver. The weather since we left Tashkurghan had been cloudy and unsettled, but this day was fine, calm, and sunny. Having rounded the snout of the Yam Bulak glacier, three or four miles from the yort, we took the long easy scree slope lying between that glacier and the Tergam Bulak to the south of it. Unencumbered ourselves, confident in our yak's prowess, we climbed comfortably to about 16,000 ft., where we sat down to await the arrival of the yak and the rest of the party. Time passed, our confidence waned. Nothing could be heard, nothing seen, for the slope, from the bottom almost to top, being as convexly regular as a schoolroom globe, limited our horizon to less than a hundred yards. Reluctantly we started down to investigate and presently came upon Gyalgen, the Turki, and the yak driver, staggering up under heavy loads. Of the yak, the party's main hope and king-pin, there was no sign. He had very sensibly struck and sat down at the very first hint of what was expected of him. The driver, too, thought no more of mountaineering than did his charge. Groaning and moaning on account of his splitting headache, and fearful of the certain death that awaited us if we proceeded, he had to be sent down at once, pursued by sounds of desultory ill-will. The rest of us struggled on with the loads,

---

*A few black hairs stretched across the eyes, while allowing one to see, are semi-effective against glare.

marveling how much better they did these things in Sven Hedin's time.

Shipton, discarding chivalry in favor of the principle of economy of force, had allowed his wife to relieve him of a sleeping-bag and a cork mattress. There was apparently more in marriage than I had yet realized, but now it was too late to repair the omission and I had to bear my own burden. We plodded on for another thousand feet and camped at 3 P.M. just below the first snow at about 17,000 ft. From here Mrs. Shipton and the Turki lad went down, leaving Gyalgen, myself, and her grateful but unfeeling husband to finish the job.

That evening we did a short reconnaissance. Just above our tent, scree gave place to snow, or rather ice, for the snow had melted from the lowest 200 or 300 ft. of underlying ice. The slope, however, was gentle, so that with care one could walk without nicking steps. Higher up was a short ice-fall which could be turned, beyond that a long stretch of crevassed snow-slope, and beyond that again unbroken slopes extending to the summit dome. Most of this, except for the actual summit whose exact whereabouts we could not locate, we had already seen from below. Our safe and methodical plan was to have a camp at about 20,000 ft. and another at 22,000 ft. from which no matter how moderately we rated ourselves, we ought to have no great difficulty in crawling to the top.

Next day we started, Shipton and I carrying very modest loads and Gyalgen rather an immodest one. The ice-fall was soon overcome by an outflanking movement, and having threaded our way through the worst of the crevassed section we camped at 3 P.M. in a snow hollow, crediting ourselves with a rise of 3,000 ft. The snow was in really excellent condition, everything was going to be too easy. This gratuitous supposition and Gyalgen's faltering under his too heavy load had already caused an alteration in a perfectly sound plan. Assuming that the snow, so good here, could be no worse higher up and might well be better, we agreed to cut out the intermediate camp at 22,000 ft. and to take only one bite at the cherry—an agreement which I, aware of my advancing years and limited high-climbing powers, had no right to make. We arrived at this pregnant decision during a halt on the way up from Camp 1, while we were pondering over ways of easing Gyalgen's burden, neither of us having the indelicacy to suggest taking some of it upon ourselves. Since this new plan meant that we should, if all went well, spend only one more night on the mountain some of the food (we had four days' supply) could be dumped. But Shipton's liberal ideas of dumping and his ruthless whittling down to a bare one day's supply led to a sharp debate. Although I may have had private misgivings about our only needing one day's food I had already agreed to the change of plan and there was little I could urge against this wholesale sacrifice beyond the desirability of keeping an ample reserve. Possibly the fact that nothing from my own load was dumped made me the more reluctant to see so much left behind.

As I had been on Rakaposhi only two months before, I expected to be better acclimatized than I proved to be; but there, though we had been twice to 20,000 ft. we had never slept higher than 17,000 ft. That night I had a violent headache and in the morning felt no more like climbing four feet than the four thousand odd which we had cheerfully set ourselves. Still it had to be done—one day being our self-allotted span—so at 6 A.M. we got under way.

Though not a breath of wind stirred in our hollow, it was noticeably cold in the bleak and pallid dawn. Merely by fumbling with buttons after some necessary business outside my thumbs and forefingers were so chilled that they never felt right for the rest of the day. Well down as we were on the west side of this considerable protuberance on the earth's sphere—almost another sphere in itself—the sun would be long in reaching us. The more reason therefore for pressing rapidly onwards and upwards to meet it, so off we went over the good hard snow. For a thousand feet we climbed rapidly and hopefully, and then conditions suddenly became worse. The snow assumed that vile consistency which necessitates one's stamping with all one's might once, twice, or even three times to ensure that the step will not give way the moment it is stood upon. Worse still, a wind started to blow. Its force seemed negligible—in the unlikely event of our wearing straw hats I doubt if we should have had to hold them on—but nevertheless it cut to the bone. The exertion of stamping steps contributed nothing to our warmth, nor did the sun when it at length reached us, so that even at this early stage the effects of these conditions became serious. Shipton was overcome by a fit of rigor and lay shaking in the snow, while we sat by shivering with a violence only a little less.

On we plodded up that vast tilted snow-field, seeing no other mountains either to north or south by which to measure our progress. Though we moved slowly we moved continuously, for it was too cold to sit and rest and eat. As early as 1 o'clock we had the impression of arriving somewhere, but two hours later all we could say was that that impression was no weaker. Still we thought the end must be very near. We reckoned we had climbed a thousand feet in the first hour when the snow was good, and having been climbing steadily since then for eight hours we argued that most of the remaining three thousand odd feet were below us. Whenever we dared to look up our eyes met the same unbroken snow horizon, maintaining its unconquerably rigid distance of two or three hundred feet. And now the long hours of cold, fatigue, and deferred hope began to tell.

Some while before this my contribution to step-kicking had become of small account and presently Gyalgen, too, found himself unable to take his turn. Shipton had still a little left in him, so that we agreed to struggle on for another half-hour until 3:30 P.M. when, if there was still no firm indication of the summit, we would give up and try again another day. Quite early in the afternoon I had suggested going back so that next day we should have the advantage of a great many ready-made steps; but this had been overruled on the ground that tomorrow the steps might no longer be there. This was true enough because, when we did come to go down, we had trouble even to find the steps, so completely had the driving snow filled them.

After a generous half-hour's extra play in this hard-fought game between the mountain and ourselves a decision in our favor seemed as far off as ever. For me the delusion of the summit being at hand had long become stale, stimulating despair rather than hope. I feared that even if we reached a point from which the summit could be seen we should find it at the wrong end of a long flat ridge, for the perversity of inanimate objects is always a factor to be reckoned with. By this time we were all pretty well on our knees. Had the summit been in sight and our remaining task measurable, some hidden reserves of strength might have been found, but there was still nothing to be seen beyond the next hundred feet or so of snow. To persevere one must have hope, and this, which had been pretty severely tried, had now perished, worn out by too long deferment.

If we allowed only two hours to get down there was still time enough to struggle on for another hour could we but force our bodies onwards. But before the clock had time to impose its decision on us we gave up. Perhaps we were weak-minded—in fact, we damned ourselves heartily later—but our wisest actions are sometimes those for which we are not fully responsible and the sequel showed that we did well to go down. Exclusive of halts for vomiting by Shipton the descent did take about two hours. Our up-coming tracks were by now obliterated, so that the finding of the way through the crevassed area was less easy than it had before been. After dark we could not have found it.

Back in the tent an unpleasant discovery awaited us. All the toes on one of Shipton's feet were frost-bitten. They were dead white that evening and black the next morning. The tips of both my big toes were slightly touched and went black, but came painfully back to life 48 hours later. I was wearing the "expedition" boots with the heavy moulded rubber soles and Shipton a pair of the heavily nailed porters' boots which I had brought out for Rakaposhi and which he maintained had got wet the previous day so that they had ice inside them before we started. Gyalgen, who was wearing lightly nailed boots, came to no harm. As a purely speculative consolation it may not amount to much, but there is little doubt that had we persevered for another hour the damage would have been much more serious. Success would have been a very considerable consolation, but it would only have been gained at a high cost. Failure with frost-bite thrown in was a tough bullet to chew.

The condition of Shipton's foot was, of course, decisive—we had to go down—but in point of fact not one of us was fit to try again next day or even for several days. The effort had taken more out of us than we realized and a week later I still found it more than usually trying to walk uphill at all.

Whether the top of the mountain is a long flat ridge or whether, as seems more likely, it is a flattish dome we still do not know. Shipton is of the opinion that we were on the summit dome and not more than a hundred feet below the top. An inexcusable assumption of the probable snow conditions, overconfidence in our powers, and the unexpected cold, had proved our undoing, and of these, only of the last had we any right to complain. In early June on the North Col of Everest one would not experience such cold. Here it was mid-August, and though Muztagh Ata is in Lat. 38° and Everest is 10° further south one would not expect that to make so much difference. We live and learn, and big mountains are stern teachers.

"GRIM DAYS ON HARAMOSH"

BY TONY STREATHER WITH RALPH BARKER

FROM
Heroic Climbs: A Celebration of World Mountaineering
CHRIS BONINGTON, EDITOR

AS WITH MANY OF THE MOUNTAINEERING EPICS THAT STICK IN OUR collective memory, the real story of the 1957 Oxford University expedition to Haramosh began after the party realized they would fail to climb the peak.

Tony Streather, a British army officer, was a Himalayan "veteran" at age thirty-one when he accepted leadership of the Haramosh expedition. He had climbed Tirich Mir in 1950, was a strong member of the ill-fated 1953 American K2 Expedition, and made the second ascent of Kangchenjunga in 1955.

Streather's four-man high-climbing party was aiming for a first ascent on Haramosh, a 24,270-foot unclimbed peak in Pakistan, south of the Rakaposhi Range. Just as the party stood at the point where the true difficulties of the peak lay revealed before them, a sudden avalanche shuffled the deck to set off one of the most haunting tragedies in the history of Himalayan climbing.

The avalanche swept two of the climbers into an inaccessible basin from which the only escape was upward through steep ice cliffs. Accident soon led to tragedy, as the rescuers themselves came to need rescuing, one climber was saved only to later walk straight off the mountain to his death, and another had to be left alive to meet his fate in the death-trap basin.

The full story of this classic tale of courage and endurance was told in the book *The Last Blue Mountain* by journalist Ralph Barker. Streather joins Barker in this condensed version, published in *Heroic Climbs: A Celebration of World Mountaineering,* Chris Bonington, editor; pages 164-167.

C ome on up!" I called. "You can't imagine what you'll see when you get here!"

For the four of us who made up the high-climbing party on Haramosh, this was a bittersweet moment. Forced to lower our sights by unseasonable weather, we had at last reached a point, between the mountain's twin peaks, from which its secrets were dramatically revealed.

After five weeks of frustration, it was some consolation to realize that even with favorable weather this 24,270-foot summit in the Karakoram would probably have been beyond us. A stronger parry, not so restricted for time, might succeed, but for each of us other commitments intruded, and tomorrow we were going to have to start the descent.

Bernard Jillott, seeking an even more spectacular vantage point, urged John Emery, our doctor, to climb to a pinnacle a little farther up the ridge, "Then Tony can take a picture of us." Roping up, the two had almost reached the pinnacle when there was a muffled, subterranean explosion, and simultaneously the snow on which they were standing started to move. With Rae Culbert, the fourth member of our group, I watched stupefied as our friends swept past with terrifying acceleration, down into the snow basin a thousand feet below. There seemed nothing to stop them being carried on with the avalanche straight over the North Face. When the snow flurries subsided, I moved across to the avalanche trail and, belayed by Culbert, peered down the slope into the basin. To my astonishment and joy, I could see two crumpled figures emerging from the snow. Jillott and Emery had survived the fall, but they were trapped in an inaccessible place. I couldn't see how we were going to get them out.

Bernard Jillott, at 23 the prime mover of our expedition, was President of the Oxford University Mountaineering Club. The year was 1957. A few months earlier he had invited me to talk to the club about my experiences on K2 and Kangchenjunga, and this was when the subject of Haramosh was broached. Three other club members wanted to go, Jillott told me, but he felt they needed a "veteran"—I was 31—to lend credibility to the project. Would I be their leader? His single-mindedness impressed me, and I soon found myself drawn into the expedition by the enthusiasm of the group.

With the leadership settled, Jillott set about the planning and obtaining permissions and sponsorship with characteristic energy. His favorite climbing partner was a young medical student named Emery, and as one of my stipulations was that the party should include a "doctor," Emery, keen to come, fitted the bill admirably. I found him less obsessive than Jillott, of wider interests and broader vision. Jillott's final choice for the high-altitude party was New Zealand forestry graduate Rae Culbert. At 25, Culbert owed his greater maturity not so much to his age as to three years surveying with the New Zealand Forest Service and a deep affinity with his work. Each of us, at various times, was to turn to Culbert for friendship. A fifth member of the expedition, though excluded from the high-altitude party by inexperience, was the American, Scott D. Hamilton, Jr., 29 and a graduate of Cornell University. Devoted to Jillott and Emery, his puritanical upbringing left him wincing at Culbert's colorful language, but he recognized in him an ally from the New World.

From Heathrow to Karachi and forward to Gilgit, 40 miles west of Haramosh, we traveled by air, all except Emery, who voyaged by sea with the expedition stores. At Gilgit we engaged porters to help carry our stores to the high camps. A day's ride to the road-head at Sussi and two days on foot brought us to the high Kutwal Valley and the Mani Glacier, where we set up base camp.

Our initial aim was reconnaissance: to explore and survey the approaches to Haramosh. But I knew well enough that I had in my party, skillful and ambitious climbers, capable, once a pyramid of camps was built, of a disciplined dash for the summit.

Starting our assault via the Northeast Ridge, we moved base camp up to the head of the valley, below the pass known as the Haramosh La. Soon we had established Camp I half-way up towards the La and found a site beyond it for Camp II.

Progress in the next few days was slow. The Northeast Ridge proved impossible for porters, and the detour forced upon us led through a grotesquely crevassed icefall, causing further delay. Then the weather broke, driving us back down. By extending our travel bookings I managed to devise a new 12-day assault plan which still gave us an outside chance of reaching the summit. But when we finally left base camp on the 29th of August, fresh snow combined with clashes of temperament to threaten cohesion. Yet gradually we were shedding something of our individualism, pooling our resources, becoming a team. Camp III was put in at 18,500 feet, Camp IV at 20,000. Hamilton retreated with orders to keep Camp III open, and on September 15th, in good snow conditions, we succeeded at last in breaking through to the Northeast Ridge.

I had watched continually for signs of avalanche conditions, and I felt perfectly safe on the ridge. But it was the first time we had stood on a slope facing northwest. A great weight of snow must have been driven against it to account for the avalanche.

Now, judging that Jillott and Emery would survive perfectly well in the snow basin for the night, I returned to Camp IV with Culbert, for sustenance, to fill thermos flasks of hot soup for Jillott and Emery, and to collect more rope. Then we set out again for the ridge, hoping to get down to the basin that night.

It was ten o'clock when we reached the ridge. The night was dark, but we had torches. Asking Culbert to keep me on a fairly tight rope, 300 feet of it, I started down the slope. Soon the snow hardened and I felt safer; I was in the track of the avalanche. The same area wouldn't avalanche twice. As the slope steepened I was forced to turn and face into it, as though going backwards down a ladder. Sometimes I half-turned and shone my torch down the slope, shouting as I did so. Soon I heard answering shouts. When the rope pulled taut, Culbert joined me, and together we resumed the descent. It was tedious work, and we were astonished when it began to get light. The second day of our traumas had begun. Now we could see Jillott and Emery waving to us, and hear their warning shouts. A line of ice-cliffs lay directly below us, and there was no way down. We would have to traverse along the top of the ice-cliffs until they petered out. The effort taxed us both, and it was late afternoon before we approached the end of the traverse, by which time we had been climbing almost continuously since the morning of Day 1.

It was at this point that Culbert lost a crampon. I already knew that Jillott and Emery had lost their ice axes. Now, as I caught Culbert's eye, we both knew how significant this latest loss might be.

From the end of the traverse we started down a 400-foot slope, which ended in a bergschrund or large crevasse at the change of levels. Again we had to go down backwards, kicking steps. But at last we reached the bergschrund. Advancing to the upper lip, we lowered a rope, Jillott and Emery tied on in turn, and a moment was spared to celebrate our reunion. But there was no time to waste. Although the light was already failing, no one doubted that we must start the climb out that night. We had almost reached the traverse, on a single rope, Culbert leading, when something crashed into me and knocked me off the slope. It was Culbert, hampered by his lost crampon. Our combined weight dislodged Jillott and Emery and we fell together in a tangled mass straight over the bergschrund and back into the snow basin. No one was hurt, but I had lost my ice axe in the fall. Taking over the lead, using Culbert's axe, I tried again. It was almost dark now, but later there would be a moon. Again we had nearly reached the traverse when I found myself falling: Jillott had gone to sleep in his tracks and dragged us off a second time. Exhausted, we spent the night jammed in the bergschrund, huddled together to keep warm.

When it began to get light—it was now Day 3—I climbed out of the crevasse. I felt fairly strong, but I knew the others had been less fortunate. We had a difficult day ahead of us. We had climbed about 300 feet, without roping up, when Emery spotted an axe sticking out of the slope; it was the axe I had been using during the night, Culbert's axe, and I could now cut much firmer steps. But on the traverse, first Emery and then Culbert felt themselves slipping. Digging in with his crampons, Emery arrested the slide. But Culbert, with his cramponless foot already frostbitten, called to me for help. I replied that I would give him a belay from the end of the traverse. Reaching it, I climbed a few feet up the slope to be sure of safe ground, then made way for Jillott and Emery and told them to go back to Camp IV. "We'll follow you shortly," I said. Almost immediately, Culbert came off the traverse. The jerk was too much for me to hold, and soon we were tumbling the lower half of the avalanche fall suffered by Jillott and Emery. But with no snow falling with us, to cushion us, we were shaken and concussed. Already it was getting dark, the end of Day 3. Jillott called down, "We'll go on back to camp and get food and drink. We'll be back to help you as soon as we can."

Culbert and I fell into an uneasy sleep. All our hopes now rested on Jillott and Emery. We would wake for Day 4, but it was plain to me that Culbert would not survive another night.

Next morning I found I was suffering from snow-blindness. I had lost my goggles and the two ice-axes, and I was also hallucinating. But we had to get going. Jillott and Emery would have reached Camp IV during the night, and

I calculated that after food and rest they would be back at the point of the avalanche by about midday. I expected to meet them somewhere on the traverse. Twice more, as we climbed the steep slope to the traverse, Culbert slipped and fell off. The second time he sat where he landed, absolutely all in. I called to him to hang on where he was. "The others will be down soon." They would bring food and drink, a spare ice axe and a spare crampon. Between us we would get Culbert out. Yet as time passed there was still no sign of them. What could be delaying them? I began to fear that something had gone desperately wrong.

When I reached the point where I had belayed Culbert across the final stretch of the traverse, I saw something sticking out of the snow; it was the axe I had been using, Culbert's axe. It gave me renewed strength.

Picking up the track back to Camp IV I realized that Jillott and Emery had taken a different route from the original, and with much trepidation I followed it. It proved to be a dead short cut. After avoiding numerous hazards I joined up with the original track. Then, with darkness falling on the fourth day since leaving Camp IV, I picked out the two tents, dreading what I might find. Emery was lying on top of his sleeping bag, shaken and distressed. There was no sign of Jillott. I asked the obvious question. "Where's Bernard?"

"He's gone."

"Gone? Gone where?"

"He's gone. He's dead. He walked straight off the mountain."

I learned with mounting horror how Jillott, driven by his determination to return as quickly as possible to the snow basin, had forged ahead, and how Emery, trying to follow, had fallen into a crevasse, lost consciousness, and lain unprotected all night. When he came to that morning he had struggled out and followed Jillott's tracks until they reached a point where, in the darkness of the previous night, he had walked off the mountain.

Emery had called repeatedly but got no answer. Later I did the same. Meanwhile Emery asked his own question. "Where's Rae?"

"I'm afraid he's still in the basin. He kept slipping off. We'll have to go back for him." Even as I said it, I saw the utter hopelessness of it. With Jillott dead and Emery so badly frostbitten that he was almost totally incapacitated, the only practical task that remained was to try to get him off the mountain alive.

To leave a comrade to his fate on a mountain was an abandonment not to be contemplated. But I had known, when I left Culbert, that he could not survive another night. I could do nothing for him now. For hour after hour I kept melting snow in an effort to slake our thirst. Then we tried to sleep. For the first time on the expedition we took sleeping pills, but they brought no rest for me. I was too preoccupied with thoughts of Rae Culbert, the man who in our separate ways we had all loved, and of the tragic end to the highly promising life of Bernard Jillott.

Emery and I fashioned a halting means of progress that eventually got us down to Camp III, where an anguished Hamilton called to us as we approached: "Are we safe?" Somehow I gasped out the truth. Hamilton, stunned by the news, broke down, as I did at that moment. I still believe that, but for the mischance of a lost crampon, we would all have got safely off the mountain.

Hamilton knew the route from Camp III to base camp better than anyone, and in the next two days and nights his help was crucial. When at last we spotted the Hunza porters coming up to meet us, Emery and I collapsed.

Haramosh was climbed in the following year by an Austrian expedition. The long ridge from the scene of the avalanche took them eight hours.

"INTERVIEW WITH JEAN-CHRISTOPHE LAFAILLE"

FROM
Kiss or Kill: Confessions of a Serial Climber
BY MARK TWIGHT

IMAGINE YOURSELF PINNED HIGH ON THE STORM-SWEPT SOUTH face of Annapurna when your climbing partner suddenly falls 1,500 meters off the sheer rock wall, taking ropes and hardware with him, leaving you with only the ringing sound of silence . . .

This life-defining moment happened to the French climber Jean-Christophe Lafaille, and climber-writer Mark Twight helps make some sense of this tragedy in a richly detailed interview.

Born near the French Alps, Lafaille was a stellar sport-climber before he expanded his experience with a number of tough solo climbs in the Alps. He trained and planned for ever larger adventures, knowing that his ultimate goal would be "something big" in the Himalaya. An invitation to join Pierre Beghin on a new route on the massive south face of Annapurna changed the course of his life.

Lafaille's story of how he overcame injury, lack of equipment, and his own near-paralyzing fear in getting himself off the face is both gripping and inspiring.

This abridged account is from *Kiss or Kill: Confessions of a Serial Climber* by Mark Twight, pages 123-131.

A fter three days of good weather a storm breaks rapidly. Spindrift makes exiting off the rock wall impossible. Jean-Christophe Lafaille and Pierre Beghin begin retreating off a new route on the enormous south face of Annapurna (8091 meters). At 7,200 meters Pierre plants a single, small-sized camming unit in a bottoming crack. He rappels 10 meters down a vertical, ice-choked chimney. Reaching the lower-angled snow-slope below he unweights the anchor. It shifts in the brittle Himalayan rock and then rips when he leans back to continue. Pierre falls 1,500 meters. The ropes and rack go with him, leaving Jean-Christophe alone two-thirds of the way up one of the most difficult and dangerous walls in the Himalayas with little equipment. Stunned, motionless, he listens through the hiss of spindrift for any sign of life. He hears nothing.

This is the most important spiritual reference point in his life. It signifies the end of one period and the beginning of another. He doesn't recognize it yet.

➤   ➤   ➤

Signs distinguishing these transitions matter to Jean-Christophe. Spiritual land-marks punctuate his life. Most relate to mountaineering. Born in Gap, with the Central French Alps looming above, he began climbing with his father at the age of six. This gave him "the opportunity to progress slowly and accu-mulate an enormous amount of experience compared to the climber who starts later." They did easy routes at first, climbing occasionally. In 1979, at four-teen, Jean-Christophe started climbing seriously. Alpinism interested him the most, but he divided time equally between the crag and the mountains.

Jean-Christophe was swept along in the Sport Climbing phenomenon. The area around Gap is isolated from more fashionable Sport Climbing venues (and their fashion victims). Rather than traveling to these, Jean-Christophe devel-oped his own "private" cliffs, such as the Roche des Arnauds. At Ceuse, the Sector Lafaille, which he and several friends developed, is renowned for its very hard but above all very beautiful routes. Jean-Christophe's individualism sepa-rated him from the "super-mediatized" course of the French climbing scene. Asked why he didn't want to be part of all that, he answers, "The leading clique among French climbers lacks ideas and initiative, whether they are alpine climb-ers or sport climbers. In 1985-86, Christophe Profit began his string of enchainments in the Mont Blanc Massif, virtually running up and down sev-eral peaks in one day. All the other leading alpinists began copying him." . . .

. . . Jean-Christophe kept to himself and worked on his own projects. In the autumn of 1986, during his military service, he placed well in several com-petitions held on natural rock, notably at Troubat and Biot. In 1987 he free-soloed Reve de Gosse, 8a+ at the Roche des Arnauds. . . . The climbing world took notice, but Jean-Christophe returned to his secret projects and unknown cliffs. This period of determined work resulted in many new routes. Perhaps the most important of these is Patience at the Roche des Arnauds. He graded the climb 8c, and although several people have worked on it, the route re-mains unrepeated.

After weeks in the claustrophobic cave repeating and rehearsing the techni-cal, dynamic movements of Patience, he longed to see the horizon stretching away toward the unknown. He drove four hours to Chamonix where he soloed the Swiss Route on the Grand Capucin (300 meters, 6b, A0). It was like flicking a switch. Recognizing he was saturated with Sport Climbing, he decided to spend more time in the mountains. Alone.

Jean-Christophe closed this period of his career with a reference point. He wanted to hang something on the shutting door. Privilege du Serpent 7c+, solo. As he described it, the 25-meter-high route has "good holds with big dynos between them. There was no way I could have downclimbed if I'd wanted to, and technically, the higher one climbs, the harder the route is." Several friends filmed him soloing it, and every time he walks beneath it now he remembers well his previous life as a Sport Climber. . . .

During the years dedicated to Sport Climbing Jean-Christophe trained for the mountains. He ran hills; taught himself to navigate with map, compass, and altimeter; and paid attention to weather patterns. On rest days he slept outside to test bivouac systems. He expressed his commitment to the hard climbs of the future by climbing easier routes in bad weather. Jean-Christophe had a plan and didn't want to confront any surprises along the way. . . .

The French climbing magazines dedicated several pages of photographs and text to [his] routes. Jean-Michel Asselin from *Vertical* magazine christened him "the Mystic of the Extreme," setting the stage for the future. Jean-Christophe signed contracts with Charlet-Moser, Millet, Beal, and Petzl. The French Mountaineering Federation awarded him their annual prize for mountaineering achievement: The Crystal. Philippe Poulet, a photographer for the prestigious Gamma agency, sold articles and pictures, organized helicopters to ensure coverage of future ascents, and sounded the Jean-Christophe trumpet. Jean-Christophe quietly acknowledged all this, knowing it a necessary tool to finance larger expeditions in the years to come.

He planned to visit the Himalayas in the autumn of 1993, believing he needed another year of experience to succeed on something big his first time out. His arduous "preparation" resulted in another important first ascent: Chemin des Etoiles (1000 meters, 6b, A3) on the Grandes Jorasses. . . .

Jean-Christophe tried the route in March, but bad weather forced retreat 600 meters up the wall. He finished the climb in April, spending four days alone.

"The bad part about succeeding was dragging my two haulbags through waist-deep, wet snow down the Italian side." Almost as soon as *Vertical* broke the news, an invitation to the Himalayas changed the course of his life. Another reference point.

➤   ➤   ➤

Pierre Beghin intended to attempt a new route on the massive south face of Annapurna. He believed the combination of Jean-Christophe's technical expertise and his own vast Himalayan experience would prove crucial for success on the difficult and dangerous line. Jean-Christophe accepted eagerly, advancing his schedule a year or so in the process. They plotted, they planned, and after the monsoon season, they flew to Nepal.

Katmandu didn't faze Jean-Christophe. He'd spent two months in the North African desert, so the Third World was nothing new to him. "It's just like any big city, really," he stated, and then smiling, "as far as big cities go, I liked San Francisco better." He didn't much like the bureaucratic hassles involved with climbing in Nepal, but the people, the countryside, and the feeling of having embarked on a magnificent adventure thrilled Jean-Christophe. He says he'd return today "as much to see the people and the land as to go climbing." Because he'd passed much of his youth hiking and camping, and purposely bivouacked on a number of routes—a rare thing among today's French alpinists—living in a tent was easy for him. He whiled away bad weather listening to classical music on his Walkman, reading, and hiking around to get a better feeling for the mountain.

Pierre Beghin expected the difficult new route, climbed Alpine Style, to be his great Himalayan statement and one of his last expeditions to the big mountains. His previous climbs, the solo of Kangchenjunga, then K2, Dhauligiri, Jannu, and Manaslu in Alpine Style, prepared him for it. Soloing the final 1,500 meters of hard, technical terrain on the south face of Makalu may have been his finest achievement.

The pair climbed the lower face at night to avoid the unbelievable stonefall generated by the rockbands. Stonefall rained perpetually during the day but

froze silent at night. "It was an impressive bombardment. I've never encountered, or even heard of anything like it." (Alex MacIntyre was killed by stonefall
attempting what became the Catalonian Route on this same face.) The initial ice and mixed terrain rose 1,500 meters, continuously 55 degrees with
passages of 90 degrees. Pierre left 150 meters of fixed rope at 6600 meters
to facilitate the descent, but otherwise they climbed in pure Alpine Style; simul-
soloing and carrying everything on their backs. The steep wall offered few
bivouac sites.

On the third day Jean-Christophe and Pierre reached a band of "curious"
Himalayan rock. "It was like bricks, or café trays stacked on top of each other.
Not really loose, and surprisingly compact in places." They free-climbed where
possible, bypassing overhanging sections on ice and hard mixed ground. An
unavoidable roof went at A2/A3. "We got around one nasty-looking wall on
a perfect, frozen waterfall, 25 to 30 meters high. Wild." According to their
photos, seven pitches up the rockband should have placed them on a ledge
above the waterfall, at 7,300 meters. Instead, they discovered a 70-degree
slope of dense, black ice. They couldn't chop a platform for the tent and had
to bivouac hanging in their harnesses. Unable to fire up the stove because of
the wind, the night trudged by slowly, foodless and bitter. "It was awful and
drained everything out of us. Luckily, we managed to slide most of our bodies into the sleeping bags."

The next morning they climbed to 7,500 meters, "within 150 meters of
the easy climbing, we could see where the angle eased back." They fought
through these final difficulties before the diving barometric pressure developed into a storm. Wind and spindrift stopped them cold. They agreed to
descend. Wasted and slightly out of control, the pair took huge risks on every rappel. At one point Pierre was willing to rap off a single tied-off ice screw,
but Jean-Christophe hammered in one of his tools to back it up.

After two more rappels, Pierre set the anchor that would allow them to
reach lower-angled terrain and arranged the gear over his shoulder.
Holstering both ax and hammer was too complicated. Annoyed, he handed
his ax to Jean-Christophe who stood on a small ledge, out of reach of the
anchor. His years of experience muddled by fatigue, the confusion of the

storm, and the need to get down quickly, Pierre leaned back on a single anchor without any backup. It failed and he fell. Jean-Christophe watched, sickened, but certain that "he would stop himself. Even though it was so steep I believed he would self-arrest . . . I won't ever forget thinking that."

He was alone; the storm raged on.

Realizing that "it would have been impossible to go up," Jean-Christophe downclimbed through relatively difficult mixed-terrain to their last bivouac and 20 meters of rope they'd left at 7000 meters. He spent 48 hours cowering there while the storm blew itself out. He ran out of food and there was little gas left for the stove. During those hours, he schemed with the cunning instinct that keeps hunted men alive. He figured, "Once I recover the extra rope, pitons, and fuel left at 6500 meters, it'll be a simple matter of rappelling and staying out of the way of the stonefall."

The following afternoon during intermittent clearings, he retreated, using a combination of downclimbing and rappelling. After Pierre's fall, Jean-Christophe found himself with two carabiners, a sling, and two ice tools. He rapped off whatever he had; the tent poles went first. He hammered in two sections at a time as far as they'd go and called it good. His long experience of soloing up (and down) routes in the Alps allowed him to clinically assess each problem, find the solution, and execute it without freaking out. "The sum of everything I'd done over the last 10 years got me out of that situation—mostly the solo climbing. Still, I had trouble getting myself going. I almost stayed at 7000 meters because I was scared—scared of falling."

About 150 meters above the ramp that led back to the fixed rope, Jean-Christophe lost a crampon. It tumbled away and disappeared from sight. He continued downclimbing, sliding one foot and then stabilizing himself with his tools and the other foot. At the top of the ramp, he discovered the crampon sticking out from behind an ice flute. It had stopped in softer snow. Hanging off his tools, he replaced the crampon. "It was a sign to me that I was going to make it, things were going my way."

He reached the rope, which was fixed in 50-meter sections, and rappelled. As he stood at the first changeover, a falling stone smashed into his right forearm, compound fracturing both bones. It swelled immediately, filling his jacket-sleeve. "My morale was high when I got to the rope because I knew I was going to live. Ten minutes later I was as down as I have ever been . . . I didn't think I could make it off the wall." He continued down to the bivy at 6500 meters and spent a sleepless night. "I'd had it. I was at the end of my reserves. I laid there in my sleeping bag, thinking that I was suffering too much. I had given everything, but I'd lost. It was a cold, cold thought, without judgment. I knew that all I had to do was roll a half-turn toward base camp, tumble off the ledge, and it would be over. I thought this thought without emotion."

The sun came up bright and hard the next morning. Jean-Christophe spent the day eating, drinking, and recharging himself. The condition of his arm hadn't worsened during the night and, hope springing eternal, he felt he just might make it. At nightfall, as the stonefall ceased, Jean-Christophe continued down. "I thought about Doug Scott and Joe Simpson and figured, those guys gave all they had, and then gave more. They fought and fought and did not give up. I should at least do the same—give everything I have. I still had a little left." From 6500 meters he rapped 200 meters, but then left the ropes because they were too hard to pull with only one hand and his mouth. He downclimbed the 55-degree ice using a single ax.

The rope they'd left to get back over the 'schrund was frozen and no amount of yanking and chopping and biting would loosen it. "This chipped tooth is from that incident," he says as he smiles and points it out. So on the morning of the fifth day after the accident, his eighth on the wall, Jean-Christophe downclimbed into the bergschrund. Sheltered from stonefall by the overhanging lip, and not far from base camp, he relaxed. After unfastening his helmet, he threw his pack off and lay down for thirty minutes. He felt that ten years had just been subtracted from his life. "I will never, ever go into the mountains again," he swore.

Before the climb, he and Pierre easily ran from the 'schrund to base camp in half an hour, but it had snowed half a meter while they were on the face. The tent they'd left at advance base camp was buried and frozen solid. Jean-Christophe practically went crazy when he couldn't get at the food cached inside. He took two tubes of honey from a Slovenian team's tent. "I was scared to take more. Now, I don't know why," he recalls, and he followed their tracks toward base camp. A helicopter overflew the glacier and he realized that others knew something had gone wrong. He was no longer alone.

Then he saw a figure. Far away on the moraine someone was running toward him carrying something in his hand. After eight days of virtual slow motion, Jean-Christophe was amazed at the runner's speed and agility. Five minutes passed before one of the Nepalese base camp staff, holding a full teapot and a sack of food, wrapped his arms around Jean-Christophe, and they both burst into tears. . . .

Despite his declaration in the bergschrund beneath Annapurna, Jean-Christophe hasn't given up on Himalayan climbing. He had plans to go to the Shishapangma with the Slovenians who helped evacuate him from Annapurna Base Camp after the accident. "I wanted to go with them because we got along well together, there were no sponsors to please, no last great problem to solve, just a climbing adventure among friends. I need to test my head to see if I've absorbed everything and can actually go on climbing. I also thought it would be a way to get out from under the pressure of the French scene. But the trip fell through, and now I'm going to Cho Oyu having bought a place on a French Commercial Expedition. It's a way to get there," he states with resignation. More eagerly he allows, "I spotted a 1,500-meter-high route I can solo if I feel good." Jean-Christophe has other plans as well, but he's keeping quiet about them. "I certainly won't be going to one of the current 'fashionable' walls. It is a joke to me; the fashion passed from the south face of Lhotse to the west face of Makalu and everyone who's anyone will be throwing themselves at it until it gets done. I have different ideas. I mean, they are attractive mountains and all, but those walls are measuring sticks for other men. To remain true to myself, I need to find my own challenges and weave my life around them. Most important at the moment is to close this chapter, to absorb it and put a name on it, build a monument to it and leave it behind. I don't want to wear the weight of Annapurna around my neck for the rest of my life."

"THE K2 MYSTERY"

FROM
*Moments of Doubt and Other Mountaineering Writings
of David Roberts*
BY DAVID ROBERTS

THE 1939 AMERICAN EXPEDITION TO K2 HAS BEEN AND LIKELY WILL remain one of the most widely talked about, written about, and disputed events in the history of mountaineering. That the party came so close but failed in its attempt at a first ascent is the smallest part of the story. What went wrong, why, and whose fault it was are elusive facts that will be researched, interpreted, reinterpreted, and argued about as long as there are mountains and climbers. What is not in dispute is the fact that this expedition was one of the greatest mountain tragedies of all time.

Fritz Wiessner, leader of the ill-fated expedition, was a complex and fascinating man with near legendary capabilities as a climber. He became a figure of controversy almost the minute the world began receiving reports of the deaths that occurred high on the mountain. While Wiessner gained as many supporters as detractors over the years, the events of the expedition and their continuing rehash dogged him the rest of his life.

Hoping to bring a more complete picture of Wiessner's achievements before the world audience, writer David Roberts worked with Wiessner for some years before receiving approval to write the following article, which, as Roberts states, had some unfortunate consequences. The article was written some years before the release of expedition member Jack Durrance's diary. Durrance had withheld even the existence of this diary until after Wiessner's death. The diary shed some new light on the matter—and created new controversy of its own (see the next selection, "Neither Saint nor Sinner").

"The K2 Mystery," originally published in the October 1984 issue of *Outside* magazine, was republished in *Moments of Doubt and Other Mountaineering Writings of David Roberts*, pages 161-179.

[Author's Note: It took some ten years of knowing Fritz Wiessner before he would consent to my writing an article about his 1939 K2 expedition. I hoped that bringing the story of his achievement to the wide audience of Outside *readers might serve as part of a long-overdue homage to the man I think of as the century's greatest mountaineer. Alas, inevitably the article stirred up the old Wiessner-Durrance-American Alpine Club*

controversy, and stirred up Fritz's feelings as well, troubling his sleep for weeks afterwards.

I suppose the bitterness will never be laid to rest. But I continue to hope that Wiessner will be credited in this country as he is in Europe, where he has been a legendary mountaineering figure for sixty years.]

t was July 19, 1939. At nine o'clock that morning, Fritz Wiessner and Sherpa Pasang Lama had left Camp IX at 26,000 feet on K2, the second-highest mountain in the world. All day long they had moved upward on slopes of snow, ice, and rock that had never before been climbed. Neither man used oxygen.

Throughout the day, Wiessner had stayed in the lead. At age thirty-nine, he was in the best shape of his life. And at that moment in history, there was no better mountaineer anywhere in the world.

Some of the climbing had been extraordinarily difficult, considering the altitude. With his crampons, ice axe, and handful of pitons, Wiessner had mastered, in succession, a couloir of black ice, a short overhang of iced-up rock, and two rope lengths of broken rock covered with a treacherous skin of ice called verglas. The air was still, however, and Wiessner had been able to take off his gloves and do the hardest moves bare-handed.

Now he made a short traverse to the left, then climbed twenty-five feet up a very demanding wall of rock. At the top of this section, he hammered in two pitons for security. With growing elation, he surveyed the terrain above. The wall continued for another twenty-five feet that, while difficult, lay back at a lower angle than the rock he had just climbed. He knew he could get up this obstacle without much trouble. Above the rock, there was an apparently easy snow slope leading to the summit. It was late afternoon. The two men had reached an altitude of more than 27,500 feet. At the very most, the top of K2 stood only 750 feet higher.

In that moment, Fritz Wiessner stood on the threshold of a deed that, had he accomplished it, might today be regarded as the single most outstanding triumph in the long history of mountaineering. By 1939, none of the highest peaks in the world had been climbed. Only the year before, the seventh major expedition to Everest had been defeated some 2000 feet below the summit, and a strong American effort on K2 had turned back at 26,000 feet. Many experts had begun to doubt that the highest mountains would ever be conquered without oxygen. There are fourteen peaks in the Himalaya that exceed 8000 meters in height. Success on an "eight-thousander" was to become the four-minute mile of climbing. Not until 1950, with the French on Annapurna, was the feat accomplished. Everest was not to be climbed until 1953; K2, not until the year after.

But that July day in 1939, Wiessner and Pasang Lama had K2 in their grasp. It would mean coming down in the night, but the weather was holding splendidly, and the moon would be out, and the two men were in superb condition. Wiessner had no qualms about descending the easy ridge from the summit during the night, if necessary.

He began to move up the last twenty-five feet of the wall. There was a tug at his waist as the rope came tight. Turning to look at his partner, Wiessner saw Pasang smile almost apologetically. As a Buddhist Lama, Pasang believed that angry spirits lurked about the summit at night. "No, sahib, tomorrow," said the Sherpa.

When he saw that his companion's resolve could not be shaken, Wiessner thought for a moment about unroping and going for the summit alone. In 1939, however, the ethics of climbing prevented a leader from leaving his partner. But there were twelve days' worth of food and fuel at Camp IX, and the good weather looked as though it would stay forever. He gave in and agreed to descend. The next day would surely bring success.

Never again would Wiessner reach such a height on K2. Instead of claiming a great triumph, he would find himself embroiled for the rest of his life in one of the bitterest controversies in mountaineering history. For reasons that remain unclear today, the camps that had been so carefully supplied as the team moved up the mountain had been systematically stripped—the sleeping bags were removed and much of the food thrown out in the snow. As an indirect result of this catastrophe, four members of the 1939 expedition perished on K2. Wiessner returned to the United States not to be laureled for his heroic attempt on the great mountain, but to be plunged into the unjust opprobrium of his peers.

Fritz Wiessner turned 84 this February. He still rock climbs regularly at a creditable standard. His long career has been crowned with achievement, both in and out of the mountains, and with deep happiness. Toward other climbers, Wiessner has always maintained a generous and magnanimous stance. For several generations of mountaineers all over the world, he has become a hero.

But K2 remains the great disappointment of his life, and when he talks about it his voice shakes with the sense of betrayal that has lingered in his memory of that expedition for the last forty-five years.

PART I:
THE MOUNTAIN AND THE CLIMBER

K2 stands at the head of the Baltoro Glacier in the Karakoram of Pakistan, some 900 miles northwest of Everest. Seen from a distance, it is a striking, pyramidal peak, more beautiful than Everest, just as it is the harder ascent. The mountain was first attempted in 1902 by a small party that included the redoubtable Oscar Eckenstein, and again in 1909 by an Italian team led by the brilliant explorer Luigi Amedeo, Duke of the Abruzzi. Both parties had to turn back a little above 21,000 feet, nowhere near the 28,250-foot summit; but for such an early era, both expeditions were remarkable efforts.

The mountain was not attempted again until 1938, when a small but strong American party of four made a late but bold assault on the Abruzzi Ridge, the line first tried by the Italians. Paul Petzoldt, a cowboy from Wyoming, and Charles Houston, a Harvard-educated medical student, pushed up to 26,000 feet before having to quit. This expedition, too, had been an exceptional feat. Wiessner's attempt would be next.

His credentials were superb: born in Dresden in 1900, he had done his first climbs as a teenager in the Elbsteingebirge, the cluster of intimidating sandstone pinnacles near the banks of the river Elbe. In the second decade of this century, probably the hardest pure rock climbs in the world were done on these towers by Wiessner and his cronies, a fact not broadly recognized until the 1960s, thanks to the subsequent isolation of East Germany from the mainstream of climbing culture.

After World War I Wiessner moved on to the Alps, where he made some of the finest first ascents of the 1920s. Two of his most memorable were the southeast wall of the Fleischbank, which a German commentator later called "the great problem of its time," and the oft-attempted north wall of the Furchetta. In 1932 Wiessner went on his first Himalayan expedition, a pioneering effort on Nanga Parbat, where he reached 23,000 feet.

By 1929 Wiessner had emigrated to the United States, where he ran a very successful chemical business. He began climbing with American friends, in effect teaching them what European alpinism was all about. As Wiessner's latter-day friend Richard Goldstone puts it, "He probably went down a little bit in standard from what he had done in Germany when he came to the U.S. But he was so far ahead of the people here, they didn't understand what he was doing."

One of Wiessner's finest American accomplishments was the first ascent of Devils Tower in Wyoming in 1937, on which he led all the hard pitches. (Goldstone: "Fritz took along his standard three pitons. He basically soloed it.") Another was the first ascent of Mount Waddington in British Columbia's Coast Range, certainly the hardest climb yet completed in North America.

It was Wiessner, in 1937, who first won official permission for an American expedition to K2, but business commitments prevented his going to Pakistan the next summer. Charles Houston took over the leadership of the 1938 expedition, while Wiessner retained permission for 1939, should Houston's party not reach the summit.

As he began planning for the 1939 expedition, Wiessner was disappointed that none of the four veterans from the previous year's attempt could go again. By spring he had recruited two other first-rank mountaineers, one of whom had led the second ascent of Mount McKinley. Only four weeks before the team's departure, however, both had to back out.

The remaining party was so weak that Wiessner pondered postponing the attempt for another year. But the American Alpine Club urged him to persevere, and so the team sailed for Europe in late spring. Two of the members, Chappell Cranmer and George Sheldon, were twenty-one-year-old Dartmouth students. Eaton Cromwell had made many climbs in the Alps and Canada, but none of great difficulty; he was now forty-two years old. Dudley Wolfe, at forty-four, was a strong skier and alpinist but had little technical experience. After the team had embarked, an AAC mentor persuaded twenty-eight-year-old Jack Durrance, a Teton guide and one of the country's best climbers, to join the expedition. To Wiessner's great surprise, Durrance showed up in Genoa with an explanatory letter from the well-meaning AAC executive.

"I was a little worried then," says Wiessner today. "I knew Jack as a great sportsman, and I knew he was strong. He had done some climbing in Munich when he lived there, and he had good climbs in the Tetons. But I also knew he was very competitive, which might cause troubles. Actually, at that time I liked Durrance, and hoped he could do well."

Wiessner lives in retirement on an idyllic country estate in Stowe, Vermont. He is a short man, perhaps five feet five. He looks extremely fit, and the barrel chest and strong arms of his best days are still in evidence. His bald pate and great-browed forehead dominate his expressive face: as he talks, strong wrinkles delineate his forehead, and his eyebrows arch with meaning. He speaks in a clear, emphatic voice; still heavy with a German accent. His manners and bearing breathe old-world civility; his smile could conquer a drawing room. But he is equally captivating when he conjures up the troubles of the past. And the troubles in 1939 began when Wiessner and Durrance met.

"After we had reached base camp," Wiessner says, "and were on our first trip up the glacier, I wanted to check a little bit on safety and roping. We had two ropes. Soon Jack's rope started to put up speed, trying to go faster than the others. Cromwell and Wolfe said to me, 'What's up? Do we have to do this running?' When we got back to base camp, I gave a long talk. I said, 'Look, fellows, I can tell you right now, we will never climb this mountain if there's competition between the members. Get it out of your head. We have to work really hard and work together.' Jack didn't say anything, but seemed to agree."

Nevertheless, during the first five weeks above base camp the expedition went much as planned. The 1939 party had the advantage of knowing where the 1938 camps had been placed and, in some of them, benefited from rock platforms that had been built the previous year. Slowly a logistical ladder of supplies was constructed up the mountain. The Sherpas were tremendously useful in stocking the camps. Each camp was equipped with three sleeping bags, air mattresses, stoves, and gasoline. "I believed," says Wiessner, "that if you climb a mountain like this, you want to be sure, if something goes wrong or somebody gets ill, you can hold out for at least two weeks in any camp. If a man had to come down in very bad weather, he ought to be able to just fall into a tent, and everything would be there."

But in other respects, Wiessner insisted on a spartan, lightweight style. Oxygen was standard on Everest, but Wiessner refused even to bring it to base camp on K2. "My ideal has always been free climbing," he explains. "I hated mechanical means. I didn't even want walkie-talkies on the mountain."

Even as the chain of supplies was being built up, some of the climbers were having trouble. Because of his late inclusion in the party, Durrance had to wait for his high-altitude boots, specially made in Munich, to arrive. Cranmer almost immediately came down with a serious illness, probably pulmonary or cerebral edema. At base camp, Durrance, who was a medical student, nursed him back to health. According to Wiessner, Cromwell had the idea that being up high for very long was unhealthy, and soon he too wanted to go down. Wiessner suspects that these worries, continually expressed, made Durrance apprehensive. Sheldon got chilblains on his toes and went no higher than Camp IV. Among the sahibs, only Dudley Wolfe kept up fully with the high-altitude work of Wiessner and the best Sherpas.

Once Durrance's boots had arrived, he started eagerly up the route with Wiessner and Wolfe. Carrying loads to Camp VI, however, he began to move very slowly. On July 12, after five days of storm, Wiessner, Wolfe, and Durrance, with seven Sherpas, prepared to ferry supplies from VI to VII. Says Wiessner, "A very short distance above VI, Jack told me, 'Fritz, something is wrong with me. I am ill. Maybe I am not well-enough adjusted to the altitude.

I will go back to VI and come up tomorrow or the next day.'" Durrance turned around and descended to Camp VI.

Wiessner, Wolfe, and three Sherpas stayed at VII. The others returned with Durrance to VI, planning to bring more supplies the next day. But on July 14, instead of coming up with loads, Durrance retreated down the mountain. Even more unfortunately, from Wiessner's perspective, Durrance took two Sherpas with him, including the most experienced, Pasang Kikuli, who had been earmarked for a summit attempt but was suffering from frostbite. Wiessner's purist refusal to use walkie-talkie radios meant that he now had no way of communicating with Durrance, who did not stop until he was all the way down to Camp II.

The advance guard pushed on and established Camp VIII at 25,300 feet. From there, Wiessner sent two Sherpas down to VII to meet up with the anticipated contingent of Durrance and several Sherpas. Left at VIII were Wolfe, Pasang Lama, and Wiessner. After two days of storm, this trio set out upward again, but immediately got bogged down in extremely deep, loose snow. Wiessner literally had to swim through the drifts. Wolfe, the heaviest of the three, exhausted himself trying to flounder up a trough Wiessner had plowed in the drifts. He decided to return to camp and make another attempt the next day with the others. (Loose, new-fallen snow often compacts after a day of sun.)

Wiessner and Pasang Lama pushed on and established Camp IX. For security, they built a rock wall completely around the tent. The next day, July 19, they made their first attempt on the summit. It ended when Pasang, afraid of the coming night, refused to let out any more rope. "No, sahib, tomorrow!" he pleaded, and Wiessner gave in.

On the way down, as Pasang rappelled over a cliff, the rope got entangled in the crampons on the back of his pack—he was carrying both men's pairs. With a furious effort, the Sherpa got the rope loose, but the crampons came loose too. Wiessner watched with a sinking heart as they bounced away into the void. The descent grew more difficult, and only at 2:30 A.M. did the men regain Camp IX. To Wiessner's consternation, no one had arrived from below.

Nevertheless, the camp was well stocked and the weather continued to be perfect. Wiessner had decided on an easier alternative for the second attempt. It was a route up a gully that he had planned originally, but had given up when avalanches from an immense ice cliff near the summit had roared over it. On July 18, on their climb up to Camp IX, Wiessner and Pasang Lama had crossed the one-hundred-foot-wide track of such an avalanche, and this had led Wiessner to choose the more difficult rock-and-ice route of the first attempt. In the middle of that attempt, however, he had had a good view of the alternative route, and could see that no more avalanches were likely to come down for some time, and so the gully route was now safe.

The men rested the whole next day. It was so warm in the thin air that Wiessner sunbathed naked! At 6 A.M. on July 21—three hours earlier than their previous attempt—the two men left Camp IX to go for the summit. The alternative route lay over hard snow that had turned, in the sun, to ice. The loss of the crampons came home with a vengeance. In the crucial gully, as Wiessner later wrote, "With crampons, we could have practically run up it, but as it was we would have had to cut 300 or 400 steps. At these heights that would have taken more than a day." Once again the two men descended to Camp IX.

Wiessner was still quite confident of making the summit, however. The team members coming up in support would undoubtedly have crampons, as well as more provisions. Thinking his teammates were probably ensconced at Camp VIII, Wiessner decided to go down on July 22 to pick up Wolfe, more food and gas, and the all-important crampons. Pasang carried his sleeping bag down, but Wiessner, certain he would return, left his in the tent at Camp IX.

Without crampons, the descent was tricky, especially since the Tricouni nails (which climbers used on the soles of their boots in the days before Vibrams) had been worn dull on both men's footgear. "Pasang was behind me," recalls Wiessner. "I should have had him in front, but then I would have had to explain to him how to cut steps. I had just got my axe ready to make a few scrapes, when suddenly he fell off. I noticed immediately, because he made a funny little noise. I put myself in position, dug in as much as possible, and held him on the rope. If I hadn't been in good shape, hadn't climbed all those 4000-meter peaks in the Alps, I wouldn't have had the technique to hold him."

Wiessner makes such a belay sound routine, but it was a difficult feat.

At VIII, Wiessner had expected to find Durrance and the other Sherpas with their precious loads. Instead, Dudley Wolfe was there alone. He was overjoyed to see Wiessner, but furious that no one had come up from below. He had run out of matches two days before and had been able to drink only a little meltwater that had run off a ground cloth.

By now Wiessner was utterly perplexed by the absence of reinforcement from below. At Camp VII, however, he knew the bulk of the reserve food had already been cached. With a quick trip down to VII for supplies, the three men could still probably climb K2 without any help from below. Wiessner could use Wolfe's pair of crampons to lead the ice.

So on July 23 the trio started down to VII. Wolfe, not the most graceful of climbers even on his good days, was tied in to the middle of the rope. Pasang Lama was ten or fifteen feet in front, Wiessner the same distance in the rear. Once again the snow got icy, and Wiessner had to go first to cut steps. As he leaned over in a precarious position, Wolfe accidentally stepped on the rope. The jolt pulled Wiessner off.

"I immediately called back, 'Check me! Check me!'" Wiessner remembers. "Nothing happened. Then the rope came tight to Dudley, and he was pulled off. The rope tightened to Pasang behind, and he too came off. We were all three sliding down, and I got going very fast and somersaulted.

"I had no fear. All I was thinking was, how stupid this has to happen like this. Here we are, we can still do the mountain, and we have to lose out in this silly way and get killed forever. I didn't think about family, and of course I was never a believer in Dear Old God.

"But getting pulled around by the somersault and being first on the rope, it gave me a little time. I still had my ice axe—I always keep a sling around my wrist—and just in that moment the snow got a little softer. I had my axe ready and worked very hard with it. With my left hand I got hold of the rope, and eventually I got a stance, kicked in quickly, and leaned against the axe. Then, bang! A fantastic pull came. I was holding it well, but it tore me down. But at that time I was a fantastically strong man—if I had a third of it today I would be very happy. I stood there and I wanted to stop that thing. I must have done everything right, and the luck was there, too."

Wiessner's belay has become the stuff of legend. Very few men in all of mountaineering history have performed the like: having already been pulled off a slope, to recover, gain a stance, and, with only the pick of an ice axe for purchase, to stop the otherwise fatal falls of three men roped together.

The men made their way on down to Camp VII at 24,700 feet. There they received an incomprehensible shock. Not only was there no one in camp: The tents had been left with the doors open. One was full of snow, the other half-collapsed. The provisions that had been so carefully carried up nine days before lay wantonly strewn about in the snow. Most of the food was missing, as were all the sleeping bags.

Utterly dismayed and confounded, the three men cleaned out one tent and repitched it. It was too late to go farther down. With one sleeping bag and no air mattresses, they huddled through a bitterly cold night. In the morning the weather was raw and windy. Wolfe decided to stay with the one bag at Camp VII while Wiessner and Pasang went down to VI. Despite all their setbacks, the trio was still of a mind to push upward. Surely there would be sleeping bags and food still at VI, and there ought to be at least six Sherpas there as well.

On July 23 the two men headed down. At VI they found only a dump of two unpitched tents and some provisions: again the sleeping bags and air mattresses were gone. Grimly Wiessner and Pasang continued the descent. Camp V, IV, III . . . still no sleeping bags. At nightfall, the men reached Camp II, supposedly the best-provisioned camp on the mountain. No sleeping bags! Utterly worn out, Wiessner and Pasang took down one tent and wrapped themselves up in it while they tried to sleep in the other. Their fingers and toes froze, and they got no sleep.

By the time the two men reached the level glacier the next day, they were dragging themselves along, often falling. Wiessner recalls the effort: "We were so exhausted. We would go 100 or 200 meters, then sit down a little. Suddenly we look, and there comes a party up the glacier. It was Cromwell with some Sherpas. My throat had gotten very sore, and I could hardly speak, but I was mad enough. I asked him, 'What is the idea?'"

"He told me they had given us up for dead. He was just out looking to see if he could find any sign of anything on the glacier. I said, 'This is really an outrage. Wolfe will sue you for your neglect.' We went on to base camp. The cook and the liaison officer came out and embraced me and took me to my tent. Pasang Kikuli and all the Sherpas came and embraced me. But Durrance didn't come for about half an hour.

"When he did, I said immediately, 'What happened to our supplies? Who took all the sleeping bags down? And why were they taken down?' Durrance said, 'Well, the Sherpas . . . ' It was blamed on the Sherpas."

It is a measure of Wiessner's intense commitment to K2 that even after such a colossal setback, he still had hopes of making another attempt on the summit. All that was needed to rebuild the logistical ladder, he reasoned, was to get the sleeping gags back into the camps and to bolster the food supplies above. Also, Dudley Wolfe was waiting alone at Camp VII. On July 26, Durrance and three Sherpas set out, hoping to climb all the way up to VII. Wiessner planned to follow in two days, after recuperating from his ordeal.

Durrance, however, could go only as far as Camp IV before altitude sickness forced him down again on the third day. He left two Sherpas at IV, with instructions to go up to VII and explain matters to Wolfe. Meanwhile, Wiessner had not recovered from his debilitating descent, and Pasang Lama was in even worse shape. When Durrance reappeared, Wiessner realized that at last all hope of climbing K2 had to be abandoned. It remained only to bring Wolfe down.

Despite his exhausted state, Wiessner wanted to try to climb up to VII himself, but Pasang Kikuli dissuaded him, saying he himself would go up to get Wolfe and bring him down. Instead, on July 29, Kikuli and another Sherpa went all the way from base camp to VI—a gain of 6800 feet—in a single day. This feat of fortitude remains virtually unmatched in Himalayan history. On the way, Kikuli picked up the two Sherpas who had been left by Durrance at Camp IV.

The next day, this rescue team of four found Wolfe in a bad state. He had lost, it seemed, the will to live. Again he had run out of matches, and he had lain apathetically in his bag without eating. He had grown so lethargic, in fact, that he had not left the tent to defecate. The Sherpas tried to rouse him, but he declared that he needed another day of rest before he could make the descent. Without sleeping bags, the Sherpas could not stay at VII, so they went down to VI, determined to try to prod Wolfe into descending the next day. A storm intervened, and it was not until the day after, July 31, that Pasang Kikuli, Pinsoo, and Kitar started out again to climb up to VII. They left Tsering alone in VI with orders to have tea ready.

At base camp, little could be known of the doings high on the mountain. Through binoculars Durrance had seen three figures cross the snow just below Camp VII. Finally, on August 2, a terrified Tsering returned to base alone. On July 31 he had brewed tea and waited. No one had come the rest of the day, nor all of the next day. After that, he could wait no longer.

Wiessner made one more attempt to go up the route. He left on August 3, with two Sherpas, and it took him two days to "drag" himself, in his own phrase, to Camp II. On August 5 a full-scale storm broke, dumping twelve inches of snow and ending any further hopes of rescue. On August 7 the expedition turned its back on K2.

The fate of Dudley Wolfe, Pasang Kikuli, Pinsoo, and Kitar has never been determined. It may be that the Sherpas reached Wolfe, and all four men perished in an avalanche or in a roped fall like the one Wiessner had barely managed to stop. No trace of any of the four has ever been found.

PART II: AFTERMATH

During Wiessner's absence in the middle of July, the mood at base camp had worsened. Sheldon, Cranmer, and Cromwell wanted nothing more than to head for home. In the end Cranmer and Cromwell left early, leaving Wiessner and Durrance to bring up the rear as the expedition left the Baltoro Glacier for good.

"We were together every day," says Wiessner. "Durrance looked after me as if I were a baby. He made pancakes for me. And every day we talked. I just couldn't comprehend what had happened on the mountain. 'I don't understand it, Jack,' I told him, 'why those sleeping bags were taken out after all our agree-ments.' He kept answering, 'It was a matter of those Sherpas.'

"I kept asking him. Finally, he stood there and shouted, 'Ah, Fritz! Stop it! Stop it! We have talked about it long enough!'"

Once the men reached civilization, they parted. World War II had broken out. Wiessner traveled from Karachi to Port Said, then took a liner back to the United States. Durrance traveled in the other direction, across the Pacific. The two men would not set eyes on each other again until thirty-nine years had passed.

Upon his return, Wiessner went into a hospital in New York City. His many nights out on K2 had caused severe arthritic problems in his knees. He was bedridden for six weeks. Durrance came to New York City, stayed in a hotel, and sent some belongings to Wiessner in the hospital. He never paid a visit.

In his bed, Wiessner brooded about the stripped camps. He had talked not only to Durrance but to the Sherpas. They tended to blame Tendrup, one of their younger men. Gradually Wiessner deduced that, after he had parted with Durrance on July 14, something like the following chain of events must have unfolded.

Durrance had immediately descended to Camp II, taking with him Pasang Kikuli and another Sherpa. This left two Sherpas at Camp VI, who were soon joined by the two sent down by Wiessner. Kikuli had appointed Tendrup the leader of this group of four. Their orders were to carry loads to Camps VII and VIII in support of the summit effort.

Tendrup, however, came down with Kitar from a ferry to Camp VII, claim-ing that he was sure the three men in the lead had been killed in an avalanche and urging all the Sherpas to descend at once. The other two Sherpas refused to go along with the story and stayed put in Camp VI. Tendrup and Kitar descended to IV, where they ran into Pasang Kikuli, who angrily ordered them back up the mountain. So the pair made another foray up to VII. There they yelled up toward VIII, but got no answer. The silence added credibility to Tendrup's avalanche story, and the four Sherpas broke open Camp VII, scat-tering the supplies on the snow—exactly why remains problematic—before heading down the mountain with the sleeping bags from VI and VII. At base camp, the other Sherpas called Tendrup a devil who wanted to wreck the expedition. Wiessner concluded, however, that Tendrup was not so much malevolent as lazy—that he had invented the avalanche story to get out of carrying loads. Even so, this explained only the missing bags at VI and VII. Why had the lower camps also been stripped? Wiessner puzzled over this point for days. Then, he says, among his personal papers from the expedition, he came across a note he had earlier overlooked. It had been left for him by Durrance at Camp II on July 19. According to Wiessner, the note congratulated him and Wolfe for making the summit, then explained that the day before (July 18, on the eve of Wiessner and Pasang Lama's first summit attempt) he had ordered the bags from the higher camps and from Camps IV and II—thirteen bags in all—taken down to base, in anticipation of the expedition's departure and to save valuable equipment. The implication was that Durrance assumed Wiessner, Wolfe, and Pasang Lama would be bringing their own bags down all the way from Camp IX. When Wiessner had found this note at Camp II, he had been too exhausted and emotionally overwrought to make sense of it. Now, in the hospital, it supplied the missing piece to the puzzle.

Wiessner says today, "As I told others, I had no ill feelings against Durrance, but I thought a man should be honest. If only he had come to me and said, 'I'm sorry, Fritz, I made a mistake. I meant the best. I wanted to save the sleeping bags,' I would have accepted this without hard feelings." But Durrance never communicated with Wiessner.

According to Wiessner, he deposited the all-important note in the files of the American Alpine Club. When he later tried to locate it, it was gone. Assuming Wiessner's interpretation is correct, what could have possessed Durrance to pull out support so flagrantly behind the summit trio? The defeatist mood of base camp must have contributed to a shared impatience to go home. Moreover, the sleeping bags were the most valuable gear on the expedition. If indeed Wiessner, Wolfe, and Pasang Lama had made the summit and descended without mishap, they would probably have brought their own sleeping bags with them, obviating the need for the bags in the intermediate camps. Sitting at base camp day after day with no news from above is a vexing business: the mind all too easily begins to invent theories about the maneuvers out of sight above. More than one Himalayan leader has felt the urge to pull out and go home while the advance guard was still high on the mountain. But another suggestion with respect to K2 is that everyone at base camp had given Wiessner's party up for dead and the survivors were retrieving the equipment. Cromwell had virtually admitted this when he had found Wiessner and Pasang Lama staggering across the glacier.

What was done was done. The loss of four men on K2 was a deep tragedy, but Wiessner's extraordinary feat in reaching 27,500 feet without oxygen, with no strong teammates except the Sherpas, ought to have been widely hailed for its excellence. Instead, one of the sorriest chapters in American climbing politics was about to unfold.

The American Alpine Club launched an investigation of the expedition, headed by some of the most distinguished men in American mountaineering. Ostensibly, their purpose was to "point the way towards a greater control of the risks undertaken in climbing great mountains." But the investigation report made some patronizing conclusions. It claimed that the expedition's "human administration seems to have been weak"; that there was "no clear understanding" of plans between Durrance and Wiessner when they parted; that it was an "error in judgment" to leave Sherpas alone in the middle camps; and that an ill climber (presumably Wolfe, who was not in fact ill) should not have been left alone to make his own decisions. The brunt of all these criticisms fell on Wiessner. Correspondingly, the committee gave Durrance's actions an implicit but total whitewash. The club sent a letter to members summarizing the report and ended by congratulating itself for the investigation, with its "valuable contribution" in the way of guidance "if Himalayan expeditions are undertaken again."

There were two significant calls of dissent. One came from Al Lindley, the strong mountaineer who had had to back out of K2 shortly before the party left for Pakistan. Lindley argued cogently that Wiessner was being dealt a serious injustice by the report, for the simple reason that "the action of the Sherpas and Durrance in evacuating these camps was so much the major cause of the accident that the others are insignificant." The other came from Robert Underhill, who as much as any American had brought the techniques of the Alps to this country. Underhill's long rebuttal came to this eloquent conclusion:

> *What impresses me most is the fact that thruout all the bad weather, the killing labor and the grievous disappointments, [Wiessner] still kept up his fighting spirit. Except Wolfe, the rest of the party were excusably enough, finished and thru—quite downed by the circumstances; toward the end they wanted only to get out and go home. Wiessner, with Wolfe behind him, was the only one who still wanted to climb the mountain. Far be it from me to blame the others; I know well that if I had been there myself I should have come to feel exactly the same way, and probably much sooner. But this leads me to appreciate Wiessner the more. He had the guts—and there is no single thing finer in a climber, or in a man.*

These wise appeals, however, fell on deaf ears. In November 1941, Wiessner resigned from the American Alpine Club.

To understand the harshness of the American reaction, one must reflect on the climate of the 1930s. The British, who had invented alpinism a century before, were becoming increasingly conservative as climbers. The best routes in the Alps were being done by Germans, Austrians, and Italians. As political tensions between Britain and Germany escalated in the 1930s, British rock climbers began to derogate their German counterparts as suicidal risk-takers. There was no more dangerous prewar climbing arena than the north face of the Eiger, where the best alpinists in Europe competed for the first ascent, at the cost of a number of lives. When four Germans succeeded in 1938, Hitler awarded them medals. These likable young men were thoroughly apolitical; nevertheless, a sour-grapes reaction dismissed them and their brethren as Nazi fanatics, throwing their lives away on *Nordwände* for the glory of *Füher* and *Vaterland*.

In this nasty debate, American climbers, who were technically decades behind the Europeans, tended to sympathize with the British. Fritz Wiessner, though he had come to America in 1929, long before Hitler had risen to power, was a German; he was a far better climber than anyone in this country; and he seemed willing to take greater risks than American climbers. The AAC reaction to K2, then, amounted to institutional conservatism tinged with the chauvinistic passions of the onset of the war.

The drama reached its nadir a few months after Wiessner was released from the hospital. "One day my secretary in my New York office told me that two men from the FBI had come by," Wiessner recalls. "I went down to the FBI office and met two very nice young chaps—they were both Yale graduates. We sat down and talked. They wanted to know my whole history, and they had the funniest questions. Such as, 'You go skiing often in Stowe in the winter, do you not? That's very near Canada, isn't it? Can you get easily over the border?' I said, 'Yes. It's quite a distance to walk, but I am in Canada very often anyway because I have a business in Toronto.' And they laughed.

"I wasn't very keen on Roosevelt then. And so they said, 'You don't like the president? You made some remarks about him.' I said, 'Well, I wasn't the only one. There are very many people who feel that way!' They laughed again.

"They asked about some of my friends. We sat there half an hour, then we just talked pleasantly. On the way out I said, 'Now look, fellows, I was pretty open to you. I have my definite suspicions. Would you tell me the names of the men who put you up to this?' They said, 'Naturally we can't do that.' So I said, 'Let me ask this question: Was it some climbers from the AAC?' They nodded. They said, 'Don't worry about it. You know who we had here yesterday? We had Ezio Pinza, the famous opera singer. It was the same thing, a little jealousy from his competitors. They complained that he was a Mussolini follower.'"

Wiessner can joke about the episode today, but it must have been a chilling encounter.

The 1939 K2 expedition began to recede into the past. In 1956, in the journal *Appalachia,* Wiessner published a brief, restrained narrative of the climb from his point of view. The editor invited any readers with dissenting versions to speak up. None did.

Sadly, the expedition itself settled into a somewhat ambiguous place in climbing history. At its worst, the second-guessing British analysis prevailed;

thus a book like Kenneth Mason's *Abode of Snow,* summarizing an utterly garbled version of the events on K2, could sermonize, "It is difficult to record in temperate language the folly of this enterprise."

Wiessner for the most part put the controversy behind him. In 1945 he married Muriel Schoonmaker, an American woman, with whom he has climbed and traveled extensively for almost forty years. Their daughter, Polly, is a research anthropologist; their son, Andrew, an adviser to Representative John Seiberling.

Most climbers tail off drastically after the age of forty or quit altogether. Wiessner has climbed steadily now for seventy years. In the United States he pioneered routes on local cliffs all over the country. As Richard Goldstone says, "There are these crags in the woods that people come upon and think they've discovered. Then they find a rusty old piton high on some route. Fritz was there in the 1940s."

Well into his seventies, Wiessner could still lead 5.9 climbs comfortably. Even today, at the age of eighty-four—hobbled by the arthritis that has plagued his joints since 1939, the survivor of a heart attack on a climb in France in 1969—Wiessner can second some 5.9s, and he regularly goes to the Shawan-gunks of New York State and solos both up and down easy routes that he "put in" forty years ago. There is no other example in mountaineering history of a climber keeping up such standards at that age.

In 1966 a number of AAC members, led by Bill Putnam, Andy Kauffman, and Lawrence Coveney, persuaded Wiessner to rejoin the club. In an act that went some way toward expiating the wrong that had been done him years before, the club soon afterward made him an honorary member for life.

In December 1978, the annual AAC banquet meeting was held in Estes Park, Colorado. The previous summer, four Americans had finally reached the top of K2. The slide shows to be presented at the meeting were accordingly focused on K2, and Jack Durrance, who lives nearby in Denver, was invited to talk. Wiessner got word of this development and flew back from a meeting in Europe in order to be present. This writer, who was present, vividly remembers the events that ensued.

All day in Estes Park the rumors flew that the long-delayed confrontation was about to take place. Durrance was finally going to tell "his side" of the story. Meanwhile, a veteran of the 1953 K2 expedition managed to talk Wiessner and Durrance into saying hello to each other. It was the first time they had met since parting in India in 1939. The meeting was curt in the extreme.

A number of AAC old-timers took Durrance aside. They managed to talk him out of making any inflammatory remarks. Their belief was that whatever dirty laundry remained from 1939, this meeting to celebrate American success on K2 was not the place or time to air it. Durrance gave in. His slide show carried the expedition up to base camp, then closed abruptly with a photo of himself in "retirement" in a cabin near the Tetons.

Later, at the banquet, Wiessner was given a special toast in recognition of his years of service to mountaineering. The crowd's reaction was deeply emotional, and the whole assemblage rose to its feet, applauding wildly—except for Durrance, who remained seated, his face fixed in a scowl.

In the course of researching this article, I asked Jack Durrance for his version of the events. Though he has never publicly told his side of the story, Durrance consented to an interview, during which that version emerged. On later reflection, however, Durrance decided against allowing his remarks to be published.

For more than forty years, the 1939 K2 expedition has lain under a cloud of criticism and rumor. Yet younger climbers the world over have come to an appreciation of it that is relatively free of the biases that animated the 1930s. And their response has been one of almost unilateral reverence and awe.

Wiessner was far ahead of his time. His refusal to rely either on oxygen or radio, criticized as cranky in his day, has come to seem an uncompromisingly high-minded example of "clean climbing." The logistical organization of the assault was utterly brilliant. Good weather helped the expedition get as high as it got, but the solid buildup of camps with tents, food, and gas amounted to the kind of textbook execution no other expedition had yet pulled off in the Himalaya.

The most astounding facet of this accomplishment is that Wiessner performed it with only one able-bodied American teammate and a group of dedicated Sherpas. The other four sahibs were of only marginal help low on the mountain. Equally astonishing is the fact that Wiessner led every bit of the route himself. On contemporary expeditions to Everest, the route had been put in only by the laborious leapfrogging of separate teams. On K2 in 1939, one man "in the shape of my life" broke every step of virgin ground himself.

Then, at his highest point, he was ready to climb through the night to reach the summit—a feat that had never been attempted in the Himalaya. There were only, at most, 750 feet to go; as subsequent parties found, those last 750 feet were mostly easy walking on a snow ridge. It is possible that even Wiessner might have lacked the strength to cover that last bit, but it seems more likely that he would have made it.

Forty-five years from his decision late that afternoon of July 19, Wiessner wonders whether he made a mistake. He considers what he might do, given another chance, at the moment when Pasang Lama balked and held the rope tight. "If I were in wonderful condition like I was then," he says, "if the place where my man stood was safe, if the weather was good, if I had a night coming on like that one, with the moon and the calm air, if I could see what was ahead as I did then . . . then I probably would unrope and go on alone." Wiessner pauses, his thoughts wrapped in the past. "But I can get pretty weak, if I feel that my man will suffer. He was so afraid, and I liked the fellow. He was a comrade to me, and he had done so well."

"NEITHER SAINT NOR SINNER"
AND
"STRANGERS AND BROTHERS"

FROM
K2: The Story of the Savage Mountain
BY JIM CURRAN

UNLIKE DAVID ROBERTS, AUTHOR OF THE PREVIOUS SELECTION ON the 1939 American K2 Expedition, British climber-writer Jim Curran had the benefit of reviewing the long-withheld diary of expedition member Jack Durrance when he began to write his definitive history of K2. Thus Curran is able to present an expanded view of both the events and Fritz Wiessner's leadership of the ill-fated expedition in the first of these two selections on K2.

In "Neither Saint nor Sinner," Curran reports and weighs the evidence on the 1939 climb with as much impartiality as an historian is able to do. The reader has plenty of food for thought about the controversy: Was Wiessner a victim of circumstances beyond his control? Of the actions of others? Was the tragedy the result of leader failure, as claimed by his detractors? Was the rancor aimed at Wiessner more a product of the times—it was 1939; Wiessner was from Germany—than of the facts?

In the second selection, "Strangers and Brothers," Curran tells of yet another expedition to K2, the American party in 1953 led by Charles Houston. This well-remembered expedition stands in extreme contrast to Wiessner's 1939 trip. While it had its share of tragedy, the 1953 expedition was marked by unequaled harmony and acts of almost unbelievable heroism, including the famous ice-axe belay by Pete Schoening that saved five climbers from certain death. Just as the 1939 Wiessner expedition holds a special place in mountaineering history, so does this 1953 expedition, but instead of a hallmark of bitterness, the 1953 Houston expedition's legacy is as a symbol of all that is the best in mountaineering.

These two selections are Chapters 7 and 8 from K2: The Story of the Savage Mountain by Jim Curran, pages 81-103.

"NEITHER SAINT NOR SINNER"

The tragic events of 1939, the recriminations and endless feuds, remain a tender scar in the annals of American climbing. So much has been written, analyzed and dissected that the events of 1939 have become to Americans what Whymper and the Matterhorn were to the British, the Franey Pillar disaster to the Italians or the 1934 Nanga Parbat tragedy to the Germans. Now, fifty-five years later, it seems pointless and cruel to try and load all the blame for what happened on any one person: a chain of events unfolded, in which several people played key roles—the interaction between them produced a terrible result.

Fritz Hermann Ernst Wiessner was thirty-nine, a stocky, immensely powerful man, whose commitment to lead and make the first ascent of K2 was absolute. Once Houston's expedition returned with the welcome news that a reasonable way had been found up the mountain, Wiessner set about organizing the second attempt. It is easy to see in retrospect how the seeds of disaster were sown, almost from the outset, for a variety of reasons. Money or lack of it came high on the list. None of the 1938 team could afford to return so soon, and none was invited, with the exception of Bill House whose wealthy Pittsburgh family might have footed the bill. House had the talent and the experience to be high on Wiessner's list of candidates. He had also climbed with Wiessner frequently and it was this that caused him to pull out. For Wiessner was, by every account, a difficult man to spend any length of time with.

With America still fighting depression, Wiessner was forced from an early stage to invite people who could help pay for the expedition. Given that the initial pool of experienced climbers in the States was so small, and the four climbers from 1938 already discounted, his team was never a strong one and over the months leading to departure his first-choice climbers all dropped out. Sterling Hendricks, Alfred Lindley, Bestor Robinson and Roger Witney were all experienced climbers. Each withdrew with compelling excuses but underneath there was a feeling that Wiessner's personality was a common problem.

It is hard to discuss this without bringing up his German background, and all too easy to fall into the trap of racial stereotyping. Undoubtedly Wiessner was a rigid, single-minded, humorless and authoritarian figure. But these are by no means exclusively Teutonic characteristics—it is not hard to think of British, French and Italian climbers who have over the years displayed the same qualities and earned themselves huge accolades in the process. Many superstar climbers are impatient, intolerant, and totally unable to empathize with lesser mortals. This was at the heart of Fritz Wiessner's problem. The very qualities he displayed that might enable him to climb K2 could also be the undoing of the whole expedition, particularly an American one, with its own culture of democratic discussion and joint decision-making.

In the end Wiessner's team was both unbalanced and weak, so much so that even before it set out, questions were being asked about its chances of success. Maybe any other leader than Fritz Wiessner would have called the expedition off. But any other leader than Fritz Wiessner might not have ended up with such a curious collection of personalities, whose commitment to success varied widely and whose comprehension of what they were letting themselves in for was blinkered by Wiessner's own tunnel vision.

The team finally consisted of Wiessner himself leading, as always, from the front. His deputy leader was Tony Cromwell, a man whose main interest was mountaineering but not at a high level, and invariably in the company of guides. His private income was doubtless a factor in his selection, but he was also an efficient expedition treasurer. His climbing inadequacies were overlooked: he had after all amassed a lot of mountain experience. Chappel Cranmer and George Sheldon were both twenty and students at Dartmouth College. Both were promising but inexperienced climbers being thrown in at the deep end. The oddest choice was undoubtedly Dudley Wolfe. He was seriously rich, described by his nephew as "being like something out of Scott Fitzgerald's *The Great Gatsby*." He had all the playboy toys: power boats, yachts, fast cars. He had taken to skiing, then mountaineering at which he was enthusiastic but almost totally without ability. It frequently took two guides to haul his ungainly bulk up easy climbs. Worse, he was incapable of descending even easy ground without constant supervision and encouragement. But he was fit, strong and determined, and totally under the spell of Fritz Wiessner, who had obviously selected him for his money. Dudley Wolfe was desperate to prove himself and find meaning in a life that had often lacked direction. It was this combination of blind devotion, misplaced ambition and lack of skill and experience that would prove to be a fatal brew.

The last member to join up (or possibly be press-ganged) was twenty-seven-year-old pre-medical student at Dartmouth, Jack Durrance. When Bestor Robinson dropped out at the last moment with Wiessner already in Europe buying equipment, Durrance was drafted in with anonymous financial backing from members of the American Alpine Club. In the summers Durrance was a mountain guide in the Tetons with an excellent record of technical rock climbs. He certainly was quite good enough to join the team, but he had not met Wiessner, nor had he been chosen by him. Their first encounter sowed the seeds of a resentment that would last a lifetime.

Jack Durrance sailed for Europe. At Genoa he boarded the ship for India before the rest of the team and bumped into an elderly Italian gentleman looking for expedition members. It was the eighty-year-old photographer Vittorio Sella, anxious to meet the men returning to his beloved Karakoram. Five minutes later Wiessner arrived, intending, as leader, to be the one to welcome Sella. Instead he found him in conversation with a stranger. Durrance introduced himself and explained that Bestor Robinson was not coming. "Can't quite forget Fritz's look of disappointment at finding insignificant Jack filling Bestor Robinson's boots," Durrance wrote in his diary.

Despite his cold welcome the expedition quickly settled down and the voyage to Bombay was a pleasant interlude with its fair share of shipboard romance. The party traveled by train up to Srinagar in Kashmir where they picked up their English transport officer, Joe Trench, and nine Darjeeling Sherpas including, once again, Pasang Kikuli as sirdar. Four of the others had also been on Houston's expedition and, on paper at least, they seemed to be one part of Wiessner's expedition that was well up to scratch.

On May 2, having found time for two weeks' skiing above Srinagar, the team set out following the by now well-known 300-mile approach march to Base Camp. This passed off uneventfully, apart from the almost mandatory porter strike at Urdokas, until on May 30, just below Concordia, a tarpaulin was lost in a crevasse. Chappel Cranmer spent an age on the end of a rope searching for it before being hauled back to the surface. This immersion at 4500 meters must have been cold and exhausting and almost certainly precipitated a far more serious problem when two days later, on arrival at Base Camp, Cranmer developed what would now be quickly diagnosed as pulmonary edema. Jack

Durrance, despite an almost complete lack of medical experience, had been appointed expedition doctor on the strength of his future as a medical student, and was faced with a major crisis.

Cranmer sank into delirium, coughing up evil, bubbly fluid and developing diarrhea as well. Interviewed years later, Durrance recalled, "I never knew anyone could be so sick and stay alive . . . from the day I entered medical school until now at seventy-five, I've never had a worse patient than my first." He did everything he could to keep his patient warm, dry and clean. "In those days I wasn't very good at that sort of thing but I did what I could, everything I thought would be of help." Durrance without doubt saved his life. After two days the crisis passed. Chappel would live but was already a non-starter for K2 itself. The team was down to five Americans, though Wiessner himself was always reluctant to accept that Chappel had been so ill.

Work started on the Abruzzi Spur on June 8. Wiessner, out in front most, if not all, of the time, quickly found out that he was the only person able to make any progress on the mountain. Unlike in 1938 the weather was poor (perhaps "typical" is a better word), with strong winds, frequent short storms, and between June 21 and 29, a big storm that had the effect of dividing the team physically as well as psychologically. Out in front at Camp IV, Wiessner and Dudley Wolfe felt that with its clearing they would be able to press on for the top. Below them the rest of the team were shaken and disillusioned by the battering they had received and, ominously, were already thinking of home. There does seem to be a sea change on every expedition when the dominant mood swings from "thinking up" to "thinking down." Ideally this should only occur when the summit is reached. Unfortunately, it sometimes happens before and once it does it is hard, if not impossible, to reverse. Wiessner was possibly the only person who possessed the sheer force of character to stop the rot, but out in front he grew steadily more fixated with the summit and less aware of the house of cards slowly collapsing beneath him.

Progress was being made, albeit slowly. On June 30 Wiessner climbed House's Chimney with Pasang Kikuli and the next day Dudley Wolfe was almost winched up to join them. Camp V was established as another three-day storm started. Supplies up the mountain were poor to non-existent. Tony

Cromwell was proving to be an inadequate deputy and vacillated at every decision, endlessly delaying carries for the feeblest of reasons that could not hide his own lack of commitment. Higher up the mountain Jack Durrance seemed to be forever caught between the Devil and the deep blue sea. Wiessner, above, was always criticizing him while driving ahead with Dudley Wolfe, the one man who Jack Durrance, with his guide's experience, was most concerned for. Below, the expedition was running rapidly out of steam. Durrance himself had found it hard to acclimatize and had been plagued early on by useless boots and cold feet. He was now suffering sleepless nights worrying about the way Wolfe was almost being conned ever higher up the mountain.

And yet Wolfe *was* still going up, slowly and clumsily, however long he spent trying to recuperate at each camp. It is important to remember that in 1939 there was still only a very vague understanding of acclimatization and the then current theory (which was to persist well into the second half of the century) was that each stage of acclimatization could only be achieved by spending prolonged time at any given altitude. Today the policy of "climb high, sleep low" is well established, even if it is still often disregarded, sometimes with dire consequences. Now it is recognized that one deteriorates faster than one acclimatizes during time spent above 6000 meters. Dudley Wolfe, once he left Base Camp, never returned, and he was to spend an extraordinary amount of time above 7000 meters. These days it is a known fact that permanent life is impossible above approximately 5500 meters and physical deterioration leading to death is dramatically accelerated above 7000 meters; so much so that the summit of Everest, at 8848 meters, is right on the limit for human survival and then only for a matter of hours rather than days. But in 1939, and doubtless thinking he was doing the right thing, Dudley Wolfe determinedly pressed ever upward in the footsteps of the seemingly indefatigable Fritz Wiessner.

Only once did Wiessner descend to Camp II to find out what, if anything, was going on. Exhorting his weary men for an all-out effort, he urged everyone capable to do a carry to the highest camp. By the time they reached Camp IV below House's Chimney Wiessner, Durrance and Wolfe were the only ones capable of further progress to Camp VI, on the Black Pyramid. Jack Durrance was now acutely worried about Dudley Wolfe's ability and fitness. He was already showing slight signs of frostbite on his feet which should, to a more experienced man than Wolfe, have spelled out the need for an immediate retreat. But when Durrance "strongly" advised this, Wolfe sought Wiessner's opinion which was predictably hostile to Durrance, assuming he was jealous of Wolfe and wanted to go higher himself.

In fact Jack Durrance would have been only too happy to see the expedition abandoned altogether. He was all too aware that Wolfe would find the descent difficult, if not impossible, without help. But his concern was to no avail, and the next day on the way to Camp VII he himself was in trouble, beginning to show symptoms of edema: a violent headache, faintness and an inability to get his breath. Wiessner, as usual, thought he would recover almost immediately but, after an appalling night at Camp VI, Durrance wisely descended to Camp IV, then all the way down to Camp II and in doing so probably saved his own life.

This left Wiessner and Wolfe out on a limb. Between Camp II and Camp VII stretched a line of well-equipped camps but with only minimal Sherpa support. Since the early Everest expeditions of the 1920s the Sherpas had shown their worth as brave, sometimes heroic porters. But they were not the experienced mountaineers they are today. They were very dependent on obeying orders, often frightened on difficult ground, easily discouraged and, on top of this, their command of English was poor. It was asking too much of them to take all the day-to-day decisions high on the Abruzzi Spur without supervision.

By July 17 after yet another short storm, Fritz Wiessner, Dudley Wolfe and Pasang Lama, the strongest of the Sherpas, had established Camp VIII just below the Shoulder, and they set out on what they hoped would be the beginning of their summit bid. As soon as they crossed a bergschrund they immediately met bottomless snow. Poor lumbering Dudley Wolfe just couldn't make any progress, floundering in the others' tracks, and returned to Camp VIII. He would either try again with "another party" in Wiessner's optimistic words, or stay and maintain contact with the rest of the team. Neither actually happened and for five days Dudley Wolfe was to be entirely on his own.

In the deep snow Wiessner and Pasang Lama only managed to gain the crest of the Shoulder before camping well short of their intended site and the next day it still took them several hours to reach a campsite on the flat top of a rock pillar, at around 8000 meters. This was presumably the site spotted by Petzoldt the year before and marked the end of known ground. Above reared the rock buttress and above that was the great frozen wave of the sérac band. Wiessner's camp was to the left (west) of the crest of the Shoulder and well out of the line of sérac fall.

His campsite and, more important, the route the following morning, were chosen because Wiessner was first and foremost a brilliant rock climber and would remain so until well into his seventies. Instinctively, rock was his first choice; he was inexperienced and uncomfortable on steep ice and the sérac band seemed to be a very obvious danger. On Nanga Parbat a sérac had collapsed under him, causing him a twenty-meter fall into a crevasse from which he was extremely lucky to escape alive. Wiessner therefore resolved to climb the broken rocks above his camp, traversing left under the steepest section of the rock buttress and turning in at its western extremity. From there he hoped to gain the much easier summit snow slopes.

The alternative would have been to bear right from the top camp and follow a snow gully, now known as the Bottleneck, cutting through the rocks directly underneath the sérac. From there a dangerous-looking left-hand traverse would lead to the same summit slopes. Understandably, Wiessner rejected it. Had he chanced his arm on July 19 it is possible that he would have changed the course of Himalayan climbing.

Wiessner and Pasang overslept and left Camp IX late, at nine A.M. This was regrettable, for the rock climbing on verglassed rock proved to be more difficult than it looked and the hours slipped by. Wiessner led all day on mixed ground far harder than anything previously climbed at that altitude. He graded it Six which was the highest grade given in the Western Alps at the time. As nobody has ever tried to repeat Wiessner's route it is impossible to verify this, but at that altitude it must have been an incredible performance.

At last, late in the day, only a short traverse separated him from the summit snows. He was at around 8365 meters, less than 250 vertical meters from the summit. In his words:

> It was six P.M. by then. I had made up my mind to go for the summit despite the late hour and climb through the night. We had found a safe route and overcame the difficulties, and with the exception of the traverse had easy going from now on.
>
> The weather was safe and we were not exhausted. Night climbing had to be done anyway, as it would take us a long time to descend the difficult route up which we had struggled. Much better to go up to the summit slowly and with many stops and return over the difficult part of the route the next morning. Pasang however did not have the heart for it; he wanted to go back to camp once he realized night was not far. He refused to go on, even did not pass my rope when I started the traverse. His reasoning and my lack of energy made me give in.

Did Pasang Lama, who had performed extremely well all day, rob Fritz Wiessner of the summit, or was his the voice of reason? It could well have been both, for had Wiessner pressed on, he would possibly have made the top, but to climb up and down through the night with no bivouac gear would have been a very hazardous gamble. Wearing leather nailed boots would have almost certainly led to severe frostbite and, however good the rest of their equipment may have been, the cruel cold air of a clear night on the summit of K2 would have tested them to the absolute limit. No wonder that it was later said that Pasang Lama dreaded the wrath of the mountain gods that inhabited the summit snows of K2!

Although forced to retreat, Wiessner told Pasang that they would try again. On their way up the broken buttress earlier in the day he had studied the gully on their right below the sérac barrier and realized that it was probably much safer than he had first thought. It would also take far less time, and he resolved to try it. But on their descent, by now in darkness, they had to make a difficult abseil. Pasang got tangled in the ropes and in trying to free himself he managed to dislodge the two pairs of crampons he was carrying on his rucksack which dropped away into the black depths below. This misfortune set the seal on their summit ambitions, though they didn't realize it immediately.

July 20 dawned fine and clear. But the pair at Camp IX were in no state to try again for the summit and they spent the day resting. It was so calm that at 8000 meters with the tent door open, Wiessner lay naked on his sleeping-bag. He was determined to set out on the 21st, this time via the Bottleneck Couloir. How realistic an attempt this might have been if they had been wearing crampons is hard to guess. Wiessner himself was always convinced they could have done it, but after so much time spent at altitude it is quite likely that he was deluding himself. Nevertheless, leaving at six A.M., he and Pasang traversed right and up towards the Bottleneck. Wiessner describes reaching "a short steep slope just beneath the ice cliff which would require step-cutting . . . a full day's work at this altitude so again we return . . . " Just how far up the Bottleneck he went is difficult to say.

After yet another night (the fifth) at 8000 meters, Wiessner decided to go down to Camp VIII and pick up spare crampons, more food and fuel and also a fresh Sherpa, for Pasang was now very tired. As they regained the camp Dudley Wolfe emerged from his tent. No one else had made it to Camp VIII, he had run out of matches, and was resorting to melting snow for water in the folds of the tent.

Wiessner was puzzled. Why had no one come up? But he did not seem as worried as he should have been that nine days had passed since they had last seen anyone else. They all decided to go down to Camp VII which was well equipped. On the way down Dudley Wolfe trod on the rope, which pulled Wiessner off. Suddenly all three were falling towards the huge 2000-meter drop to the Godwin-Austen Glacier, and only a desperate ice-axe arrest from Wiessner managed to stop them twenty meters short of disaster. Wolfe lost his sleeping-bag in the fall, and only Pasang had carried his down from Camp IX. Wiessner had left his, thinking he would be returning the same day. In twilight they reached Camp VII to find it abandoned. The tents were full of snow, the poles of one tent had broken and there were no sleeping-bags or mattresses.

The three had a miserable night and the following morning Wiessner made the fateful decision to leave Dudley Wolfe and descend with Pasang Lama to Camp VI to see what was happening. By doing this Wiessner split his team and left the weakest member on his own with everyone else below him. Whether or not Wolfe wanted to stay there for another attempt, as Wiessner later claimed he did, it was, at best, a lapse of responsibility by the leader quite likely caused by his prolonged stay at altitude. Wiessner must have known that Wolfe would be unable to descend unsupervised from so high on the mountain, and it seems almost unbelievable that, given the state of Camp VII, he still did not appear to realize that something was seriously amiss below. The only explanation must be that Wiessner was still fixated by the summit and just not prepared to accept the need to plan a safe retreat. Judgment, reflexes and perception were dulled by being too high for too long. A situation that would occur again on the Shoulder of K2.

All through July 23 Wiessner and Pasang descended, passing through four more abandoned camps. No sleeping-bags, no mattresses, and no American members or Sherpas. After another grim night at Camp II they managed, by this time on their last legs, to make it back to Base Camp. Barely able to speak but apoplectic with rage, Wiessner laid into the hapless Tony Cromwell. Why had they been abandoned? Why had the tents been stripped? What had happened to the Sherpa support?

The answers to these questions and the accusations that followed were to haunt the American climbing establishment for years to come. But at the time Wiessner, despite his exhaustion, seemed to be mainly concerned that he had been temporarily robbed of the summit. For several days after his return to Base Camp Wiessner planned another attempt, even hoping it would be possible to pick Dudley Wolfe up on the way. Gradually, though, it began to dawn on him that not only would he not be able to regain his high point but that saving the forlorn Dudley Wolfe was the only thing that mattered.

By now only the Sherpas were in any sort of condition to go high. Jack Durrance tried, but soon developed signs of the pulmonary problems that had beset him before. Wiessner was still unable to set out and in the end only Pasang Kikuli, by far and away the most experienced Himalayan climber on the expedition, Tsering Norbu, Pasang Kitar and Phinsoo were still willing and, what's more, fit enough to return. Pasang Kikuli and Tsering Norbu in fact climbed from Base Camp to Camp VI in one day—over 2000 meters of ascent! It was an astonishing performance, more in keeping with the "speed ascents" of the 1980s. On July 29, almost a week after Wiessner had left him, three of the Sherpas regained Camp VII and found Dudley Wolfe still alive but in a bad way. Bodily waste soiled the tent and he had again run out of matches. The Sherpas made him tea and managed to get him outside the tent but he refused to go down and told them to come back again the following day when he would be ready. The Sherpas, for whom blind obedience to the Sahibs was still ingrained, didn't argue, and went back to Camp VI, where it stormed for a day. On July 31 the same three, Pasang Kikuli, Pasang Kitar and Phinsoo set out one last time, either to rescue Dudley Wolfe or at least make him write a note that absolved them of any further responsibility. They were never seen again.

Whether they reached him and all four fell or were avalanched on the descent or whether the three Sherpas failed to make it to Camp VII is academic. What is virtually certain is that the attempt was doomed to failure from the start. Dudley Wolfe would be incapable of helping himself and three men would never have managed to lower the sick man all the way down to the Godwin-Austen Glacier. Anyone who has been involved in mountain rescue, and its complex techniques evolved since the Second World War, is aware that unless the victim can move himself it takes more men and equipment to evacuate a casualty than Wiessner's team could possibly muster. During the first week of August the weather had broken down completely and on August 8 any faint hope that there would be survivors was finally abandoned. K2 had claimed its first four victims.

The recriminations were not long coming. As is almost inevitable in disasters of this nature the arguments were compounded by guilt, sorrow, revenge and ignorance. Time and time again, the same potent brew would surface over accidents on K2, producing long-running sagas in which the original, often complex, circumstances were buried under huge volumes of half-truths and prejudice.

The 1939 controversy was particularly vitriolic and soon to be com-pounded by Wiessner's German origins and the outbreak of war. At its heart were two simple issues. Why had the camps on the Abruzzi been abandoned and stripped of their sleeping-bags and, given that set of circumstances, why was Dudley Wolfe left on his own?

To attempt to answer the first question let us return to July 18, the day Fritz Wiessner and Pasang Lama are establishing their final camp. At the bottom of the mountain Jack Durrance is still recovering from illness. At Base Camp Tony Cromwell is preparing for the imminent return journey and por-ters from Askole are due to arrive on the 23rd. Jack Durrance receives a note from Cromwell asking him to bring down "all the tents and sleeping-bags you can." This is actually easier said than done, given the limited manpower, but Durrance, safe in the knowledge that there are still Sherpas high on the mountain above Camp IV, and all the camps are well stocked, does what he can—the more gear removed from lower down the mountain now, the less to be carried down by the (hopefully) successful climbers in a few days.

But unknown to Durrance, the Sherpas above, unsupervised, unclear as to their role, with little understanding of English and with rapidly sinking morale, have failed to keep supplies moving upwards. On July 20 Tendrup is the only porter to venture above Camp VII. Alone and nervous he shouts up to the site of Camp VIII and (not surprisingly) gets no reply.

Convincing himself that everyone above is dead, there is now no point in staying up. Tendrup persuades the other Sherpas at Camp VII that the best thing to do is descend with as many of the most valuable bits of gear as they can carry. Sleeping-bags have always been the most precious commodity on expeditions for Sherpas, to be traded or used later at home. Once persuaded, the deed is done rapidly. And so, almost by accident, the mountain is stripped simultaneously by two teams, both hoping they are doing the right thing, but all obeying their natural instincts which are to go down and go home.

A mystery which has never been resolved concerns a note that Fritz Wiessner alleges Jack Durrance wrote to him, congratulating him on reach-ing the summit and saying he had had all the sleeping-bags brought down from Camp IV by Kikuli and Dawa and that they would descend with these and the ones from Camp II to Base Camp. There would be no sleeping-bags at all from Camp IV down as Wiessner, Wolfe and Pasang would have their own with them. This note was allegedly left at Camp II for Wiessner on his way down.

The problem was that no trace of the note has ever been found, and Jack Durrance has no recollection of writing it. Andy Kauffman and Bill Putnam surmise in *K2, the 1939 Tragedy* that there are three possible explanations. First that Wiessner made the story up; second that Durrance *did* write it and it was later lost or thrown away and third that Wiessner mistook the note that Tony Cromwell wrote to Jack Durrance. Wiessner didn't mention the note at all until 1955. It seems unlikely that he deliberately lied, though it is just possible. Durrance on the other hand is certain that he didn't write it. Perhaps the most likely explanation is that Wiessner wrongly assumed that a note addressed to Jack Durrance was *from* him not *to* him. In the aftermath of such a fraught expedition it is easy to give the note more meaning and importance than it deserves.

After the expedition Cromwell became the focus of all Wiessner's anger, he in turn held Wiessner totally responsible for the deaths—adding fuel to the flames by stating publicly on his return to America that Wiessner had murdered Dudley Wolfe. On his own return Wiessner tactlessly told reporters that "on big mountains, as in war, one must expect casualties." Given that war had just broken out in Europe, this remark gave his detractors, many of whom were anti-German, another stick to beat him with. Perhaps the most outspoken critic of Wiessner was Kenneth Mason who wrote the classic Himalayan history, *Abode of Snow.* "It is difficult to record in temperate language the folly of this enterprise" was his summing-up of a very one-sided account of what happened.

Jack Durrance was appalled at the feud between Wiessner and Cromwell and decided from an early stage to keep a dignified silence. This he maintained for fifty years, during which time both Wiessner and public opinion turned against him instead of Cromwell. The American Alpine Club was torn by the controversy and in 1941 Wiessner resigned. He was readmitted in 1966 after a lot of persuasion from his friends, becoming an honorary member for his services to American climbing generally. But he never returned to the Himalaya. He died in 1988.

Durrance, in the end, emerges with credit. His diaries show that his concern with the performance of Dudley Wolfe was motivated by responsibility not jealousy and that the sleeping-bag removal was instigated by Cromwell and compounded by the Sherpas' lack of direction.

In the end Wiessner must be judged as neither saint nor sinner, but as a brilliant, single-minded climber, who was temperamentally unsuited to the demands of leadership. Chris Bonington, who has had more experience of leading major Himalayan expeditions than most, is firmly of the opinion that the leader must be prepared to carry out his role by spending most of his time behind and below the lead climbers, whose drive and commitment will invariably prevent their having a totally objective view of the whole venture. By leading from the front Wiessner cut himself off from his team both physically and psychologically.

And yet it could so easily have turned out differently. If Wiessner had decided that the Bottleneck Couloir was worth risking on July 19, K2 might have been climbed. The descent would have been carried out with Sherpas still placed in high camps and most of the tensions existing within the team would have been forgotten in the euphoria of success. The ascent, without oxygen, would have made K2 the first of the fourteen 8000-meter peaks to be climbed and could well have changed the course of Himalayan climbing after the war. Ironically, the choice of route was a decision that Fritz Wiessner made for the best possible reason—safety. How sad that it should, albeit indirectly, have provoked such a terrible outcome.

"STRANGERS AND BROTHERS"

The Second World War put an end to any further expeditions and after the war came the Partition of India in 1947 and the creation of the Muslim nation of Pakistan. In the turmoil of its birth, expeditions to K2 near the controversial new border with Kashmir were out of the question. This did not deter Charles Houston who had wanted to return since 1939. Despite his constant efforts it was not until 1952 that he made any progress. Even then it took the influence of the American Ambassador to Pakistan before permission was at last granted for an attempt in 1953. By this time Charlie Houston was one of America's most experienced Himalayan climbers. He had taken part in the first reconnaissance of the south (Nepalese) side of Everest in 1950 when with Bill Tilman they reached the foot of the Khumbu Icefall that bars access into the Western Cwm of Everest. This was to be the key to the eventual success.

On K2, Houston was again accompanied by his oldest and best friend Bob Bates. William House had to pull out but Houston and Bates were still able to select a strong and experienced party of eight men, two more than 1938, and for a very good reason. After Partition, Sherpas were unwelcome in Pakistan and local Hunza porters would have to take their place. Hunzas had already proved themselves on pre-war Nanga Parbat expeditions and were a hardy mountain race, though not quite as experienced as the Sherpas were rapidly becoming. Houston guessed that they would find the Abruzzi Spur beyond their ability and only planned to use them for carries from Base Camp to Camp II. So the team was increased, but not doubled or trebled, for Houston and Bates knew that campsites on the Abruzzi were difficult to find and more numbers would not necessarily make the climb easier. It was a lesson that other teams would have done well to heed in the future when some truly colossal expeditions would arrive at Base Camp. But Houston and Bates remained true to their pre-war alpine-style ethic.

They interviewed a lot of good people, trying to choose a compatible, rather than a brilliant, team that would work together. Choosing the right people was one of the reasons that they were later able to survive an appalling and protracted ordeal. Their team was made up of Bob Craig, mountaineer and ski instructor, from Aspen, Colorado; Art K. Gilkey, a geologist from Iowa; Dee Molenaar, also a geologist and artist; Pete Schoening from Seattle; George F. Bell, a physics professor at Cornell University; and an English army officer, Captain H. R. A. Streather, who would be transport officer. Since Partition Streather had served with the Chitral Scouts and had already climbed

Tirich Mir with a Norwegian expedition, though on his own admission he was then a complete novice. Tony Streather was considered for the 1953 Everest expedition, but turned down because of his lack of Alpine and technical climbing expertise. Charlie Houston's invitation to K2 arrived almost the same day as his rejection letter for Everest. Ironically, he had been turned down for an expedition to a technically simple route, and invited instead to attempt a far harder one.

Like Houston's 1938 expedition it was a harmonious and happy party that gathered in Rawalpindi towards the end of May. After picking up their liaison officer, Colonel Atta Ullah, and Tony Streather and completing a hectic week of engagements, they flew to Skardu and in all hour and a half did what in 1938 and 1939 had taken two weeks of hard walking. Since Partition the old approach from Srinagar was out of the question. Now Skardu had trebled its population, both civilian and military, acquired a hospital and an airport, and become the jumping-off point for all future Central Karakoram expeditions.

The day they left for Skardu the expedition heard that the British had succeeded on Everest, They must have had mixed feelings about this and certainly the motivation for Houston's comparatively small expedition to succeed must have been turned up a few notches.

The walk-in seems to be unique in that there is no record of a porter strike! Twenty-six days after leaving America they arrived at Base Camp in good spirits and soon work on the lower part of the Abruzzi Spur was smoothly under way. To see if he was technically up to it, Charlie Houston diffidently asked if anyone would mind if he led House's Chimney and, with its ascent, felt that he could cope with anything else K2 had to offer. A pulley system was rigged at the top of the Chimney to haul loads up the outside walls. The weather was much worse than in 1938, with frequent short storms. Nevertheless progress was slow but sure, as the old campsites from 1938 and 1939 were reached and made habitable.

The higher they climbed the more apprehensive they became, for the mystery of Dudley Wolfe and the three Sherpas had never been resolved. Tony Streather remembers his unspoken fear that they would find their remains. At the site of Camp VI, which the Sherpas had left on their last attempt to rescue Wolfe, they found some sad remnants. Inside the wrecked tents were the Sherpa sleeping-bags neatly rolled up and ready to be carried down with the stricken Wolfe. A stove, fuel and a small bundle of tea wrapped in a handkerchief were the only other poignant reminders of the three brave men. Nothing else was found higher up to shed light on what might have happened.

As on the previous expedition the Black Pyramid provided sustained and precarious climbing. The expedition had taken longer to reach Camp VI than in 1938, and supplies, while not becoming critical, were certainly starting to cause some anxiety. Even matches, which had been such a problem in 1938, were beginning to get low and Houston had nightmares about running out again. The climb was becoming a struggle. "Gone were most of the jokes; the banter had become more serious. We were more determined than ever, but the picnic was over."

By the end of July Schoening and Gilkey had pushed the route out in poor weather to establish Camp VIII just under the Shoulder of K2. On August 2 the whole team arrived there, all safe and well with enough food for a serious summit bid. But the weather was breaking down and soon a full-scale storm was raging.

Much has been written about the monsoon not reaching the Karakoram. But it seems clear that in heavy monsoon years, of which 1953 was certainly one, the weather on K2 is affected by it and there have been some prolonged and ferocious storms on K2 in the last days of July and the first ten days of August. 1986 is another case in point.

At first Houston's little team were in good spirits: "Bob Bates read aloud to us for hours. Dee Molenaar painted. We all wrote diaries." They were still thinking upwards, so much so that Houston, true to his democratic roots, took a secret ballot to decide on the summit teams. ". . . When I crawled back from the other tents through the blizzard I was prouder than ever before of my party. When the ballots were counted Bell and Craig were to be the first team, Gilkey and Shoening the second." As on Nanda Devi all those years before, Charlie Houston hoped that the names of the would-be summiteers would be kept secret. "We hoped to report, 'Two men reached the top'—no more, no less."

During the fourth night of storm George Bell and Charlie Houston watched their tent start to disintegrate. At dawn it collapsed completely and Bell crawled in with Molenaar and Craig, while Houston remarked, "Streather and Bates pretended to be glad to have me crowd into their tent, a French model with lining which made it very cramped even for two."

By the afternoon of August 6 they were dispirited and discussed a partial retreat for the first time. They had radio contact with Colonel Atta Ullah at Base Camp with whom they had all become very close. He was tuned into Radio Pakistan weather forecasts which were grim. Could they descend to Camp IV, regroup, rest, rehydrate, then have another attempt? It seemed a forlorn hope and was to be cruelly dashed the next day.

August 7 was less windy and brighter. Everyone crawled from their tents and "stumbled around like castaways first reaching shore." But Art Gilkey suddenly collapsed and passed out. He came round quickly: "I'm all right, fellows; it's just my leg, that's all . . . I've had this charley horse [cramp] for a couple of days . . . I thought it would be gone by now. It's sure to clear up in another day—isn't it?"

Houston examined him and knew that disaster had struck. Art had developed thrombophlebitis—blood clots in the veins of his left leg. At sea level his condition could be serious with a possibility of clots breaking off and being carried into the lungs. But at that height, around 7800 meters, Gilkey's chances of survival were virtually nonexistent. Houston tried to reassure Gilkey while "trying to hide my awful certainty that he would never reach Base Camp alive."

Now thinking downwards was all they could do. Tony Streather, interviewed forty years after the event, summed up his own feelings then, feelings that were almost certainly shared by everyone else.

> *I think we had deteriorated to the extent that we didn't think anything very logically, we just did what was obviously necessary at the time. We thought Art was going to die. We didn't think he would ever live. I don't think we kidded ourselves or didn't admit it to ourselves. As far as we were concerned, while he was*

*still alive, we were trying to carry him down . . . in retrospect I
don't think there was ever any chance.*

Despite everyone's deep foreboding there was never any question of leaving
Art Gilkey. Somehow every effort must be made to save him. They discussed
their options: 1. try to get Gilkey down; 2. Gilkey and Houston to stay in
camp while the others went down for more supplies; 3. all sit it out until the
weather cleared, by which time Art Gilkey might be dead.

Hastily they packed up. Charlie Houston with ingrained good habits
attempted to clear the campsite, throwing supplies of food away and disman-
tling the tents. He was stopped—no time for that now—and they started down.
After a very short time it became obvious that they were pulling Gilkey on to
textbook avalanche-prone slopes: feet of powder snow lying on hard ice with
no chance to consolidate. There was no choice but to return to the camp—
mercifully still intact. But it took a major effort to get Gilkey back up.

By now they had spent seven nights at Camp VIII and faced an even longer
stay at an altitude which would eventually kill them all if they remained there.
In despair Bob Craig and Pete Schoening explored the descent of a steep rock
rib that seemed to lead eventually to Camp VII and give some security from
avalanches. The next day was slightly better and Houston thought that the
weather was now on the change. They decided to wait one more day in the
hope that it would really improve. As a last gesture of defiance Craig and
Schoening set out on a forlorn gesture—climbing up the Shoulder for some
150 meters before returning to the tents.

On August 9 the storm returned at full force. No one could move and for
the first time Houston thought that they might all die. During the night Art
Gilkey had begun to cough and his pulse rose to 140 per minute. Clots seemed
to have carried to his lungs. Art apologized for being a burden and talked about
the others making a further summit bid: "Art said nothing of himself. He had
never talked about his death, though he was too wise not to see its imminence."

August 10 dawned cold, grim and windy. Conversations had to be yelled
to be understood. Art *had* to descend, a clot was forming in his other leg and
he couldn't survive much longer at that height.

Quickly the others packed up, taking the lightest of the tents, "in case of emergency," as Bob Bates wrote. (One has to wonder just what *would* constitute an emergency, if not their present predicament.) Then they set off. "Each of us realized that he was beginning the most dangerous day's work of his life."

The nightmare descent began. In freezing, numbing spindrift Gilkey was first pulled through deep snow then, when the angle increased, lowered. Every maneuver demanded the utmost concentration and the seven battered men began to realize the enormity of their task. Art Gilkey, strapped into a makeshift stretcher of a wrapped tent, a rucksack and a rope cradle, was uncomplaining but silent, his face a bluish gray. But whenever anyone asked how he was he would force a smile. "Just fine . . . just fine."

Painfully slowly they lost height. At one stage they set off a powder-snow avalanche which nearly swept Craig and Gilkey away, but the rope from above held. At last they got to a point on the rock rib where they could start to traverse across to the abandoned site of Camp VII. Pete Schoening was belaying Art Gilkey and Dee Molenaar. Above them were Houston and Bates and Bell and Streather. Craig had unroped from Gilkey and crossed to the shelf on which the camp had been placed.

Suddenly George Bell slipped on hard ice and fell out of control. Streather was pulled off and the two of them cannoned into Houston and Bates who were traversing below them. All four hurtled down the slope with nothing to stop them going all the way to the Godwin-Austen Glacier—nothing, that is, except the rope from Art Gilkey to Dee Molenaar, which somehow caught and snagged Tony Streather. Molenaar was plucked off and all five carried on falling until the strain came on to Art Gilkey and that in turn came on Pete Schoening belaying him above with an ice-axe jammed into snow behind a rock. Miraculously, Schoening held them all. Miraculously, no rope broke.

The whole jumble of tangled rope and bodies slid to a halt in total confusion. Far below George Bell minus rucksack, glasses and mittens staggered in confusion. Bob Bates and Dee Molenaar were tangled together and were almost cutting Tony Streather in half. And Charlie Houston lay crumpled and unconscious on a ledge poised over a huge drop. Bob Bates soloed down to him and Houston came round, concussed and confused. "Where are we?" he kept repeating. "What are we doing here?"

Bob Bates, knowing that if Charlie Houston couldn't help himself no one else could, looked his old friend in the eye. "Charlie, if you ever want to see Dorcas and Penny [his wife and daughter] again, climb up there *right now!*"

Mechanically Houston obeyed and climbed brilliantly. Bates followed slowly to reach Dee Molenaar, trying to answer Charlie's insistent question, "What are we doing here?"

Stunned, shocked, facing frostbite and, above all, exhausted, it was essential to get a tent up quickly. Gilkey, who had not fallen and was probably the warmest of them all, was anchored securely by two ice-axes in the gully he was being lowered into when the accident had occurred. The others moved across and tried to get Bell and Houston warmed up in the tent. Now Pete Schoening, the strongman of the party, seemed on the verge of collapse and was coughing uncontrollably. Art Gilkey had been shouting to them but in the wind they couldn't understand what he was saying. At last Bob Bates and Tony Streather returned to the gully to try and bring him down. Bob Bates wrote, "What we saw there I shall never forget. The whole slope was bare of life. Art Gilkey was gone."

It has often been surmised that Art Gilkey had somehow cut himself free in an attempt to save the others, but Charlie Houston firmly believes this to be impossible.

> *Memories aren't clear about Gilkey's shouting. If he did it was only once or twice and muffled by the gust of wind. He was almost unconscious the last time I spoke with him (and, I believe, I gave him another shot to ease his pain) . . . there was no way he had the strength, freedom or intention to struggle himself free: he was almost dead by then—at least that's what I believe and the others feel similarly.*

There seemed to be a faint groove in the gully that had not been there before. Gilkey had been avalanched. The two men, disbelieving and crushed by this last and biggest blow, returned to the tents.

The survivors had a horrendous night. Charlie Houston was severely concussed, hyperventilating and trying to cut a hole in the tent saying they would die from lack of oxygen. He kept asking the same questions: "How's Pete? How's Tony?" Somehow the long night passed and the seven exhausted men emerged to fight another day.

Art Gilkey's death, however harrowing, undoubtedly saved them. Now they only had to fight for their own survival and it would take them the whole of the next day just to get down to Camp VI, which was still over 7000 meters. On the descent Tony Streather recovered a small bag, believing it belonged to Art Gilkey. But it didn't, it belonged to George Bell and miraculously contained a spare pair of unbroken glasses which cheered him up immensely. There was no sign of Gilkey except for some blood-streaked rocks, a tangle of ropes and an ice-axe shaft jammed in some rocks. No one mentioned this on the way down and it was not until the team was reunited that they all admitted they had seen those remnants.

George Bell's feet were badly frostbitten and, as Houston's concussion faded, Bell became the one to worry about. All the next day they descended carefully, aware that they were still not safe. At the top of House's Chimney Houston, insisting as leader on "first up, last down," belayed everyone down in the dusk and supervised the lowering of all the rucksacks. By the time everyone else was safe in Camp IV just below it was dark.

Houston then had to abseil into the void but couldn't tell which, amongst the remnants of old ropes that littered the chimney, was the new one. He knelt in the snow and recited the Lord's Prayer, then climbed clown without using them. Thankfully, he rejoined his companions in the camp below.

The descent to Camp III was more tedious than dangerous and there the exhausted men found plenty of food. After a decent meal they decided to go on to Camp II. Here the Hunza porters were waiting and, in an emotional reunion, many tears were shed and the Hunzas spontaneously said a prayer for Art Gilkey. It was, said Bob Craig, "the deepest experience I've ever had with a human being."

Back at Base Camp at last they received another heartfelt welcome from Colonel Atta Ullah, who, through regular radio contact, had become a vital part of the team. They made an hour-long tape-recording that evening of all that had happened. As Charlie Houston concluded, "We entered the mountain as strangers, but we left as brothers."

The day after their return, the Hunza porters built a memorial cairn that still stands on a tiny saddle of an outlying spur of rock at the confluence of the Savoia and Godwin-Austen Glaciers. It commands a superb view down to Concordia and across the South Face of K2. The team limped the four hundred meters to the cairn. They laid mountain flowers, the flags they had hoped to take to the summit, a favorite poem and Art's own ice-axe which he had given to Bob Craig just after the multiple fall. Bob Bates read a passage from the Bible and said a prayer. Then they turned away and began the preparations for the long journey home. George Bell had to be carried in a makeshift stretcher, but in the end lost only one small toe and half a big toe.

Unlike the bitterness surrounding the Wiessner expedition, the 1953 American K2 expedition became a symbol of all that is best in mountaineering. Today the team are still united in friendship and their shared ordeal brought them a depth of understanding and insight that is very apparent in their reunions. For Houston himself the expedition was a turning point. For many years he found it hard to come to terms with Art's death and suffered depressions, even, on one occasion, amnesia on the anniversary of the accident. Initially, he wanted to return in 1954 and was mortified to find that "his" mountain had been booked by a large Italian expedition. Although he had permission for 1955 he didn't take it up and 1953 marked the end of his serious mountaineering. Instead he turned to the study of high-altitude medicine and in the last forty years he has become one of the world's greatest authorities on every aspect of the subject. It is surely no accident that his desperate attempt to save Art Gilkey has in a sense continued, for his research has surely saved many, many more lives since then.

Exactly forty years later, in 1993, Art Gilkey's remains were found just above the site of the present day Base Camp. Several pieces of clothing, including a down jacket, and fragments of skull and other bones were positively identified as his. Eight years earlier an old ice-axe had been found at the base of the mountain, its shaft snapped below the head. It was in all probability the other end of the shaft that the 1953 team noted on the descent. Gilkey's bones were returned to the United States for burial in the family plot. As well as Gilkey's remains, the bones of a very small Asian were found further up the glacier. They were almost certainly the remains of Pasang Kitar who was apparently well below the average size of Sherpas. . . .

"THE WESTERN APPROACH AND DEFEAT"
AND
"ATTEMPT TO REACH SUMMIT RIDGE"

FROM
Everest 1938 in *The Seven Mountain-Travel Books*
BY H. W. TILMAN

THE TILMAN-LED BRITISH EXPEDITION TO EVEREST IN 1938 WAS THE seventh party to visit the mountain, but only the fifth to attempt the ascent. Tilman himself had been there on a reconnaissance foray in 1935, after which he pronounced, "No one would choose to go there merely for a mountaineering holiday."

Tilman was already becoming an advocate of small, lightly equipped expedition parties. Possibly he actually did say "the best expeditions are those that can be planned on the back of an envelope." While the 1938 trip wasn't quite to this pattern, Tilman was proud to point out that it consisted of only seven members, all climbers, bringing one-fifth of the gear and spending one-fifth of the money of previous expeditions.

As in all Everest expeditions between 1921 and World War II, the 1938 party came in from the north side (it was on the North Face route that George Mallory and Sandy Irvine were lost in 1924). Tilman's party traveled up the East Rongbuk Glacier to a Camp III at the foot of the North Col, alternatively trying the more eastern Kharta Valley approach as well, and would advance and retreat a number of times before finally being turned away by extreme cold weather, short of the summit ridge.

It would be more than twelve years following the unsuccessful 1938 attempt before the way to the summit began to open. Tilman's reconnoitering of the Khumbu Valley in 1950, with American mountaineer Charles Houston, and Shipton's 1951 passage through the Khumbu Icefall and his entrance into the Western Cwm, led the way for John Hunt's British expedition finally to achieve the summit, in 1953, via the South Col.

This is an abridgement of Chapters 8 and 9 from *Everest 1938*. Considered one of the finest classic expedition books ever written, *Everest 1938* was first published by Cambridge University Press, 1948. The book was republished in *H. W. Tilman: The Seven Mountain-Travel Books;* this selection comprises pages 482-494.

"THE WESTERN APPROACH AND DEFEAT"

Lake Camp is only about 11½ miles from Camp I; the approach to it is across the East Rongbuk valley, below the glacier snout, and then up the moraine shelf on the right bank of the main Rongbuk glacier. Camp I is as good a camp as one could expect at 18,000 ft., but Lake Camp is better. Of course there is no fuel, but it is warm and sheltered, for it lies tucked away between a high moraine bank and the bounding wall of the valley; a stream of clear water meanders through a grassy lawn to empty itself into a little lake which is pleasant to look at if not to bathe in. Because of the sheltering slopes the morning sun reaches it rather late in the day, a disadvantage which is offset by the fact that it is open to the sun until a late hour in the afternoon. No one, I imagine, who visits this camp is likely to grow tired of looking at grass, for as the shadow of a great rock and water [are] in a thirsty land so is grass to the sojourner among ice. But should he do so he has only to climb the moraine bank to see Everest with its stupendous north-west ridge sweeping down to the Lho La, the fascinating pinnacles of the main Rongbuk glacier, and the striking group of mountains, Pumori and the Lingtren group, lying between the West Rongbuk and the upper main Rongbuk glacier.

[Eric] Shipton, [Frank] Smythe, and [Peter] Lloyd, who had now recovered, were on their way up to the west side of the Col; but having heard that we had come down became uncertain what to do and were toying with the idea of making an excursion up the West Rongbuk glacier. However, this change in the weather kindled fresh hope in us all. By stepping a few yards from the camp we could see the north face of the mountain, and, through breaks in the flying scud, snow being whirled off it in the most encouraging manner. If this continued we might yet accomplish something, but while the wind promised to clear the mountain it also threatened to form wind-slab snow on the east or lee side of the Col. Bowing to Smythe's repeated warnings, we decided to abandon that side altogether and to concentrate on an approach from the west. I attached myself to Shipton's party in order to make up two climbing parties of two, and we brought up our porter strength to seventeen by sending for two good men from Camp I. The remaining fourteen porters were left to bring down some necessary loads from Camp III, and then, with the three Europeans, were to follow up as quickly as possible.

The wind having blown for 48 hours dropped on the 3rd, a very fine, almost cloudless day, with very little wind at all except high up. The march to the next camp is a rough one; at first over moraine boulders and later along a trough on the right bank of the glacier. The camp is close to the point where the short glacier leading to the west side of the Col joins the main glacier. Tents were pitched on the glacier itself, the coolness of the ice being tempered by the layer of stones which covered it. Some debris left by the 1936 expedition, including a wireless aerial, still lay about—evidently the Tibetans have not yet heard of this departure from the usual route. This place was called North Face Camp but perhaps Corner Camp would be a better name. It was so mild that afternoon that we sat about on the moraine boulders talking until after 5 o'clock; the ancient philosophers sat on stone seats expounding their systems, and no doubt our topics—the absurd height of Mount Everest and the evils of processed foods—were so congenial that we too were indifferent to comfort.

Some snow fell in the night, and the morning was cloudy when we left at 9:30 o'clock. Turning the corner we proceeded, roped, up the glacier, steering a course close to the slopes of the North Peak above us on our left. The snow was good. The clear view we had of the north-west ridge of the mountain again impressed us with the difficulty a party would have in setting foot on it. When we had made about a mile up the glacier an icefall compelled us to bear to the left still closer under the North Peak, but as we changed direction mist came down to obscure the route and at the same time we noticed a lone figure hurrying after us up the glacier. The figure proved to be Lhakpa Tsering, who, as he had not been able to join us yesterday, was now coming straight through from Lake Camp. Leaving some men here whom he could join on the rope, for there were a number of crevasses about, we pushed on through the mist with eyes and ears cocked for anything which might fall from the North Peak so unpleasantly close above us.

By now the snow was rapidly deteriorating, but, as the many big crevasses were adequately bridged, soon after 1 o'clock saw us camped in the middle of the wide snow shelf above the icefall, two or three hundred yards from the foot of the slope leading to the Col. On account of possible avalanches it was advisable to keep as far away as possible from the snow-slopes surrounding us on three sides. The height of this West Side Camp must be about the same as that of Camp II, about 21,500 ft. The afternoon was fine and hot; on the Col snow was still being blown about, and the rocks of the Yellow Band looked deceptively free from snow. The outlook, in fact, was encouraging.

We breakfasted at 5 o'clock and left at 7 o'clock on a bitter cold morning, already chilled to the bone by the inevitable waiting for loads to be adjusted and frozen ropes disentangled. The sky had a curiously dull glassy look against which, to the west, the beautiful Pumori (the "Daughter Peak" of Mallory) appeared flat as if painted on gray cloth. Smythe and Lloyd went ahead to make the track, the rest of us following on three ropes. As we made our way to the foot of the slope the most phlegmatic might have remarked on the fact that we were walking over the debris cone of the father and mother of all avalanches, the tip of which reached nearly to the camp. This had apparently fallen a few days before—possibly on the day on which I had suggested two of us should descend this way from the Col. One result of this fall was that the first five hundred feet of our route now lay up bare ice, thus entailing much hard work for the leaders step-cutting; and in order to reach snow which was still in place, and which at that early hour, if our pious hopes were fulfilled, might possibly remain in place, a long traverse had to be cut across the ice, in crossing which it was impossible adequately to safeguard the porters. Two of us were roped to the porters, but this was done in the hope of inspiring confidence and not in the expectation of checking a slip. All that one could do really was to urge caution and pray that no slip occurred. Having reached the snow we were faced with about 800 ft. of steep slope; but the snow was of doubtful integrity and of a consistency that gave us plenty of hard work. The appearance of the sun over the Col, warned us of the need for haste, so we pressed on with all the speed we could muster. When we reached the top at 11 o'clock the sun, feeble though it was, had been on the slope for an hour and from its effect on the snow I felt it was high time for us to be off it. It was fortunate that the sun that morning was but a pale reflection of its usual self, for it peered wanly through the glassy sky surrounded by a double halo. Surprisingly enough no abnormal weather followed these alarming portents. Some snow had accumulated round the tents which we had abandoned on May 30, but nothing had blown away. We re-pitched the dome tent, and four Europeans and sixteen Sherpas (one was left behind sick) were once more in occupation of Camp IV.

June 6 dawned fine. As one of the porters had gone sick we had only fifteen available for load carrying, but this was just sufficient if they carried between 25 and 30 lb. Some time was spent making up loads which had to contain all that was required for Camps V and VI; that is to say, tents for two Europeans and seven Sherpas at Camp V, and for two Europeans at Camp VI; sleeping-bags and food for three days for two Europeans and seven Sherpas at Camp V, and sleeping-bags and three days' food for two Europeans at Camp VI. We took two pyramid tents to Camp V. They make heavy and awkward loads but would enable a party to sit out any bad weather in reasonable comfort; a similar type is used in the Arctic where their great advantage is that the four poles have merely to be brought together to enable the tent to be placed on a sledge ready for traveling. Pitching is equally quick and simple, but this is not possible when the tent has to be carried by a man, for then the poles have to be taken out and disjointed.

We finally got away at 10 o'clock to make good progress up board-hard snow. A week ago we had sunk to our knees in the snow of this north ridge, but now it was so hard that a strong kick was needed to make a nick for the edge of the boot. The question of the behavior of snow at high altitudes is difficult. For example, this hard snow extending up to 25,000 ft. gave us some reason to expect fair snow conditions higher up, but above Camp VI it was loose and soft and apparently quite unaffected by the wind. A variety of factors have to be considered besides the mere force and direction of the wind which may of course vary greatly in different places and at different heights. Mr. Seligman, who is an authority on Alpine snow conditions, believes that if some evaporation of snow cannot take place no packing can occur. That is

to say, the wind must be dry. Further, the lower the temperature the less easily does snow evaporate so that it is possible that above a certain height tem-
peratures are too low for any evaporation to take place.

Lloyd was wearing the "open" type oxygen apparatus in which he went well
once he had mastered the technique of breathing. Not that he climbed any
faster, but perhaps he did so more easily. The hard snow-bed which afforded
such excellent going comes to an end at something below 25,000 ft. Here
there is a momentary easing of the slope where a party can sit comfortably
while it summons up the little energy remaining for the next 800 ft. of mixed
scree, rock, and snow. Above this two of the men, who were feeling the height,
struggled on for only another 100 ft. before giving in altogether. They had to
be left where they were together with their loads. Tensing was going very
strong, but none of the others seemed at all happy. When still some 300 ft.
below the site for Camp V (25,800 ft.) a sudden snowstorm sapped their
resolution so much that there was talk of dumping the loads and going down.
By now Smythe and Lloyd were nearly up; they must have wondered what
Shipton, myself, and the porters, were doing, strung out over the ridge in
various attitudes of despair and dejection hurling remarks at one another. In
the end better feelings prevailed. All struggled on, and by 4 o'clock reached
the fairly commodious snow platform of the Camp V site.

Unluckily one of the two abandoned loads was the second pyramid tent.
Consequently, the sole accommodation for two Europeans and seven porters was a small Meade tent (later to go to Camp VI) for the former, and one
pyramid which at best would take five Sherpas. The prospect of sleeping seven
in a tent made to hold four was bleak, but that of going down and returning
next day was worse. Lloyd and I started down with six porters at 4:15 o'clock,
but we had not gone far before shouts floated down to us from above. I could
not understand what was said, but apparently it was a request to us to bring
up the other tent which had been dumped six or seven hundred feet below.
The only possible reply to this was the Sherpa equivalent for "Sez you"; for I
do not think that any of our party, had they been willing, were capable of
doing it. We carried on, picked up the two sick men, and continued the descent very slowly; for the men were too tired to be hurried and called frequently

and successfully for halts by the simple expedient of sitting down. The snow, too, was now very soft. Looking back at one of these halting places I saw, descending from Camp V, two men whom our Sherpas recognized as Pasang and Tensing coming down to retrieve the abandoned loads. To descend and ascend with loads another seven hundred feet, on top of the toil they had already endured, was a remarkable example of unwearying strength and vitality gallantly and unselfishly applied. We reached Camp IV at 6:15 o'clock, pleased at having at length established Camp V. For my part I was very hopeful that something might yet be done. The last entry in my diary for that day runs: "Frank and Eric going well—think they may do it," which showed how little I knew.

Camp V was established on June 6; the party's activities in the following days may best be told in Shipton's own words:

> On June 7 a heavy wind was blowing from the east; this prevented our advance up the ridge. The weather, however, had been fine for a week, and as there had been a lot of wind we hoped that the snow would be coming off the mountain. The following day was calm and fine. We started at 8 o'clock. The whole party was fit and full of hope that we were going to be granted a chance for an attempt at the summit, which had been denied us for so long. The upper part of the mountain was very white. It had always been presumed that when it presented such an appearance there was little chance of success. But no one had ever climbed far above the North Col during the monsoon, and this idea had been founded on pure conjecture. Conditions on the ridge as far up as Camp V had led us to hope that with the recent fine weather and cold winds the snow on the upper slabs might have consolidated; for now it was clear that at this time of year (on account of the increased humidity) no amount of sun and wind would remove it.
>
> We had not gone far before we found that our hopes were vain. The rocks were deeply covered in snow, which, unlike that

below Camp V, showed no tendency to consolidate and was as soft and powdery as it had been when it had fallen about ten days before. The ridge which in 1933 had not caused us the slightest trouble now demanded a lot of very hard work. It was almost unbelievable that such a change could take place on such simple ground. There was one small step that both Smythe and I failed to climb, and we wasted a considerable time making a way round it. It was hard work, too, for the porters, and our progress was lamentably slow. It was 1 o'clock before we reached the site of Norton's and Somervell's old camp at 26,800 ft. The porters worked splendidly and without any complaint. They were determined to put us in the very best position possible from which to make our attempt, and would not listen to any suggestion that they might have difficulty in getting back before nightfall. Previously it has always been rather a question of driving these men to extreme altitudes; now the position was almost reversed. I do not think future expeditions need worry about the establishing of their higher camps provided they choose the best men. Pasang was not well and his comrades went back to help him with his load more than once. Ongdi, too, showed signs of great exhaustion.

At the top of the north-east ridge, we reached at 4:15 o'clock, a gentle scree slope below the Yellow Band. Here we pitched our tent at an altitude of 27,200 ft. I have never seen the Sherpas so tired, and they must have had a hard struggle to get back to Camp V before dark.

The weather was fine, and the sunset over hundreds of miles of monsoon clouds far below was magnificent. But all we wanted to do was to lie quietly down in the drowsy condition which seems to be a permanent state at great altitudes. It was a big effort to cook and eat any supper, and all we could manage that night was a cup of cocoa and a little glucose. I had brought a small book with me against the possibility of a sleepless night.

But the meaning of the words kept becoming confused with a half-dream, as when one is reading in bed late at night before going to sleep.

We started cooking breakfast at 3:50 o'clock, and started before the sun had reached the slabs of the Yellow Band. But we were surprised to find the cold was intense. Very soon we had lost all feeling in hands and feet, and it was obvious we were in serious danger of frost-bite. We returned to the tent and waited until the sun had arrived, and then made a second start. Norton's route below the Yellow Band was quite out of the question for there was an enormous deposit of snow on the gently sloping ground. Also conditions in the couloir were obviously hopeless. Our plan was to try to make a diagonal traverse up to the ridge which we hoped to reach just before the First Step. At best it was a forlorn hope, for the ridge in any condition must be a tough obstacle, and it now looked really villainous. The only chance lay in the remote possibility that some unexpected effect of wind and sun at these little-explored altitudes had produced firm snow on the steep slabs and on the ridge.

We started flogging our way up the steep ground, through powder snow, into which we sank up to our hips. An hour's exhausting work yielded little more than a rope's length of progress, even on the easy beginning on the slabs. We went on until, on the steeper ground, we were in obvious danger of being swept off the rocks by a snow avalanche. Then we returned, completely convinced of the hopelessness of the task. It was bitterly disappointing, as we were both far fitter at these altitudes than we had been in 1933, and the glittering summit looked tauntingly near.

There can be no doubt that one day someone will reach the top of Everest, and probably he will reach it quite easily, but to do so he must have good conditions and fine weather, a combination which we now realize is much more rare than had been supposed by the pioneers on the mountain. It is difficult to give the layman much idea of the actual physical difficulties of the last 2,000 ft. of Everest. The Alpine mountaineer can visualize them when he is told that the slabs which we are trying to climb are very similar to those on the Tiefenmatten face of the Matterhorn, and he will know that though these slabs are easy enough when clear of ice and snow they can be desperately difficult when covered in deep powder snow. He should also remember that a climber on the upper part of Everest is like a sick man climbing in a dream. . . .

"ATTEMPT TO REACH SUMMIT RIDGE"

Down at Camp IV on June 7 we were almost as inactive as the party at Camp V—but with less reason, for here there was no wind and the day was fine. The temperature at night outside the tent had been 5°F. We rose late, and after a leisurely breakfast Lloyd put on the "closed" type oxygen apparatus and started to walk towards the foot of the north ridge. I watched with interest and soon saw that all was not well. When he was about 200 yards from camp he sat down, took it off, and came back. The feelings of suffocation which he experienced were exactly similar to [Dr. C.B.] Warren's. I put the thing on for myself for a few minutes and executed a light fandango in the snow with such remarkable feelings of sprightliness that I resolved to give it a proper trial. I regret to say that this resolution, like so many others made at high altitudes, was not kept; but there is no reason to believe that my experience would have differed from that of Warren or Lloyd who had both given that apparatus a fair trial. They could find no mechanical defects at the time, but whatever faults may have since been detected, and whether or no they can be remedied, I think the most obvious lesson to be learnt is that the only trials and experiments of any value at all are those carried out by mountaineers themselves at heights of over 23,000 ft., but not necessarily on Mount Everest.

We were up very early on June 8 in order to take three sick men down to the West Side Camp; they were not exactly sick but were incapable of acclimatizing sufficiently to go higher. Therefore they were better out of the way. As Lloyd and I had to return it was important to start early in order to have safe snow conditions on the way back. . . .

Next day, June 9, saw us moving up to Camp V in accordance with a prearranged program. We took with us six porters lightly laden with a little extra food and five oxygen cylinders. Lloyd again wore the "open" oxygen apparatus while I was without. Thus we constituted rather a hybrid party but such a party might function quite well for an attempt on the summit. The reason that I was without was not solely one of high principles or an intolerant scorn for the use of oxygen apparatus, but because if we were to use it all the way, as Lloyd intended, then there would not be enough cylinders to supply the two of us.

As we began the ascent of the north ridge we saw the rear party—[Noel] Odell, Warren, [Capt. P.R.] Oliver—accompanied by two Sherpas coming up from West Side Camp. They had crossed the traverse, but as we could not afford the time to wait and exchange news we continued on our way. A little later we met the seven men coming down from Camp V, very tired; their names were: Ongdi Nurbu ("Ashang"), Pasang Bhotia, Rinsing, Tensing, Lhakpa Tsering, Da Tsering, Lobsang. About this time Shipton and Smythe must have been leaving Camp VI, so altogether the mountain presented such a scene of activity that morning that it reminded one of Snowdon on a Bank Holiday. On reaching the top of the snow slope one of our men, whose cough was troubling him, dropped out, but the rest of us reached Camp V at 3 o'clock almost simultaneously with the arrival of Shipton and Smythe from above. Their report of conditions up there effectually quenched any hopes we may have entertained of reaching the summit. A valuable plan was to investigate the possibilities of the north-east or summit ridge, and, if we could reach it, to have a look especially at the Second Step. In any case, with such snow conditions, the ridge was undoubtedly a safer place than the slabs.

After some tea and talk they went down, taking with them three of our porters. Kusang Namgyal and Phur Tempa stayed with us; the former needed no prompting, electing to stay as of right and privilege, but some persuasion was required before one of the other four volunteered. It is of course a matter for wonder, no less than thankfulness, how much these men will do and how far they will go with, one imagines, few of the incentives which act as a spur to us. There is, as Shipton remarks in the passage I have quoted, no longer any need to drive them to go high if care is taken to pick only the best. It was not always thus. Amongst other factors which have brought about this change, and to which we are chiefly indebted, are the care, sympathy, and mountaineering skill, with which the porters of earlier Everest expeditions have been handled. The value of the confidence which a leader and his party now derive from the knowledge that the porters will carry a camp as high as need be cannot be over-estimated.

We slept little if at all that night. We were warm enough, in spite of having only the tent floor between our sleeping-bags and the snow, but from sunset until four in the morning it blew so hard that the noise made by the flapping of the double-skinned pyramid tent kept us awake. The night temperature was −1°F. We got away soon after 8 o'clock with Kusang and Phur Tempa carrying between them two oxygen cylinders and the little extra kit and food we needed. Camp VI was already provisioned and equipped with sleeping gear. With snow lying everywhere the climbing for the first thousand feet was not easy, and the tracks of the first party had for the most part been filled by the wind. Lloyd went ahead making the track while I followed roped to the two porters. Although it was naturally harder work making the route, Lloyd reached the camp some half an hour before us, and, by the time we arrived, had re-erected the small Meade tent which the others had struck for the sake of safety. As was to be expected the higher we went the more benefit he felt from the oxygen. On the other hand, I was roped to the two laden porters, and though at this distance of time I like to think I was accommodating my pace to theirs I should not like to have to take my oath upon it. For the short distance we went next day he again went better than I did, but perhaps under the circumstances that is not such a valuable testimonial for the oxygen apparatus as it might seem. It is conceivable that a better man, or a man who had had less sickness during the previous month, might have gone as well as or better than

Lloyd, who, it must be remembered, was carrying a load of 25 lb. I am inclined to think that any benefit likely to be obtained from the use of oxygen is cancelled by the weight of the apparatus. But this may not always be the case—a very much lighter apparatus is probably only a matter of time. It is well known that the effect of great altitudes is to sap not only the powers of the body but also of the mind. To say that the resolution of every man who goes high is thereby weakened to some extent would be too sweeping, but the will, or even the urge, to ascend and to overcome the difficulties standing in his way, which is the instinctive feeling of every mountaineer, is less strong than at lower levels. What I did rather hope and expect, therefore, was that the revivifying effect of oxygen might be sufficient to overcome this disquieting tendency, and that a few whiffs of oxygen would boost Lloyd up those rocks which next day so easily defeated us—and of course would enable him to pull me up too. But, as will be seen, there was no such effect; oxygenated and unoxygenated man acquiesced tamely in defeat.

Shortly before reaching the 1924 camp site (26,800 ft.) we untied the rope as here there was little likelihood of a slip having any serious consequences; but it was needed again on the smooth slabs just below the tent, which a covering of snow made very awkward indeed. At the top of these slabs the angle eased off, and a gentle slope of small scree, almost free from snow, continued for nearly a hundred yards up to the foot of a steep rock wall. For thirty or forty feet this wall was very steep—steep enough that is to necessitate the use of the hands—until the angle eased off where broken slabby rock led to the north-east shoulder (27,500 ft.) and the summit ridge, about 300 ft. above our camp. Fifty yards to the left (east) of the scree patch the north ridge fell away steeply to the big snow couloir which has its origin almost directly below the shoulder. On the right (west) at the same level a wide bed of snow ran up to the foot of the heavily snow-covered rocks of the Yellow Band, the wide band of light-colored rock running almost horizontally across the face of the mountain. The whole face looked steeper and more formidable than I had imagined. We had placed Camp VI two or three hundred yards to the east of and about 200 ft. below the 1933 camp site owing to the impossibility of getting there. Ours was less advantageously placed for making an attempt, but otherwise it is probably the best site on the mountain; reasonably flat, and, even at this time, free from snow except for a little hard patch close to the tent from which we drew our supply for cooking.

We were all up by 12:30 o'clock. Having sent the men down we collected snow for cooking and turned in, for the wind was already rising. It blew all afternoon and continued for most of the night, so that again we slept little. For supper that evening we each had the best part of a pint mug of hot pemmican soup which we swallowed with equanimity if not with gusto; nor did I think it was this, and not the wind, which accounted for the rather miserable sleepless night which followed. To drink a cup of pemmican soup is very well, and to do it at that height is indeed a triumph of mind over matter; but the whole cupful does not amount to more than 4 oz. of food. This was probably more than half of our total food intake for that day which again was only a quarter of the amount considered necessary for men doing hard work. Pemmican and sugar have high calorific values—the former the highest of any food—but to provide the requisite number of calories, supposing only these two foods were taken, one would have to consume $1/2$ lb. of pemmican followed by 1 lb. of sugar which would at any rate help to keep it down. Perhaps this could be accomplished easily enough in the course of a day; but how many pounds of caviar, quails in aspic, chicken essence, sweet biscuits, jam, dried fruit, tinned fruit, pickles, and other things beloved of those who believe this high-altitude food problem could be solved by the tempting of the appetite, would be required to do the same? In many counselors there may be wisdom, but in many foods there is neither sense, nourishment, nor digestibility. There are several foods still to be tried out, but I believe the fact will have to be faced that at these altitudes it is impossible to eat very much and that one will have to be satisfied with eating as much as one can of some food of high value, even if not very palatable, rather than pecking at kickshaws. In spite of having been inhaling oxygen for most of the day Lloyd had no more appetite than I had, but perhaps he ought to have taken alternate sucks at his mug of pemmican and his tube of oxygen. Proverbially difficult though it is to blow and swallow at the same time, no doubt in the near future some genius will produce an apparatus which will make possible the assimilation of oxygen and food simultaneously.

We rose early on the 11th; not so much because we were panting to be off, like hounds straining at the leash, but because being up would be less wretched than trying to sleep. To say that we rose conveys a wrong impression; we did nothing so violent, but merely gave up the pretence of trying to sleep by assuming a slightly less recumbent position. Then one of us had to take a more extreme step—sitting up, and reaching out for the stove; and for the saucepan full of snow, waiting in readiness at the other end of the tent. Once the stove was lit an irrevocable step had been taken, for it had to be tended. But once lit it burnt well considering that it was laboring under the same difficulty as ourselves, anoxemia—not so well, however, that one could afford to leave it to its own devices and pretend to go to sleep again. Occasionally it would splutter, which was the signal for going out altogether, or for a long tongue of flame to lick the roof of the tent playfully—an emergency calling for some deft work with a pricker and a match until it was burning normally again. In the course of half an hour or so the lifting of the saucepan lid reveals no merrily bubbling water, but a murky pool of slush or half-melted snow, its surface coated with the remains of last night's pemmican. Feelings of impatience for a hot drink and thankfulness for further respite in bed are mingled equally. If patience is bitter, its fruit is sweet. Presently the water bubbles feebly and breakfast is served—a mug of tea, not completely valueless as it contains a good quarter pound of sugar, a few biscuits, and possibly a fig. None of us has been able to face porridge above Camp III, nor is there time for making both porridge and tea.

By morning the gale of the night had died away, but it was not until 8 o'clock that we considered it warm enough to make a start. (All times given, by the way, are relative and not absolute. It was 8 o'clock by my watch, but by the sun it might have been 7 or 9 o'clock.) While waiting we dressed by putting on wind-proofs, and boots which had been kept more or less unfrozen in our sleeping-bags. The sun was still below the ridge but the morning was fine and calm except for what appeared to be a gentle zephyr from the west. In reality it may have been blowing hard for I suppose if the atmospheric pressure is only one-third of normal, wind strength is also reduced. On our arrival the previous afternoon I cannot say that the rock wall which we proposed climbing as the most direct way to the summit ridge had made a very good impression. Like boxers confidently announcing their victory on the eve of a fight we told each other it would "go," comforting ourselves privately with the thought that rocks sometimes look worse than closer acquaintance proved them to be. But now, in the cold light of morning, as they looked still less prepossessing we decided not to waste time but to turn the wall on the right where it merged into the easier angle of the face, and where a shallow depression filled with snow led diagonally upwards to the summit ridge. As we moved slowly up the scree towards the right-hand end of the wall I kept changing my axe from one hand to the other thinking it was that which was making them so cold. But before we had been going ten minutes they were numb and I then began to realize that the gentle zephyr from the west was about the coldest blast of animosity I had ever encountered. I mentioned the state of my hands to Lloyd who replied that his feet were feeling very much the same. We returned to the tent to wait until it was warmer.

We made a second brew of tea and started again about 10 o'clock by which time the sun had cleared the ridge, although it was not blazing with the extraordinary effulgence we should have welcomed. In fact at these heights the only power which the sun seems capable of exerting is that of producing snow-blindness. It was still very cold, but bearable. We skirted the snow lying piled at the foot of the wall and took a few steps along our proposed route, where Lloyd, who was in front, sank thigh-deep into the snow. I believe it was somewhere about there that Shipton and Smythe had tried. Without more ado we returned to the rocks. There seemed to be three or four possible ways up, but first we tried my favored line of which Lloyd did not think very highly. It was one of those places which look so easy but which, through an absence of anything to lay hold of, is not. I did not get very far. A similar place was tried with like result and then we moved off to the left to see if there was any way round. This brought us to the extreme edge of the north ridge where it drops steeply to the gully coming down from the north-east shoulder. There was no way for us there. Retracing our steps along the foot of the wall Lloyd had a shot at my place which he now thought was our best chance; but he too failed. It was not really difficult; at least looking back at it now from the security of an armchair, that is my impression, but the smooth, outward-sloping rocks, covered in part by snow, very easily withstood our half-hearted efforts. I then started up another place which I think would have "gone," although the first step did require a "shoulder." Very inopportunely, while I was examining this our last hope, there was a hail from below and we saw Angtharkay, presently to be followed by Nukku, topping the slabs just below the tent. I had left word for him to come up with the oxygen load abandoned by the porter who had failed to reach Camp V with us. We wanted to have a word with him, and of course to go down to the tent was a direct invitation to go down altogether— a course which I am sorry to say was followed without any demur.

It will be a lasting regret that we never even reached the summit ridge, but I think the information we would have brought back had we reached it would have been mostly of negative value. From the point we were trying to reach close to the north-east shoulder, the Second Step is about 1,200 yd. distant; the summit itself is a mile away, and 1,500 ft. higher. The ridge, on which there was plenty of snow, did not look easy, while the Second Step looked really formidable; so much so that the only chance seemed to lie in the possibility of making a turning movement on the south face, which of course we could not see. The only reason for preferring the ridge route to Norton's Traverse would seem to be when there is snow about; but since under such conditions the ridge itself is not easily attainable little remains to be said for it as an alternative route.

We descended to Camp V in a storm of snow and wind which made the finding of the best route a matter of difficulty. Kusang and Phur Tempa were still in residence. After some tea and an hour's rest we started again at 4 o'clock for the Col. The Sherpas were roped together, while we went ahead making a track for them down the snow; but they went so slowly that we had constantly to wait for them. The storm had blown itself out and the evening was now calm and fine, so near the bottom we pushed on ahead leaving them to follow at their leisure. Amongst the crevasses at the foot of the ridge, where the storm had obliterated all old tracks, we had a discussion, about the right route, which threatened to be interminable until Lloyd settled the matter, or at any rate pointed out the wrong route, by falling into one; thus bringing an inglorious day to its appropriate conclusion. As we were unroped at the time, this slight mishap will possibly evoke neither surprise nor sympathy. In response to my inquiries a muffled cry from below assured me that he was unhurt and had not fallen very far; but as nothing could be done until the porters arrived with the rope, I had to leave the victim down there for a good ten minutes—possibly penitent, certainly cold. It should never happen, but if one does fall into a crevasse in free unfettered fashion (I speak from experience), as one does if the rope is not being worn, it is a question which feeling predominates—surprise, fear, or disgust at having been such an ass. I could see the Sherpas up the ridge and they could see me, but they neither heard my shouts nor took any notice of my gesticulations except to sit down once again and ponder at this new form of madness. At length one of them, who was possibly a better arithmetician than the others, must have totted up the number of Europeans who had left Camp V that afternoon and discovered that there was one short. Down they came, and Lloyd was hauled out none the worse.

Only Odell, Oliver, and seven porters remained at Camp IV as the others had gone down that morning by the old route to Camp III. Warren was obliged to go too in order to look after Ongdi who on his return from Camp VI had suddenly developed pneumonia; at least the symptoms pointed to pneumonia, but his recovery was so speedy that it may not have been. They went down by the old route because for a sick man that was the easier. Another Camp VI man, Pasang Bhotia, was lying there alone in a tent, sick. The first report was that he had gone mad for he was unable to articulate, but it soon became clear that his right side was completely paralyzed and he was therefore incapable of movement. They had attempted to take him down that morning, but two sick men in one party were too many. The other Sherpas seemed rather to wish to shun him than to assist him in his piteous plight; he could neither dress himself, put on his boots, feed himself, talk, get out of his tent, nor even out of his sleeping-bag. They regarded this misfortune as a judgment, either on him or on the whole party, for supplicating too perfunctorily the gods of the mountain.

With this sick man on our hands, with some anxiety about the safeness of the descent, and since there was now no hope of climbing the mountain and the weather was not improving, we decided on the prudent course of going down. Oliver was keen to go to Camp VI, more for the sake of treading classic ground than for any good he could do. I sympathized, and was sorry to disappoint him, for dull indeed must be the man whose imagination does not quicken at the thought of treading that ground which in its short history of sixteen years has been the scene of so much high, even tragic endeavor. . . .

"LAST ATTEMPT"

FROM
Ghosts of Everest: The Search for Mallory & Irvine
BY JOCHEN HEMMLEB,
LARRY A. JOHNSON,
AND ERIC R. SIMONSON

EVEN THE MOUNTAINEERING PRESS HAD BEGUN TO DEVELOP A HO-hum attitude about expeditions to search for the bodies of Mallory and Irvine on the North Face of Everest. These trips were becoming almost an annual event, and the snow-plastered rocks of Everest were far from yielding any secrets about this great mystery. Lost somewhere high on the summit ridge in 1924, British climbers George Mallory and Andrew "Sandy" Irvine may—or may not—have reached the top of the world's highest peak before they disappeared. If only some artifacts could be found from the lost climbers, if only the camera that Mallory was reported to be carrying could be located . . .

The American expedition that took off for Everest in spring 1999, led by Eric Simonson of Seattle, had some ammunition that previous such expeditions did not. Jochen Hemmleb, a young German climber and mountain historian, had spent years analyzing every bit of published and unpublished information about the north side of Everest, and especially the tragic 1924 expedition. Hemmleb fastened on the report by an Asian climber some years previously about spotting "an English dead," and was sure he knew where to locate this body.

Hemmleb and Simonson joined forces, hoping to advance the knowledge of what may have happened to the two climbers. The expedition team assumed the body, if found, would most likely be that of Irvine, the less experienced of the two climbers. With almost eerie ease, the expedition located a body near where their information led them to search—and shocked themselves and the world when they discovered the body was that of the legendary George Mallory!

Both the body itself and the letters and artifacts found in its clothing have given mountain historians enough information to ponder for years. Still unanswered, at least definitively, is whether or not either Mallory or Irvine stood on the summit before the fatal fall. Absent proof, then, their story remains one of the most glorious failures in the annals of mountaineering.

The story of Hemmleb's research and of the discovery of Mallory's body is told in *Ghosts of Everest: The Search for Mallory and Irvine,* by Jochen Hemmleb, Larry A. Johnson, and Eric R. Simonson. This selection, the book's prologue (pages 11-19), tells the story of the 1924 expedition that was started in such high hopes, only to end in haunting sadness.

For three-quarters of a century, this is all that has been known with any certainty:

Just after dawn on the morning of June 6, two members of the 1924 British Everest Expedition, George Leigh Mallory and Andrew Andrew Comyn Irvine, crawled out of their simple canvas tent on the North Col, a wind-savaged, 23,180-foot- (7,066-m-) high saddle of snow, ice, and rock between the hulking mass of Everest itself and its lesser northern peak, Changtse, and took the first steps in what would become a climb into history.

They were not alone on that brilliant but bitter-cold morning. Two of their colleagues, Noel Ewart Odell and John de Vere Hazard, had prepared them a hearty breakfast of fried sardines, biscuits, tea, and hot chocolate, which, Odell would later complain, they "hardly did justice to." In another tent draped with sleeping bags to keep it dark, Colonel Edward Felix Norton, the expedition leader, utterly snow-blind and in excruciating pain after an unsuccessful sum- mit attempt two days earlier, awaited help down to Advance Base Camp, some 1,700 feet (500 m) below the col.

The men said little to each other. There was little need. They all knew the situation was critical. It had been more than two months since they had walked out of Darjeeling, India, toward Tibet, and more than a month since they had arrived at their Base Camp at the terminal moraine of the main Rongbuk Glacier on the Tibetan plain to the north. Twice in that preceding month, they had to push higher on the mountain—once as far as Camp III at the base of the Col, once to Camp IV on the col itself—and twice, miserable weather and haps drove them all the way back down to Base Camp. Finally, in the first few days of June, the expedition team succeeded in establishing two higher camps, Camp V at 25,300 feet (7,710 m) and Camp VI at 27,000 feet (8,230 m) but two attempts to reach Everest's 29,029-foot (8,848-m) summit had failed. They were running out of supplies and Sherpa support. Many of their native porters were too sick to climb, and the expedition team itself had been whittled down to a few hardy souls. Most of all, they were running out of time. In a matter of days, perhaps even hours, the annual monsoon would sweep up from the humid Indian subcontinent to the south and bury the high Himalaya under wave upon wave of snowstorms.

➤   ➤   ➤

Mallory had seen it all before. Twice. The 1924 Everest expedition was in fact the third British attempt in four years. The English had failed to be the first to reach either the North or South Pole, and were now determined that "the Third Pole," Everest, would be theirs. Spurred on by a well-publicized talk by Himalaya explorer Captain John Noel, who had made a clandestine foray into Tibet in 1913, a final expedition was organized for 1921, primarily as a reconnaissance trip into the unmapped Tibetan territory north and east of Everest. Yet the lure of the summit had been strong even before the expedition team left England and Mallory had complained that the composition of the team was inadequate to that task. Except for Mallory's friend and climbing partner Guy Bullock, most of the other expedition members drawn from the Alpine Club's "old-boy net-work" were just that: old, and generally unfit for climbing at high altitude. Indeed, one expedition member died on just the approach walk.

After weeks of reconnaissance, Mallory sighted a route to the summit from the northeast. A last-minute summit attempt was mounted, but the climbers could get no higher than the North Col before appalling weather forced them down. Ill-equipped and ill-prepared—"I doubt if any big mountain venture has ever been made with a smaller margin of strength," Mallory wrote—it was a historic achievement nonetheless.

Even before the 1921 expedition team returned from Tibet, officials in London had begun planning another expedition for the next year. This time there were several experienced climbers involved besides Mallory. On that expedition, the first summit team established a Camp V at 25,000 feet (7,620 m), but only reached 26,700 feet (8,130 m) before exhaustion and illness turned them back. A second team, using oxygen, succeeded in establishing a fifth camp at 25,500 feet (7,770 m), but trouble with the oxygen apparatus forced that team to retreat from a height of 27,500 feet (8,380 m). Finally, Mallory led a third attempt on the peak, but this effort failed even to reach the North Col; an avalanche on the snow slope above Advance Base Camp killed seven of their porters, and the expedition was over.

➤   ➤   ➤

Now, on this promising June morning, as Mallory and Irvine struggled into their primitive, unreliable, and brutally heavy oxygen apparatus, Noel Odell snapped their picture. In it, Irvine, a strapping young man only twenty-two years old, stands calmly with his hands in his pockets, his head tilted slightly as he watches Mallory fuss with his oxygen mask. Mallory, while certainly the finest English mountaineer of his day, is at age thirty-eight getting "a bit long in the tooth" for Himalaya expeditions. Yet he is driven, almost to the point of obsession, by this mountain and is determined to conquer it, for himself and for his country. This will be the third and last attempt to reach the summit during this expedition. If he fusses with the oxygen device, therefore, it is understandable: everything must be perfect. They have run out of chances. If they are to become the first human beings to reach the highest point on earth, they must succeed on this attempt. It is do or die.

Moments after Odell took the picture, at 8:40 A.M., Mallory and Irvine, accompanied by eight Tibetan porters carrying provisions, blankets, and additional oxygen cylinders, set off up the North Ridge toward Camp V. A little more than eight hours later, four of the porters returned to Camp IV with a note from Mallory: "There is no wind here and things look hopeful." The next morning the two climbers and the remaining four porters pushed higher to Camp V. At the same time, Odell and two other porters headed up from the North Col Camp V to support the summit team should they require assistance on their descent. Odell climbed without supplemental oxygen; he was no fan of the experimental and controversial apparatus and, in any event, the oxygen set he had worn on an earlier occasion appeared to give him little benefit.

With Mallory and Irvine established at Camp VI, their remaining four porters descended, carrying with them two notes from Mallory scribbled in pencil on the torn-out pages of a small notebook. One was addressed to Captain John Noel, the expedition cinematographer who would attempt to film the summit assault from Camp III at the base of the North Col:

Dear Noel,

We'll probably start early to-morrow (8th) in order to have clear weather. It won't be too early to start looking for us either crossing the rock band under the pyramid or going up skyline at 8.0 P.M.

Yours ever,

G. Mallory

The "8.0 P.M." was obviously an error; Mallory meant 8:00 A.M. The "rock band" refers to a belt of gray limestone that girdles the summit pyramid and ends in a prominent outcropping on the Northeast Ridge called the "Second Step."

The other note was addressed to Odell. Ever the English gentleman, Mallory apologized for the condition in which they'd left Camp V; asked him to bring up to Camp VI a compass Mallory had, with characteristic forgetfulness, left behind at Camp V; instructed him to descend the next day to the North Col, as he planned to do the same thing and there was insufficient room at VI for the three of them anyway if he didn't; and filled Odell in on their oxygen use:

Dear Odell,

We're awfully sorry to have left things in such a mess—our Unna Cooker rolled down the slope at the last moment. Be sure of getting back to IV to-morrow in time to evacuate by dark, as I hope to. In the tent I must have left a compass—for the Lord's sake rescue it: we are here without. To here on 90 atmospheres for the two days—so we'll probably go on two cylinders—but it's a bloody load for climbing. Perfect weather for the job!

Yours ever,

G. Mallory

Having sent his ailing potters down with the others, Odell spent the night alone at Camp V. The North Ridge of Everest is notoriously windy, pummeled by gales even in good weather, but this night was relatively calm and the morning dawned clear.

Though Camp VI was only some 2,000 feet below the summit, Mallory and Irvine faced a series of daunting hurdles when they began climbing the next morning: a crumbly "Yellow Band" of steeply rising, scree-strewn limestone slabs; a nearly vertical 100-foot wall of harder rock called the "First Step"; a dicey and exposed ridge walk; the 100-foot "Second Step," far more difficult than the first and described as like "the sharp bow of a battle cruiser"; then a broad, gently rising plateau leading to the snow-covered summit pyramid itself. If they attained the summit, they then faced perhaps the most daunting hurdle of all: descending safely in what would almost certainly be a state of extreme exhaustion.

Mallory and Irvine would have been well on their way by the time Odell pulled on his boots at 8:00 A.M., shouldered a rucksack stuffed with the errant compass and additional provisions for the summit team, and began climbing toward the Northeast Ridge and Camp VI. Odell, a geologist, had achieved a remarkable level of acclimatization to the thin air of Everest's upper reaches (one-third as much oxygen as at sea level), was clear-headed and strong, and planned to spend the morning exploring the geology of the mountain's northern face. By midmorning he noticed the weather had begun to change: "rolling banks of mist began to form and sweep from the westward across the great face of the mountain." He was not worried for the climbers above him, he later wrote, because "There were indications . . . that this mist might chiefly be confined to the lower half of the mountain, as on looking up one could see a certain luminosity that might mean comparatively clear conditions about its upper half."

In no particular hurry to get to Camp VI, Odell wandered happily about the mountainside, a scientist at work. At one point, he scrambled to the top of a rock outcropping to take a look around. Then,

> *at 12:50, just after I had emerged from a state of jubilation at finding the first definite fossils on Everest, there was a sudden clearing of the atmosphere, and the entire summit ridge and final peak of Everest were unveiled. My eyes became fixed on one tiny black spot silhouetted on a small snow-crest beneath a rock-step in the ridge; the black spot moved. Another black spot became apparent and moved up the snow to join the other on*

the crest. The first then approached the great rock-step and shortly emerged at the top; the second did likewise. Then the whole fascinating vision vanished, enveloped in cloud once more. There was but one explanation. It was Mallory and his companion moving, as I could see even at that great distance, with considerable alacrity, realizing doubtless that they had none too many hours of daylight to reach the summit from their present position and return to Camp VI by nightfall. The place on the ridge referred to is the prominent rock-step at a very short distance from the base of the final pyramid.

Concluding that his colleagues were now perhaps three hours from the summit, Odell climbed up to Camp VI to make it ready should they need it upon what was now certain to be a late return. As he reached the camp, a snow squall blew up and he ducked into the two-man tent for shelter, finding it strewn with food scraps, clothing, the climbers' sleeping bags, oxygen cylinders, and spare parts of oxygen apparatus.

Concerned that the camp, perched on a ledge and backed by a small crag, might be difficult to find in the swirling snow, Odell left the tent and scrambled another 200 feet up the mountain, whistling and yodeling as he went, to guide Mallory and Irvine back to the safety of their tent. After taking shelter behind a rock from the wind and driving snow, however, he realized that it was still too early for the climbers to be returning from the summit and that his calls were pointless. As he arrived back at Camp VI, the squall ended as suddenly as it had started and the snow that had fallen simply evaporated in the dry, cold air and brilliant sunshine. At 4:30 P.M., leaving behind Mallory's compass and the extra food he had brought for them, Odell descended to Camp IV, as Mallory's note the day before had instructed him.

When he arrived, glissading part of the way down the snow slope to speed his descent, Hazard greeted him with hot soup and tea: "What a two days it had been. . . . A period of intensive experiences, alike romantic, aesthetic, and scientific in interest, these each in their various appeals enabling one to forget even the extremity of upward toil inherently involved, and ever at intervals carrying one's thoughts to that resolute pair who might at any instant appear returning with news of final conquest."

But they did not appear.

Odell was not deeply concerned. After all, they had been late on their ascent; it was only reasonable that they would be late descending and that, like as not, they would shelter in one of the higher camps. The night was clear and Odell and Hazard stayed up watching for signs of movement—or flares of distress.

But they saw nothing.

Peering through binoculars at the tents at Camps V and VI the next morning, Odell and Hazard could detect no sign of movement. At noon, Odell once again began to climb, accompanied by two reluctant porters. It was a heroic performance. The man had been in what climbers today call "the Death Zone" for days. He had climbed and carried loads repeatedly during that time. And now he was at it again, struggling against the vicious western crosswind that made life so miserable on the North Ridge. When they reached Camp V at day's end, Odell found it exactly as he had left it two days before, empty and untouched. As darkness approached, "fleeting glimpses of stormy sunset could at intervals be seen through the flying scud, and as the night closed in on us the wind and the cold increased."

The next morning, the porters refused to go higher. He sent them back down and once again climbed alone toward Camp VI. He carried a spare oxygen set from Camp V but, as before, seemed to receive no benefit from it. Like Camp V, Camp VI was as he had left it, except that the unrelenting wind had collapsed one of the tent poles. Ditching the oxygen set, he immediately began climbing toward the summit along the route he thought Mallory and Irvine would have taken. After another two hours in the fierce wind and bitter cold, he had found nothing. Thinking to himself that "this upper part of Everest must be indeed the remotest and most inhospitable spot on earth, but at no time more emphatically and impressively than when a darkened atmosphere hides its features and a gale races over its cruel face," he finally relented and returned to Camp VI. He laid the climbers' sleeping bags out on a snow slope in a pre-arranged signal to Hazard, below, signifying he had found no one, then began the arduous descent to the North Col. He glanced back over his shoulder at the summit: "It seemed to look down with cold indifference on me, mere puny man, and howl derision in wind-gusts at my petition to yield up its secret—the mystery of my friends."

Mallory and Irvine had vanished.

         ➤   ➤   ➤

Their disappearance created one of the most enduring and puzzling mysteries in exploration and mountaineering history. Did they reach the summit? Did they do it together? If they did, what became of them? Did they, singly or roped together, their guards down after their historic effort, make one false step on the descent and tumble through the gathering darkness to their deaths? Or were they, exhausted and oxygenless (as their cylinders would have been long since empty), forced to spend a night that never ended on the rooftop of the world?

In the months, years, and finally decades since their disappearance, theories have been proposed, debated, and debunked; calculations have been made of their possible departure time from Camp VI, climbing speed, and oxygen use rate; speculations have been raised about the characters of the two climbers and how they might have responded to a range of potential summit crises; tantalizing new clues have from time to time been discovered. The net result? Three-quarters of a century after their disappearance, the world knew little more about the fate of these two Everest pioneers than it did on June 21, 1924, when *The Times* of London published expedition leader Norton's terse telegraphed announcement:

"MALLORY AND IRVINE KILLED ON LAST ATTEMPT."

PERMISSIONS

We have made every effort to trace and contact copyright holders and gratefully acknowledge all those who gave permission for material to appear in this book. If an error or omission is brought to our notice we will correct the situation in future editions. For information please contact the publisher.

Excerpt from *Mt. McKinley: The Pioneer Climbs* by Terris Moore, © 1967, 1981 by the University of Alaska. Used by permission of Katrina Moore.

"Masters of Understatement" excerpted from *Postcards from the Ledge* by Greg Child, © 1998.

Excerpt from *Deborah: A Wilderness Narrative* in *David Roberts: The Mountain of My Fear; Deborah: A Wilderness Narrative* by David Roberts, © 1991.

Excerpt from "Advent of Mountaineering" in *The Land That Slept Late* by Robert L. Wood, © 1995.

Extract from *This Game of Ghosts* by Joe Simpson, originally published by Jonathan Cape. Used by permission of The Random House Group Limited, U.K.

Excerpt from "Second Diary: 1 January 1942 to 21 November 1943" and "Third Diary: 21 June 1944 to 3 August November 1943" in *Hermann Buhl: Climbing Without Compromise* by Reinhold Messner and Horst Höfler, © 2000. Used by permission of Weltbild Ratgeber Verlage, Germany.

Excerpt from *Summits and Secrets* by Kurt Diemberger, later republished as *The Kurt Diemberger Omnibus* by The Mountaineers Books, © 1999 by Kurt Diemberger. Used by permission of the author.

"The German Assault on Nanga Parbat," by Erwin Schneider, excerpted from *Peaks, Passes, and Glaciers,* edited by Walt Unsworth, © 1981. Used by permission of Walt Unsworth.

"Muztagh Ata" excerpted from *Two Mountains and a River* by H.W. Tilman, first published by Cambridge University Press in 1949 and later republished in *H. W. Tilman: The Seven Mountain-Travel Books,* © 1983 by Joan A. Mullins and Pamela H. Davis. Used by permission of Baton Wicks, U.K.

"Grim Days on Haramosh" by Tony Streather with Ralph Barker, excerpted

Other titles you might enjoy from The Mountaineers Books:

GHOSTS OF EVEREST: The Search for Mallory & Irvine, *Jochen Hemmleb, Larry A. Johnson, Eric R. Simonson*
The exclusive team story of the 1999 Mallory and Irvine Research Expedition. Chronicles what the expedition discovered on Everest and provides clues to the enduring mystery: Did Mallory and Irvine make it to the top? And, if they did, what happened to them?

IN THE ZONE: Epic Survival Stories from the Mountaineering World, *Peter Potterfield*
True-life accounts of three climbers who faced the ultimate challenge in passionate pursuit of their sport.

K2: The Story of the Savage Mountain, *Jim Curran*
Formidable K2 has challenged the greatest names in climbing—and often won. Curran mines the rich history of this mountain, from the experiences of early nineteenth-century pioneer explorers to the present.

NANDA DEVI: The Tragic Expedition, *John Roskelley*
A young woman is determined to climb the peak for which she was named in this story of strong emotion, conflicting ambitions, death and victory, desire and regret.

POSTCARDS FROM THE LEDGE: Collected Mountaineering Writings of Greg Child, *Greg Child*
Sharp, incisive, and irreverent, this masterful storyteller entertains even as he plumbs the art and culture of the sport of mountaineering.

REINHOLD MESSNER, FREE SPIRIT: A Climber's Life, *Reinhold Messner*
Chronicles the career of one of the world's most innovative and disciplined climbers, the first man to summit Everest without supplemental oxygen.

SHERMAN EXPOSED: Slightly Censored Climbing Stories, *John Sherman*
A collection of biting satire, parody, and serious reflection on climbing's unsung heroes. Features the best of Sherman's *Climbing* magazine column "Verm's World."

A LIFE ON THE EDGE: Memoirs of Everest and Beyond, *Jim Whittaker*
Whittaker highlights the major events in his career: first American to summit Mount Everest; first CEO of REI; intimate of JFK; leader of the 1990 International Peace Climb; sailor circumnavigating the world with his family; and more.

K2: The 1939 Tragedy, *Andrew Kauffman & William Putnam*
Contemporary evidence sheds new light on the story of the 1939 American K2 expedition, which was marred by mystery and death.

THE MOUNTAINEERS, founded in 1906, is a nonprofit outdoor activity and conservation club, whose mission is "to explore, study, preserve, and enjoy the natural beauty of the outdoors. . . . " Based in Seattle, Washington, the club is now the third-largest such organization in the United States, with 15,000 members and five branches throughout Washington State.

The Mountaineers sponsors both classes and year-round outdoor activities in the Pacific Northwest, which include hiking, mountain climbing, ski-touring, snowshoeing, bicycling, camping, kayaking and canoeing, nature study, sailing, and adventure travel. The club's conservation division supports environmental causes through educational activities, sponsoring legislation, and presenting informational programs. All club activities are led by skilled, experienced volunteers, who are dedicated to promoting safe and responsible enjoyment and preservation of the outdoors.

If you would like to participate in these organized outdoor activities or the club's programs, consider a membership in The Mountaineers. For information and an application, write or call The Mountaineers, Club Headquarters, 300 Third Avenue West, Seattle, WA 98119; 206-284-6310.

The Mountaineers Books, an active, nonprofit publishing program of the club, produces guidebooks, instructional texts, historical works, natural history guides, and works on environmental conservation. All books produced by The Mountaineers Books fulfill the club's mission.

Send or call for our catalog of more than 500 outdoor titles:

The Mountaineers Books
1001 SW Klickitat Way, Suite 201
Seattle, WA 98134
800-553-4453
mbooks@mountaineersbooks.org
www.mountaineersbooks.org

The Mountaineers Books is proud to be a corporate sponsor of Leave No Trace, whose mission is to promote and inspire responsible outdoor recreation through education, research, and partnerships. The Leave No Trace program is focused specifically on human-powered (nonmotorized) recreation.

Leave No Trace strives to educate visitors about the nature of their recreational impacts, as well as offer techniques to prevent and minimize such impacts. Leave No Trace is best understood as an educational and ethical program, not as a set of rules and regulations. For more information, visit *www.LNT.org,* or call 800-332-4100.

Foreword writer **John Harlin III** is the northwest editor for *Backpacker: The Magazine of Wilderness Travel,* and the author of several books on mountains, climbing, and backpacking, including *Mount Rainier: Views and Adventures, Making Camp,* and *The Climber's Guide to North America.* He has climbed, skied, and kayaked extensively throughout North and South America and Europe.

Introductions to the individual selections in this anthology were written by **Donna DeShazo,** Seattle, who admits that her own climbing achievements fell short of the heights reached by the mountaineers whose work is extracted here. In her fifteen years as Director of The Mountaineers Books, however, she was privileged to meet and work with some of the finest climbers, writers, and climber-writers in the genre, and developed an abiding love of mountaineering literature.

ACKNOWLEDGMENTS

Extraordinary thanks to Bill Fortney, Geoffrey Nichols, Connie Pious, Deborah Easter, and Laura Drury.